Mennonites Encounter Hinduism (Hindu Thought and Practice)

An Annotated Bibliography

By Dorothy Yoder Nyce

Previously published:
Multifaith Musing: Essays and Exchanges

Published by:

Dorothy Yoder Nyce, DMin

1603 S. 15th St.

Goshen, IN 46526-4558

dyodnyce@bnin.net

Cover design by Benjamin Thapa

Library of Congress

Catalog No. 2015908677

ISBN 978-0-991-42129-9

Printed in the United States of America

Contents

Dedication

This resource is dedicated to the many Mennonite writers who have learned in order to inform readers about the complex world religion known as Hinduism. Many of those whose writing appears here have died; more people will pursue the task in the future, to counter conflicts and increase interfaith rapport. The book also honors those who claim something of the diversity that is Hinduism. With hopes that further information will enable good will, rather than negative, continued stereotypes between Christians and Hindus, annotations from an extensive bibliography are but one step. For someone to annotate what Hindu loyalists have written about Mennonites is welcome. Religious difference will remain but motivation to learn from the other can prod members of each faith group to better serve our world. The One "God of all nations" wills for conviction, respect, and justice to prevail.

Acknowledgements

The task of writing a book depends on friends and professionals. The writer wishes to thank those who encouraged this resource to emerge; they conveyed faith that such a venture was worthy. She also thanks Mennonite missioners who lived in India from 1962-1965 when she taught at Woodstock School in the Himalayan foothills. Friendship with Hindus began then through shopkeepers, travel, temple visits, and books. During decades since, Hindu students have come to Goshen College, Goshen, Indiana, where the writer lives. To engage them and learn from their families has been a unique step toward interfaith integrity for this Mennonite. Others to note with this project include:

- Gretchen Nyce and Phyllis Davenport Hostetler for reading early drafts of the manuscript to make suggestions. Inconsistencies and decisions remain the responsibility of the writer.
- Archivists and librarians for assistance with finding resources: Archivist Colleen McFarland and assistant Tillie Yoder (Mennonite Church US Archives Goshen, IN); Archivist John Thiesen (General Conference Mennonite Archives North Newton, Kansas); Eileen Saner (Anabaptist Mennonite Biblical Seminary, Elkhart, IN); Joe Springer and assistant Victoria Waters (Mennonite Historical Library, Goshen College, Goshen, IN); Archivist Martha Lund Smalley and Special Collections Assistant Kevin Crawford (Yale Divinity School Library, New Haven, CT) with recommendation from Edgar Metzler for access to United Mission to Nepal archival materials.
- John D. Nyce for assistance at the Newton and Yale libraries plus technical help with computer and formatting the manuscript. On-going conversations provided perspective too.
- Lewis Brubacher for gifting Ronald Neufeldt's book *F Max Muller and the Rg-Veda* and several Xeroxed articles.
- Benjamin Thapa graphic design for the book's cover.
- John Smith for managing the printing at Duley Press, Mishawaka, IN.
- Jamie Pitts for editing the writer's "Glimpses of Mennonite Engagement with Hindu Thought and Practice," *Anabaptist Witness* (2, no. 1 April 2015) 77-98.

Introduction

Why annotate what Mennonites have written about Hindu thought and practice?
- because few people have documented such information;
- because Christians live among Hindu people in India and North America;
- because Mennonites who have studied Hindu thought deserve to be read by Mennonites and others today;
- because Mennonite and Christian interfaith bonds need to be broader than with Islam and Judaism, valid as those are;
- because Hindu history, scriptures, and current expression have distinct religious aspects from which others may learn;
- because the One God welcomes religious difference and Truth.

Responses from people who learn of this project have been diverse. "Why expect reader interest in annotations of a bibliography with that theme?" You likely will not find much material for such a topic." "I would not expect western Mennonite mission workers to have done serious study of Hinduism over fifty years ago." "With Hinduism being so complex, how do you expect to present it fairly?" "How will you avoid comparison that negates some people or patterns, as among different Mennonite groups, time periods or academic background?" The writer has pondered similar questions and comments.[1]

The task to address the theme of Mennonite writing about Hinduism persists. Ever since college days, my interest in research has continued. I valued as a secondary school English teacher units called the Research Paper. To prod college students in "Bible and Sexuality" classes to be diligent in delving textual study alongside skill to evaluate writers mattered to me. To discover insight beyond the expected or to lose interest because of limited access to possible material verifies the usefulness of bibliography. Here then is bibliography with annotations, some being no more than minimal comments, some more extensive.

What becomes obvious is inconsistency. Most comments made about either Mennonites or Hindu thought or practice could be countered with other examples or explanations. What people write emerges from their experience. One person's experience varies from another's whose experience is similar; from one year or era to another year religious meanings may shift. Receive these writers as reflecting their backgrounds, their views of difference, their bias, their appreciation for tradition or things new. Some writers will not have been exposed earlier to ways to be religious different from what they inherited. Some had not attended to the complexity and integration of cultural and religious patterns. Others grew up alert to the strange or exotic, to diversity of ethnicity, language, and meaningful study.

Inconsistency and bias also mark decisions that formed this collection. As researcher, compiler and annotator I would have wished for more Indian national writers' views, more women's perceptions, and more word from Mennonite Brethren (MB). Attempts were made. Being of Mennonite Church (MC) heritage (that has now merged with General Conference (GC) Mennonite) my longer term knowledge of people and places centers with MC. I first lived in India for three years in the 1960s as a teacher at Woodstock School in the foothills of the Himalayas, without ever visiting an MB location. Nor did I get to MB archives in California to delve into personal correspondence or anecdotal gems or trivia. Whereas the MC archives is but a few blocks from my home, even a few days in the GC archives in Newton, Kansas, conveyed impressions. Gaps become clear. My intent is to learn more from MB writers and experience in order to share it. Regarding identity from the three largest Mennonite groups in North America, writers are generally named with one; changes in membership unknown to me have likely also occurred.

What might you the reader expect as you get into this wealth of information? Regarding in which chapter a given resource is annotated, a reason for its being in a different location could be justified. Some writers appear in several chapters depending on content or date of publication. While materials in the *Academic* chapter have all been published, many others have also been in print. Most *Academic* writers have been professors. More extensive annotations appear for writing centered in Hindu *thought*. Hindu *practice* appears often, though not exclusively, with *Anecdotes*. Between these covers keep *bibliography* in mind. The dated chapters clearly reflect time periods—the *Early Era* includes the 1940s, *Middle Era* from the 1950s through the 1980s, and *Later Era* from 1990s through the present. Shifts in time periods reflect how Hindu content has been approached or how people in Mennonite locations in India differed culturally. Over the years engagement with Hindu thought or practice broadens from basic information to more in-depth attention to patterns and particulars. Analysis awaits the historian, anthropologist, sociologist or teacher of world religions.

Several more points of explanation come to mind. Numbers in parentheses refer to page. Some resources are not annotated; more resources could be included. Perhaps content dealt less with the Hindu particular; perhaps the writer's time had limits. For a person's name to be underlined indicates that she or he appears elsewhere in this resource. Using the word *Hinduism* in the title accommodated to space; the preference would have been for *Hindu Thought and Practice*. The term *Hinduism* can be debated along with its history. Then too the term *missioner* appears rather than *missionary*—a personal choice of the writer's. When writer names differ, such as George J., or Jay, Lapp, the usage follows what appeared with the given article or book. As a woman who prefers using her 'maiden' and married names, I regret knowing too few full names of women here. With apology for failure to have an index for a hundred names, the reader will find alphabetical listings of writers within each chapter. Mistakes remain the writer's fault; she resisted adding more personal comments.

Readers may wonder why a given Mennonite known to have engaged with Hindu thought or practice does not appear here. While what is here is extensive, not all was known or could be gathered. Other projects beckon the writer. Perhaps a person who wrote did not include content focused on Hinduism. Perhaps the family of the person readers have in mind continues to have original papers in their possession. For example, the writer knows where Ruth (Blosser) Miller's diaries and extensive papers of Milton and Esther (Culp) Vogt are. Their family members wish to peruse materials before offering them to archives.

Three Mennonite groups receive attention here—the three largest. Several Mennonite Brethren (MB) members first met Hinduism when going to India in 1889; Mennonite Church (MC) missioners first arrived there ten years later, and the General Conference (GC) Mennonites sent representatives a year after that. (MC and GC groups merged in North America in the mid-1990s.) Brethren in Christ and United Missionary members also exist in India. The first two MB couples—Abraham and Maria Friesen and A. J. and Katharina Huebert— went from Russia to India. For nearly fifty years MBs joined American Baptists with mission efforts that had begun in the Telugu language area of Hyderabad State in 1875. The earliest MB missioners from the United States, N. N. and Susie (Wiebe) Hiebert and Elizabeth S. Neufeld, arrived in 1899. The first MB church was begun in 1904; in part due to mass conversion movements, 964 church groups with roughly 200,000 members now exist.[2]

Whereas Dutch Mennonites established a mission organization in 1847 for work in Indonesia, famines and philanthropy prompted North American Mennonite missions. Individuals concerned about the 1894-95 famine in India preceded missioners from MC and GC agencies. George Lambert (MC) from Elkhart, Indiana, and David Goertz (GC) of Halstead, Kansas, had gone separately to observe conditions before returning to India to oversee the distribution of tons of aid gathered by North American Mennonites. After the great Indian famine of 1897-98, the first MC missioners William (a physician) and Alice Page and Jacob Ressler arrived in the Hindi/Chhattisgarhi-speaking state of Central Provinces. The first GC Mennonite missioners—Peter A. and Elizabeth Penner and John F. and Susanna Kroeker (the latter couple from Russia) also went to CP state. While finding a region in which to locate, those four lived and studied Hindi for ten months with MC missioners already located in Dhamtari, CP.[3]

Several paragraphs provides examples of content for the reader to anticipate in this resource. As the chapter titled *Gandhi* includes annotations of Mennonite writing about that noted Hindu, *Anecdotes*, as is expected, highlight diverse personal experiences. For example, missioner P. W. Penner (GC)[4] reports about a Hindu custom that was not permitted to take place in churches—"sharad khana," a feast for the dead. Belief in salvation for the departed depends upon this feast, Penner explains. A personal note[5] from Jonathan Larson (GC) expresses his fascination with missioner Ramoth Burkhalter's (GC) friendship with the *mahant* (owner) of the Hindu Hanuman temple in Varanasi (Benares) during her last years in India. He made frequent visits to Burkhalters at Ellengowen (the housing for GC families located "on the hill" near Woodstock School), and Ramoth visited him in Varanasi (1997) with a group after attending Mennonite World Conference in Calcutta.

Chronology determines in which chapter most writings appear. Because this resource gives attention to three Mennonite groups—MB, GC, and MC—an account of interest by Amos Dick (Brethren in Christ) is excluded. His story titled "Missionaries and the Independence Movement in India"[6] reflects missioner risk in the context of conflict with Hindu neighbors. Historically, this piece would fit along with other accounts from the 1940s, near the end of the *Early Era*. Readers will also find reference to a consultation held in January of 1998 (*Later Era*) of the Mennonite Council of International Ministries titled "Encounters with Hindus and Hinduism." Findings from that event include statements about Hinduism for readers to ponder.

4 – Because of Hindu complexities, Christians will reflect care for Hindus by being informed of their religious heritages and by expressing the Gospel through indigenous expression.

5 – Because of global Hindu growth and influence in the west, Christians will need clear and deep understanding of Hinduism.

8 – Relating to Hindus calls Christians to have clarity of personal faith along with an integrated (not dualistic), holistic approach.

10 – While Hindu *avataras* (descent of a divine figure to earth) "came to destroy sinners and save the righteous, Jesus came to save sinners." [Such comparison suggests bias or a distinct feature of Christian grace.]

11 – Activated by the Spirit, Christians present the hope and life of Jesus to those caught in the "fatalistic world view of Hinduism."

The Findings Committee encourages publication of Consultation papers presented to enable people who encounter Hindus to "understand and respond to" their pervasive influence.

Annotations for James Pankratz' (MB) PhD dissertation (McMaster University, 1975) titled "The Religious Thought of Rammohun Roy" (1772 – 1833) could appear in *Middle Era* or *Academic* chapters, had it been read by the writer. Chapters by Pankratz appear in books edited by Robert Baird and Harry Huebner—"Rammohun Roy" in the former and "Mennonite Identity and Religious Pluralism" in the latter. In addition to countering Hindu features like *sati* (burning of a widow on her husband's cremation pyre) and the system of idolatry, Roy founded the *Brahmo Samaj* organization and was known as the "Father of Modern India," Pankratz reports.

Pankratz' chapter in Huebner's book explains how choice of faith, often referred to as voluntarism, "is a fundamental principle of pluralism."[7] Without discussion of Hinduism, this writing by Pankratz fits within the *Theology of Religions* section. Pankratz says that Mennonite' advocacy for pluralism is based on assumptions like "each person must choose a spiritual direction and most available spiritual options are misleading." (308) The early Christian confession "Jesus is Lord" emerged also within a world of religious pluralism. Although divisions within Christianity and with other religious traditions have continued, this confession does not sanction triumph over others or imply that other people are "bad." It simply expresses "good news." Love of neighbor and enemy apply to the same plural world; Mennonites will confess or proclaim news while living that love ethic, Pankratz explains.

Enjoy your read and discuss your observations and learnings!

---

[1] Wherever "the writer" appears in this book it refers to Yoder Nyce.

[2] This south central state of Hyderabad, later called Andhra Pradesh, was more recently divided with Telengama. See I. P. Asheervadam. "Mennonite and Brethren in Christ Churches in India," in *Churches Engage Asian Traditions: A Global Mennonite History*, eds. John Allen Lapp, C. Arnold Snyder, *et al.* (Kitchener, ON: Pandora, 2011) 135.

[3] CP was later named Madhya Pradesh; it is now divided between MP and Chhattisgarh States. Historian Asheervadam observes that early Mennonite missioners in CP seemed unaware of the Russian MB work that was already active in India.

[4] Box 4, Folder 4, Archives of the General Conference Mennonite Church, Bethel College, Newton, KS.

[5] June 17, 2013.

[6] *Brethren in Christ History and life*, (20, no. 1, April 1997) 119-38.

[7] James Pankratz. "Rammohun Roy" in *Religion in Modern India*, Robert D. Baird, (Manohar Publ.s 1981, 4th Revised Edition 2009). Huebner's book titled *The Church as Theological Community* honors Mennonite Bible scholar David Schroeder (GC). (Winnipeg: CMPC, 1990) 301-13.

Early Era - 1900-1940s

Block, Tina. (GC) "'That They May Know Him': P. A. Penner's First Term in India, December. 9, 1900 - March 10, 1908" (Seminar paper, North Newton, KS, 1965), 38 pp.

After Tina Block (later Ediger) worked for a year as secretary-treasurer at the evangelical seminary in Yeotmal, India, where Mennonites both studied and taught, she returned to Newton, Kansas. In a paper for a Mennonite history seminar, she describes P. A. Penner's early encounters with Hindu practices. Some troubled him; others humbled him. On one occasion of the festival of Dashera, the local *zamindar* (village owner) sent the missioners greetings and gifts: rice, flour, sugar, salt, lentils, peppers, bananas, and a goat. Recipients gratefully received such generosity, aware of the Hindu need to gain merit or find favor with deity. (28) But Penner agonized on seeing Hindus pay hard-earned rupees for images or god forms, intent to worship them, Block explains.[1]

Block further reports the time that a Hindu begged Penner to come to where a mother of the Kurmi caste lay dying. Her small room was full of people. After water and sour milk were poured into the dying woman's half-open mouth, her husband sprinkled sandalwood ashes into her mouth. Then a calf was brought into the room, and its urine poured into her mouth while the woman held to its tail. Penner could only reflect, "Poor, blind people." He recalled another occasion of death when people called upon "Ram-Ram" for assurance and performed a religious dance, each movement of which was significant. (29, 32)

Brunk, Aldine C. (MC) "A Missionary Administers an Indian Village," *Mennonite Quarterly Review*. (4, no. 1 January 1930) 60-67.

Brunk explains how an Indian village was organized decades ago. Usually a Hindu landlord would choose a committee to employ a priest to attend to religious life and idol worship within the village. A tax charged from each farmer proportionate to the person's land owned became payment for that priest. Money was also collected to pay for sacrifices made—goats, chickens, or coconuts. Brunk notes the difficulties that such a village scheme could make for Christians. If Hindus chose to fault Christians for interfering with their worship practices or for displeasing village gods, the landlord could refuse Christians admission into a village.

For such reasons, missioners requested the American Board (MC) to enable them to buy the village of Balodgahan, initially for the welfare of very poor folk. Missioner Mahlon Lapp (MC) served as a very wise—fair and motivating—landlord for Balodgahan from 1905 until his death in 1923. Of the village's eight hundred acres the mission at first bought what the previous landowner had owned and gradually purchased more land from people who were ready to sell. In turn more Christian farmers bought land; twenty-eight Christian families owned and lived there when Brunk wrote. He tells of the difficulties faced by the landowner who replaced Lapp. Although Indians do not resent a landlord scheme (they value having a hero), advice from the newcomer held little weight until he 'proved' his worth. But he chose not to enforce authority through some methods used by traditional Hindu landlords, Brunk adds. (61-63)

During a cold season non-Christians chose to organize a Ganpati dance for the Balodgahan village. They had not had enough money to celebrate that festival during the previous twenty-five years they said. Brunk explains that the seven-night dance and ceremony is expected to be held for three consecutive years. With it often comes drumming, carousing, and stealing. When the Hindus realized that the Christians did not approve of such an event, they went to the police and a local lawyer. The latter advised the missioners to permit the ceremony rather than have the complaint be taken to higher government officials. Brunk describes the mud image of the god-form Ganesh that was set up in the house of a leading Hindu along with the crowd, music, and dancing that followed. However, on the first night the only son of the Hindu leader became sick and died. The event ended abruptly. On the first night of the Ganpati dance the next year a leading farmer died. By the third year no one would offer money or a place to gather. By then, the Hindu villagers were more ready to follow the landowner's advice too. (64-65)

Brunk tells of another encounter with Hindus in Balodgahan village. Newly determined, some Hindus acquired a young *baiga* (priest) to help once again to look for two children of an idol named Takurdeo who had been "lost" for over twenty years. On hearing drums from near the location of their church, missioners learned that the "lost" children, one a white round stone and the other a brown one, had been "found." Hindu worshippers, busy washing the stones in milk before drinking the milk, reported that the god Takurdeo wished to live with the two children under the tree next to the church. The landlord countered, responding that since worship of the idols—the drum beating and all— would take place on Sundays, it would disturb the Christian worship service in the church. After a trance-like experience among some Hindus with the priest, they decided that the god was willing to be moved to the back of the village.

Several years after the missioner landlord gained a valid reputation, smallpox broke out among Balodgahan Hindus. When smallpox spread to multiple Hindu families, including with several deaths, they noticed a contrast. Individuals of a couple Christian families who started with smallpox soon recovered; they treated it as a disease that needed medicine. Aware of thirteen deaths among Hindus, they presumed that the smallpox goddess was angry. They chose to call in a witch doctor to locate where in the village a witch might be hiding but active. Whereas before the British controlled India, Indians might have put such a "discovered" witch to death, Brunk realized that at their time a helpless widow would likely be targeted, stripped, beaten, and cast out of the village. Instead, local Christians selected a day for fasting and prayer. About half of the Hindus joined them. Brunk saw that participation as a sign that some Indians were gaining courage to acknowledge Christian ways, including trust of medicine. (66-67)

Brunk, A. C. "Farm Labor in an Indian Village," *Christian Monitor*, (January 25, 1925) 781.
In this short account Brunk includes brief statements of Hindu practice among men: that Hindus often smoke before a farm labor meeting begins and that the pepper tree under which they met is thought to be sacred. Because of the tree's holy feature farmers were afraid to either express a lie or break an agreement made under the pepper tree.

Burkhalter, Martha R. (GC) *A Fragment of Missionary Life* (Being an account of our trip to Phuljhar, Thursday, Sept 16-22, 1926). A 2" x 4" booklet. (Bluffton, OH: Women's Missionary Society, 1927) 33 pp. http://mla.bethelks.edu/books/266 00954 B918f.pdf; John Thiesen Archivist (General Conference Mennonite Archives, Bethel College, Newton, KS) gave the copy.
Burkhalter served in India over forty years, retiring in 1959. A Bluffton College graduate, she also received the advanced B. R. E. degree in education from New York Biblical Seminary in 1934.

Using verse "in the complex meter of Longfellow's *"Hiawatha,"*[2] she describes a week-long trip of forty miles by spring-less wagon (and walking) with missioners S. T. and Metta Moyer (GC), plus four Indian helpers, two buffalo, and assorted *saman* (baggage). Read a few excerpts from the journey.

> . . .One would never choose this method
> Traveling simply for the pleasure,
> Going in a spring-less wagon
> Loaded with our bags and baggage. . .
> Yes, we found an empty mud-hut,
> Built for travelers, by the kindness
> Of the Hindoo village owner.
> It was small, had only one room,
> But this night, not less than seven
> Weary, hungry, rain-soaked travelers

Found in it both rest and shelter. . .
But what happened? Late one evening
Came a crowd of angry natives
Pelted tent with stones and mud clots,
Tried to drive the missionaries
From the place with angry violence . . .
Finally, it was decided
That a tract of wooded acres
Would be given in the jungles . . .

Burkhard, Mary Yoder. (MC) *Life and Letters of Jacob Burkhard Missionary to India*. (Goshen, IN: Self-published 1936).

Dester, Herbert. (GC) *About Hinduism*. 2 ½" x 5" booklet, (Newton, KS: Women's Missionary Association of General Conference Mennonites, 1946), 10 pp.

Missioner physician Dester packs numerous accounts into this small resource. He describes Hinduism as "not to be concise." It can be vague, elusive, lacking in facts, as well as expressive of deep longing, he says.

Dester reports incidents related to Hindu understanding of salvation as reward for actions in current life (*karma*). When missioner Peter Penner bought a large quantity of rice, he asked the merchant for a donation for the leprosy home. The merchant replied, "I'd rather give for the upkeep of a *guy shalla* (home for old cows) than for those with leprosy who are being punished or 'getting their due' from God."

On one occasion Dester asked a *sadhu* (Hindu holy man), "Have you received salvation?" the man replied, "Salvation is far away." On another occasion Dester and two other missioners trekked 125 miles to a source of the Ganges River at an altitude of ten thousand feet. There a nearly naked, silent *sadhu* lived year-round. Asked by one of the three what merit the *sadhu* expected, his *chela* (disciple) explained his hope for release from present existence and rebirths. He expected his body to be offered to the Ganges River. (5-6)

Dester's religious bias is clear too. Whereas at one point fifteen non-Christians had failed to clearly express the meaning of their faith, two Christians forthrightly verbalized "Jesus' saving power and grace," Dester observed. When missioner Miss Schmidt took a difficult child birth case into her home to provide close care, the patient's husband concluded that during some previous life Schmidt must have been related to the forthcoming child. Why otherwise would she have shown such care and interest? Aware that twenty low-caste, Christian families in a village twenty miles from Basna had cooperated to sponsor the education for one of their sons, Dester asked: "What religion other than Christian would so unite to empower a person?" Although he could credit Hindu India's religious strengths, hospitality, and care for caste members, perhaps limited knowledge prompted his other comparisons.

Dester observes how Hindus shape their understandings. Due to Hindu belief in many ways to attain the ultimate goal, Christian dependence on Jesus alone was often hard for Hindus to comprehend. Further, that a sore would not heal for a Hindu boy who fell out of a *pippala* tree (sacred fig tree) did not surprise a Hindu: divine punishment followed the child's earlier desecration of that *pippala*. Dester's wife reports seeing a merchant release a rat from a trap without killing it; many Hindus might be concerned that due to actions in a former life a relative might have been reborn as that animal. Dester also reports that stones or idols may be clustered alongside a dusty road or jungle path to provide a neighbor, pilgrim, or bus driver a reason to stop before it to perform a ritual of worship. The rite might also involve breaking open a coconut to leave some of it as an offering.

Graber, J.D. (MC) Multiple boxes in HM I 503, Mennonite Church USA Archives, (Goshen, IN, n.d.) Graber's mission articles appeared in MC *Gospel Herald* series like: "Across my desk" and "By the Way." Sermon notes and 'clippings' appear in Box 2, folder 24.

Joe D. and **Minnie** (Swartzendruber) were (MC) missioners in India from 1925-42. They also did relief work in China during 1943-44. J. D. was MC Overseas Missions Secretary 1944-67 and did famine relief work in Bihar State (India) part of 1967-68. Graber's notes here refer to Hinduism.

- "Jesus is Lord" undated, Box 4, folder 39. Many Hindus honor Jesus; some call him "Mahatma Isa" (Great Soul Jesus).
- "A Personal Witness" – January 2, 1960, p. 1
  A Hindu explained that Hindus achieve the goal of finding God through arduous search and many births.
- Untitled article regarding India – April 1974, p. 3
  In a crowd gathered in a bazaar
  a <u>Brahman priest</u> asks a Christian: "Who is the Father of Sin?"
  <u>Christian</u>: "The Devil."
  <u>Brahman priest</u>: "What is sin?"
  <u>Christian</u>: "Actions, like to lie or steal."
  <u>Brahman priest</u>: You forget an important one—to kill animals being the greatest sin. "Even in a drop of water or germs within disease there is life, are animals." He quoted from the Vedas.
  <u>Christian</u>: "Rather than argue, let's consider problems of justice and peace or fellowship with the True God."
  <u>Brahman priest</u>: "You stop killing animals and eating meat; then we can agree to pursue other issues."
- From "Class Notes" (about Hinduism) – Eastern Mennonite College 1968, Box 2, folder 42, pp. 7-9

A person meets sincere, devout people in all faiths.

A Hindu temple or shrine houses idols. When one who worships idols stored on a "god shelf" at home becomes a Christian, such idols or magic paraphernalia is thrown out or burned.

God is at work in world religions; God hears non-Christians when they pray, Graber adds.

Asked whether people are saved without Christ, Graber responds that God is the judge and makes no mistakes whereas people are not God; they lack full light.

- "I am the Way, the Truth, the Life" in Box 4, folder 29, p. 5
  Way – Within Hinduism are many gurus, pilgrimages, holy places, temples, priests, and offerings. Their ways, methods, and superstitions fail to enable God's light or presence.
  Truth – Christians deny the Hindu belief that "all roads or religions lead to God." Hinduism finds truth in all religions; they cannot understand the church's exclusive claims for Christ. They believe in many incarnations; Jesus being one.
  Life – Jesus extends eternal life, provides power to avoid hell.

Graber, Lena (MC) – HM I 380, Box 1, Folder 2, Mennonite Church USA Archives, Goshen, Indiana.   Missioner nurse Lena's letter to Esther Graber on August 17, 1947.[3]

"Well, India's Independence Day has been celebrated!" Graber exclaims in her letter written two days after the big event. Characterized as "nice celebrations" Graber was impressed by the overall tone of solemnity— "I guess the final realization of the responsibility is sobering."

Details of the brightly decorated Dhamtari town (population toward 20,000 then) and the day's experience, for which "Mrs. King and I wore saris," included:

Many people were awake through the night, "making ready."

First parade began at 4:30 a.m.

Flag-raising at 7:00 at the high school with all present saluting while it was pulled up the pole.

Parade to the grounds near the government buildings where more flag-raising; ("Typically, ropes were not fixed right.")

Back at the Mennonite schools at 2:30: all received sweets that were distributed by the *Taksildar*.

At the 3:30 special church service: Dr. Jonathan Yoder gave a very fitting speech titled "Ye are the salt of the earth."

Graber then celebrated further by going with Yoders to Rudri for a picnic. "We got into a large parade with all kinds of floats, placards, and *beil garries* (ox carts) en route. One float was outstanding with Pundit Nehru's picture being fanned; horns of *beil* were all painted." That night there were *diyas*, just like at *divali* holiday time. One store had an arch with brass pots piled high. Dhamtari 'big shots' wore ties; only Joseph Mukut [among Mennonites?] donned the typical "Congress cap," Graber adds. Missioners bought a flag and Graber bought peanuts to distribute among the school children. Students presented a program at the school which they had spent time decorating. A government man came to oversee the school celebrations; he was "surprised that missioner George Beare already had a flag and pole."

That the new Indian government at Delhi took over at midnight "reflected a typically Indian way," Graber says. She presumes that Gandhi was indeed grateful to see this day; he was living in a disturbed area of Calcutta at the time. Hoping that fighting is now over, she acknowledges that new government officials discussed "peace and its value" at their first meeting.

"Villagers don't seem to know what it's all about," she adds

See historian **C. J. Dyck's** (GC) account about Lena Graber (MC) in *Twelve Becoming Biographies of Mennonite Disciples from 16-20th Century* (Newton, Kansas: Faith and Life Pr, 1973) 97-108.
After a decade of being a nurse and Nursing School superintendent at the Dhamtari Christian Hospital in central India, Graber accepted the invitation in 1959 to begin a nurses' training school in Kathmandu, the capital of Nepal. Dyck includes Graber's description of patients cared for and distinct correctives for problems, such as villagers' use of cow's urine because it is thought to have sacred power. She met Nepal's charming Queen and King; he is known as a reincarnation of the Hindu god Vishnu. After death, Hindus have their cremated ashes thrown into a nearby river that flows into the Ganges River in India, Dyck reports.

Jantzen, Lubin. (GC) "From Landour to Champa in Disturbed India," *India Calling* GC Mennonite Newsletter (ix/iv, December 1947) 4
In August of 1947 when India formally gained independence from Britain, Muslim leader Mohammed Ali Jinnah persuaded officials to allow Indian Muslims to form a separate country, Jantzen explains. In the dreadful process of transition called Partition thousands of Hindus and Sikhs needed to leave their homeland to move into India while Muslims from India needed to shift with comparable meager belongings to their newly designated areas of East and West Pakistan. On meeting each other en route and triggered by latent, religious hatred, perhaps a million people died.

Lubin and Tillie Jantzen were involved in Hindi language study that August in Mussoorie, located in the foothills of the northern Himalaya Mountains.[4] Their Muslim vegetable sellers disappeared, fearful for safety. Sikhs and Hindus were known to loot Muslim shops and to threaten or kill owners. Busloads of people careened over mountain sides, some of those 'accidents' perhaps planned. From their hillside height Jantzens observed Muslim villages on the plains below in flames. Eager to return to Champa in central India, Jantzen reports delays for diverse missioners on their journey home. The journey included 'living' in a train station in the city of Dehra Dun (where over a thousand people had been killed) for ten days, grateful for U.S. army surplus tins of food and two station rooms in which seventeen people slept. Their experience provided new empathy for all refugees, most of whom know worse conditions. After bridges were repaired trains could again move; the travelers then found their next main stop, the Calcutta train station, "flooded with Hindu refugees."[5]

Jantzen, Lubin and Tillie (GC). *Guided Lives, Memoirs of a Mennonite Missionary Couple to India. An Autobiography*, (Newton, KS: Mennonite Pr. Inc. 2004).
After background chapters that introduce their broader Jantzen and Mueller families, this couple provides pleasant reporting. Their chapters alternate between traditional, prayer-oriented dedication to mission "station" efforts while living in India with blocks of time spent in the States called 'furlough.' Both Jantzens write the account; more is reported about Lubin's engagement as school administrator, evangelist, and financial treasurer for the Mission than about Tillie's use of time while in India. Later, in 1972 Lubin spent four months' time transferring Mission property rights to Evangelical Trust Association of North India.

Although living in a predominant Hindu context, little discussion of Hindu practice, belief, festivals, or friendship with Hindus appears. Aware that individuals convert to Christianity, with brief reference to "mass movements," readers learn little about people's prior religious loyalty. How Indians previously practiced sacred rituals or how prior views or meanings continued to influence lives does not appear. Perhaps Jantzens presumed that readers would have little interest in that prevailing context. Their limited reference to Hinduism receives focus here. For example, in telling about the destruction by fire of the Christian Gass Memorial Center in Raipur (which Center Mennonites frequented when in that city for business or travel) one sentence implies cause. "The State inquiry showed that the rumor about kicking the idol, which had infuriated some Hindus, was completely false." (170)

The Jantzens' accounts can be confessional or respectful. The Edward Ambrose family lived with Jantzens at Janjgir while Ambrose did his PhD research in Asia Studies from the University of Pennsylvania. Ambrose' research enabled his being better informed about caste issues and more aware of Janjgir society than were missioners, Jantzens report. He helped missioners understand local church members who had come "from two quite different caste backgrounds before becoming Christians." (223-24)

One direct reference to a Hindu involves Lubin's seeing the noted, Indian social reform leader Vinoba Bhave when in the city of Raipur. Like his friend Mahatma Gandhi, Bhave walked extensively to carry concerns of his Gramdan and Bhoodan Movement. Jantzen and several teachers from Janjgir were grateful to see this leader who "worked to get rich landowners interested and willing to donate some of their land to poor citizens of India to enable them to earn a living by farming, or for land to build their homes." (219)

Two other themes with Hindu influence that Jantzens describe are village property patterns and rituals that follow death.[6] The former makes caste difference clear. High-caste Brahmans lived in a village's center followed in the next round of homes by rulers and chiefs. Merchants and craftsmen occupied the next ring of dwellings; beyond them lived farmers and cattle raisers. Outcaste people who fulfilled other tasks—like water carrying, wood cutting, or serving as day laborers—lived near to the edge if not outside a village. Often with no place for Christian Indians within that caste scheme, they and missioners might settle beyond village outskirts, Jantzens explain. (266)

Reporting the death of a Hindu man who worked in their Mission school, Jantzens knew the importance of body disposal on the same day as death. (240-41) A Hindu priest performed last rights in Mr. Venkateshan's home before men present followed the bier (village bed) with Venkateshan's body to the river. After a pyre of logs was formed on the sandy shore, the naked body and then more logs were added to the pyre; *ghee* (clarified butter) was also shaken on it. Holding an earthen pot of water, the Hindu priest circled the pyre multiple times before, with a sharp stone, tapping the pot to let the water leak out while he kept circling. Emptied, the pot was thrown by the priest to the ground. Once the logs were set on fire the oldest son struck the body's head to release its spirits. When only ashes remained they were tossed into the river.[7] Jantzens' later visit with Mrs. Venkateshan and family was appreciated, they report.

Kaufman, J. N. (MC) HM I-356 Boxes with Folders, Mennonite Church USA Archives, Goshen, IN.

Kaufman began his thirty-four years in India in 1905. He married Elsie Drange in India in 1908; she died in 1939 in the US. Over the years Kauffman served 240 boys in the orphanage, was manager for the home with patients who had leprosy,was a bishop, and mission treasurer. In 1941 he married Dr. Lillie Shenk who had been a missioner in Africa. They together served in India from 1945-48. References to Hinduism recur within archival box materials.

- Box 1, folder 18
  "Despite sin and superstition and ignorance rampant in the land, India is full of beauty in nature."
- Box 2, folder 1
  All animals were thought to be sacred due to transmigration of a person from life to life based on the principle: "as you have sown, so you will reap."
- Box 2, folder 9

Indians are primarily religionists, Mohammedan or Hindu, Kaufman observes . . . In order to force the British government to concede to Indian ambitions, they have conceived of the use of non-cooperation, Kaufman explains. They wish to have nothing to do with a foreign government. They seem to paralyze the government—like advocate resigning positions and boycotting. Mr. Gandhi and Ali Brothers are the leading spirits in this non-cooperation movement; others fail to understand.

Both Hindus and Muslims have always resisted the onslaught of Christianity or western civilization . . . increased national consciousness regarding foreign Christians appears . . . Hindus acknowledge the truth of all religions . . . When a national resolution "urged foreign missionaries to quit India" Kaufman created a questionnaire to give to 22 Indian Christian leaders of the Mennonite community. Fourteen honest, straight forward replies encouraged them not to quit, he says.

Gandhi wrote on 23 April 1931: "Certainly the great faiths (not meaning Christianity and Judaism) are held by the people of India to be adequate. India stands in no need of conversion from one faith to another."

"Revival of Religion at Dhamtari" 1 p - All activities are understood within terms of religion, Kaufman says. Dhamtari has numerous Hindu temples—sufficient for all varied Hindu sects. Formerly neglected, temples are being renovated with new "godlets" being set up along with new temples. The "Billai Mata" temple, devoted to the smallpox goddess, is being enlarged with a new tower of stone masonry, largely the gift of a pious Hindu woman, Kaufman explains. The Mohammedan "praying place" (mosque) has several times been enlarged to accommodate the "faithful." A new mosque several stories high is the biggest structure in town. . . . Hindu religious acts that accumulate merit for the person include giving offerings to priests or gifts and donations for new temples. With no active attempt to "boycott" our Christian religion, we believe that revival will work to favor the church, he says

"Mahanadi – The New Evangelistic Station" - To get to the village of Mahanadi the Mahanadi River bed needs to be crossed. Wishing to save his engine as much as possible, Kaufman previously arranged with a Hindu owner for a buffalo team to pull him across the river. While the buffalos worked their way across the hot sands with a strange load, the engine rested. The friendly Hindu landlord who furnished the team of buffalo refused rupees (payment) for the help and offered to send his team any time needed. All he wanted was "my well wishes."

• "Emergency Three Years in India" – 1945-48 – Box 2, folder 4
Kaufman reports about sugar being rationed, train strikes, and communal (religious) riots, as when five thousand were killed and 10,000-30,000 wounded during one five-day period. Muslim leader Jinnah desired that Muslims and Hindus have separate nations—India and Pakistan—after Independence. In Kaufman's eighteen-page account of this three year period, his only other direct reference to Indian religion is about the Hindu Divali holiday.

• Letter to Prime Minister Jawaharlal Nehru – 5/18/57
Kaufman thanks Nehru for the "favorable mention" of Mennonite, Quaker, and Church of the Brethren in an American religious press release.

> As Prime Minister you are serving your people with significant success. As a lover of India, I pray for your continued success and recommend to you with all my heart the Christ "Whose I am and whom I serve."
> Signed, Bishop J. N. Kaufman.

Lall, K. Jiwan. (MC) "The Hindu Home," *The Youth's Christian Companion,* July 31, 1949, 659.
Although Lall acknowledges that great change had followed what he describes, annotations reflect characteristics at the time when he grew up in a Hindu home. Whereas a woman was to be chaste and loyal to her one husband, husbands were free to have more than one wife. As part of his property a wife was to "live and die" for him, to know him as her god through whom she gained salvation. Lall reports also that Tulsidas, the Hindu poet writer of the great Hindu Ramayana epic, justified a husband's despising or mistreating a wife. Multiplicity of children could lead to poverty and to contention within a family, he adds. The exalted father performed religious ceremonies and engaged in festivals. Lall recalls washing his grandfather's feet to be forgiven of sin; he also became a disciple of a *sadhu* (holy man) as his *guru (teacher)* at age twelve. Lall contrasts his understandings about home life after becoming a Christian.

Lapp, George Jay. (MC) HM I – 143, Multiple boxes with folders Mennonite Church USA Archives, Goshen, IN. Several boxes in this collection contain articles alphabetized. For example, those with titles beginning with *A-B* appear in box 4, folder 9 while titles *D-E* appear in box 4, folder 14.

Lapp and wife Esther (Ebersole) arrived as missioners to India in 1905. They returned for a first furlough in 1912. Both Esther and daughter Pauline later died in India; Lapp includes accounts of those experiences. He later married Fannie Hershey; they eventually left India in 1945. Lapp's informative writing includes both human interest incidents and appreciation for his disciplined study of Hindu thought and practice. An intellectual and alert observer, Lapp wrote for diverse occasions and in numerous journals. He knew about caste, transmigration of the soul, Hindu scriptures and mythology, philosophical schools, religious fears, and Hindu practice with images and festivals. He valued Hindu *pandits* (teachers) for missioners when they studied Hindi, and he promoted ecumenical ties. During his forty years in India, Lapp absorbed religious and cultural features at a profound level; his writing communicates them effectively. Some details—like the town name of *Dhamtari* being from *Dharam Tarai* meaning "collection of religious devotion"—are briefly noted; other aspects deserve more extensive annotation.

Box 5 includes copies of numerous book reviews written by Lapp, his visits with notable Indian men and women, and details from his memoirs. He understood a great deal about India—its culture, religion, and people—those from whom he learned and with whom he shared faith. He wrote articles for several series that appeared in the MC *Gospel Herald*: "Refreshing Streams of Living Water" and "The Unusual in Missionary Experience." "On the Gripsholm" reports his journey via ship to the US after serving 40 years in India.

Lapp's visit to the site of Pandita Ramabai's noted efforts with more than 1500 Hindu widows in Kedgaon (south of Bombay) took place in 1907. Widows benefited from printing, weaving, handiwork, and cooking schools, Lapp observed. Indian Ramabai, who had experienced lengthy pilgrimage with her Hindu parents, was at the time of Lapp's visit translating the Bible into the Marathi language, based in her study of Greek and Hebrew. More than two thousand people sat on the floor for Sunday morning worship with Ramabai leading. A "blessing" that Lapp noted from his visit was Ramabai's modesty as she, through prayer and patience, "waited for God in the context of opposition." She enabled unfortunate people without a word about her eternal reward.

Another encounter of Lapp's occurred in 1912 with Sadhu Sundar Singh an Indian, former Sikh. Like early, secret believers Sundar Singh met with others for early prayer (complete prostration) and scripture study. He walked extensively and provided a living example for meeting people of diverse religions. When asked by an Indian Hindu priest to prove that "Jesus was the only savior," Lapp noted the Sadhu's response. Instead of presenting "proof," he validated the priest as a sincere "inquirer after truth" who carried the "burden of proof" of his own question. The Sadhu "blessed" Lapp as a poised, courteous example of Jesus his Master—a saint.

In Lapp's "Memoirs of an India Missionary" written as a series for *Youth Christian Companion* journal, chapter VII is titled "Learning— Religious Observations." Lapp carefully read Walkin's *Hindu Mythology*, Dubois' *Hindu Manners, Customs and Ceremonies*, a section of Max Mueller's *Collected Works* about Hinduism's six philosophical systems, and more. Intent to enable future work in India, "to adapt his approach to Christian witness," Lapp directly observed practices of diverse Hindu, Muslim, Gond (tribal folk), and gypsies, in their homes and temples.

Aware of Hindu longing for an end to transmigration of the soul at death, to be finally absorbed into "the sea of eternal existence," Lapp watched ceremonies for birth, marriage, or death as well as holiday festivals. How Hindus might venerate their ancestors in animals became clear during the "Piter Pakshe" holiday, he says. People might garland, paint, and feed specially cooked food to their cattle during that day set aside to symbolically honor forebears. The idea of transmigration of the soul of a dead relative prompted such concern; Hindu priests led worship exercises to promote such occasions of remembrance.

Lapp judged some Hindu practices as less than worthy. Their "religious response" to an unusual phenomenon like an eclipse of the moon, which they credited to a good or evil deity, could prompt them to make intense noise to frighten away the god. A Brahman asked Lapp to shoot an owl that hooted repeatedly on his roof. The Brahman presumed that the owl was intent to learn family names in order to cause their death. When Lapp explained how "people are in God's hands," the man left disappointed. Lapp wished for Christians to bring a higher ethical dimension to life, so that fear and superstition could not cause such delusion. Lapp also grew sensitive to the "hold" that a heritage of spirit worship could have on those who later followed Jesus.

Lapp names two other specific problems for some new converts: the person who was married to more than one spouse prior to choosing to follow Jesus and the sincere believer in Christ who wished to continue to be an idol maker. The ancestral tradition of using molten brass or copper to make images of gods provided good income, Lapp learned.

Lapp emphasized thorough Bible training for Christians, in part to deal with opposition. He describes Hindu mendicants who—with long hair often spiraled at the top of their head, scant clothing, and their body covered with ash or dust—would sit tailor fashion by a river or under a tree to teach or pronounce a blessing upon devotees who passed by. Such a *sadhu* or "holy" man might have been a disciple of a religious teacher for years. Lapp adds further that such ascetics may have memorized entire sections of sacred Hindu writings—Vedas,

Ramayana epic or Bhagavad Gita. Hindus have little respect for religionists who fail to know their sacred writings; they reflect "great pride in showing sacred books handed down" Lapp adds.

Lapp also gave attention to cultural customs linked with religion. For example, he avoided using the left hand for work above the waist—as to greet another—while he used the left hand to take off his shoes or do 'unclean' work. He avoided touching high caste people and was careful about drinking water or dealing with raw vegetables. Lapp's articles found in box 4, folder 13 include material about India's musical, poetic Hindu expression. The noted epics—Ramayana and Mahabharata—might be sung. Or *sanyasis, sadhus*, or pandits might lead the masses to approach every act or relationship with sacred devotion. A village priest might be thought to receive oracles of the gods that he then needed to interpret for people.

From Lapp's articles starting F-H in box 4, folder 15 is one titled "Gandhi's Gospel." Gandhi clearly opposed people being called "Untouchables"; he preferred the label "Children of God." While he valued Jesus' Sermon on the Mount,' Gandhi confessed: that he "receives more spiritual help from the Gita; that salvation for him is possible only through the Hindu religion; that he opposed telling others about personal faith with intent to convert the other," Lapp quotes.

Occasions for reflection mark Lapp's writing. In box 4, folder 16 appears an article titled "What have the years 1905-45 in India Taught and Wrought" written for *Mennonite Weekly Review* readers. First, he said that the years taught that, "due to misguided religious loyalty, [many] people of India have become socially and morally depraved." For example, through his reading of sacred, ancient writings like Vedas, Upanishads, and Mahabharata epic, a part of which is the Gita, he found a thread of depravity and fatalism. Second, from such a mentality India can be emancipated. and third, the church will assist such evil forces to diminish. Other articles focus on "Questions and Answers," "Problems and Possibilities." In the latter Lapp reports a nine-day hike over the Himalaya mountain foothills to the west and north of Darjeeling. On the fourth morning as the hikers watched the sun rise and clouds nestled in the valleys dissipate, Mt. Everest and Mt. Kinchun Junga opened in full view before them. Their shout "What hath God wrought!" contrasted with some mountain dwellers whose incantations more likely indicated fear for spirits thought possibly to be in the same hills and stones.

Content in folder 25 of box 4 conveys Lapp's view of deeply religious Indian nationals. His study revealed that every detail of life for them was to be done religiously—eat, work, sleep, die—that every means of livelihood possessed some power. Among liberal-minded religious leaders, including Christians, Lapp encouraged their joining to study each others' religious systems in order to contribute to each others' cause. He calls all to remain empathetic to the good seen in all religions but, without compromise, to stand for the right—for salvation from sin. God forms worshipped are often feared; homage is rendered to avert calamity due to their wrath. Idols become mediums of communication with deities that they represent. That "no god of love" is found in non-Christian religious systems seems, to this writer, a more negative judgment than usually characterizes missioner Lapp. But it appears here and again in box 3, folder 1 when he suggests that Hindu philosophy "ignores the idea of God being love and incites worship through fear."

Reflecting something of the breadth of missioner Lapp's writing is a two-page piece titled "The Order of the Star of the East." (III-53) He explains that this "Order" is known as the Theosophical Society in India. Lapp saw theosophists in America, England or Australia to "clothe their contentions in Christian garb" while those in Ceylon (Sri Lanka) utilized Buddhist 'garb' and in India avowedly Hindu or a mixture of Buddhism and Hinduism. Annie Besant's strong English influence in India inculcates Christian ethics along with Indian views of caste, idolatry, astrology and transmigration of souls. While Lapp says that the name "The Order of the Star of the East" suggests cooperation of liberal forces from all religions, he believes that only Christ's teachings, not a person like J. Khrishnamurti of Adyar, India, can bring needed change.

Notes for a course that Lapp taught in 1948 for professor Pannebecker's class at the Mennonite Biblical Seminary (GC) in Chicago appear in box 2, folder 20. His outline identifies: India's Geography, the Ancient period including early Aryan religion of the Vedic type, Hindu and Mohammedan periods, British East India and Modern History. The latter segment includes: India's Religions, Christianity, Nationalism, and Present conditions and Personalities.

Lapp, George Jay. (MC) *The Christian Church and Rural India*. (Calcutta: YMCA Publ House, 1938).

Lapp, George J. (MC) *Our Mission in India.* (Scottdale, PA: Mennonite Publ House, 1921). Chapter 1 titled "This is India," section III of 19 pages, as found in Mennonite Church USA Archives box 3, folder 13 includes content similar to this book as does another, likely early draft titled "Religious and Social Customs." Notes about Hinduism are lifted from the three versions.

Lapp explains that Hindu religion—based on ancient Vedas, two epics, philosophical writings, plus ritualistic observances through worship— later shifted to veneration of certain deities represented by images. These combined to form the base of India's idolatrous system. He quotes an unnamed writer:

We worship the Deity with symbols when we bow before an idol. But we worship the power or virtue or characteristic for which the idol stands. In showing our veneration for cattle or reptiles or other animal life we think of them as representing some force or energy possessed by the Almighty. We believe in universal soul force which pervades all creation and therefore leads us to worship and venerate all forms of life.

Lapp understands that statement to be true for educated Hindus while poor, more ignorant Hindus accept the idols themselves as objects of worship. He suggests that Brahmin priests can deceive ignorant "heathen" worshippers to think that they (priests) "consecrate" images—give life and power to the idol itself through garlanding and blowing into their ears and mouths—knowing full well that they do not. Priests expect suitable offerings and gifts for themselves in turn or so that worshippers avoid a god's anger. Lapp identifies a few gods and goddesses like Rama, Shiva and Sita, like Kali the goddess of blood and fertility, or like Ganesh who is honored with a yearly, major procession from the Jaggernath temple in Puri. After investigating the real origin of images Lapp concludes that "idolatry has developed unspeakable traditional customs on poor, depraved worshippers." Bindranath is just one of the great places for Hindu pilgrimage that he notes.

Lapp discusses the four general caste groups. He explains how deeds that Hindus perform lead to a nobler or more disdained next birth; he knows also the holiday that honors ancestors. Then follow other features of Hindu thought and practice: the sacredness of all forms of life, limited intermarriage between castes, vegetarian diet, and worship patterns. With little corporate gathering, many temples and shrines remain ever-open for individuals. Home altars are used daily too. Hinduism involves for many Indians worship or fear of evil spirits, spirits and demons to be guarded against lurking almost anywhere.

Lapp sees how deep-seated, religious prejudice can become difficult to counter. Yet, infiltrated by other religions, Hindu practice has been reformed in waves by devout men and women, he says. A twelfth century, southern reformer named Ramanuja tried to "supplant idolatry by spreading the teachings of mystical idealism." In 1772 Raja Ram Mohan Roy of eastern India faulted idolatry and called for social reforms such as allowing remarriage for widows. A progressive follower of Roy's named Keshab Chundra Sen carried on his reforms after 1857. But opposition to reforms followed as with the Arya-Samaj group that promoted ancient Hindu Vedic teachings and radical corruption. Lapp judges Hinduism as resistant to "progress." He then provides information about Indian experience with Muslims, Buddhists, Lamaists (fusion of Buddhism and Hinduism in Tibet), Sikhs, Parsees (when driven out of Persia), Jains, Jews (likely in India as far back as the time of Solomon), and different groups of Christians.

Lehman, M. C. (MC) *Our Mission Work in India* (Elkhart, IN: Mennonite Board of Missions and Charities, 1939).

Perhaps 1800 years Before the Common Era, passages appeared in sacred books of those who later came to be known as Hindus. Such texts "graphically describe the extermination of barbarians (aborigines now known mostly as Dravidians) by civilized (Aryan) races." Lehman identifies details of principle documents of Hinduism as:

1. The One yet Many concept of deity: three major god forms named Brahma, Vishnu, and Siva along with sub deities and incarnations.
2. Written texts: belief in four Vedas—Rig, Atharva, Sama, and Yajur—in addition to Brahmanas, Puranas, Upanishads, the epics called Ramayana and Mahabarata, and Suras.
3. Transmigration of the soul up or down within the caste system, is determined by *karma*. Lehman explains how *karma* results from good or evil actions.
4. Final salvation: rebirths, in part through observing caste rules, until released into oneness with Brahma.
5. Obedience to what religious teachers (*gurus*) teach.
6. Worship of gods, sacrifice, and observance of ceremonies required with holidays. (10-11)

Lehman exposes readers—primarily Mennonites in the United States and Canada—to the religious context for those engaged in "mission endeavor" in India. He commends and integrates knowledge of what centrally matters in India. He introduces realities that both differ from and resemble missioner attention to doctrines. Both God-concept and salvation matter, writes Lehman; how each is explained is important in a missioner's presentation. For a missioner to tell biblical stories without listening to and learning from Hinduism's two main epics creates a gap in understanding. Lehman proposes two steps: 1. Effective communication of Christian thought to God's people immersed in Hindu belief and culture, and 2. A new capacity among western Christians to examine their convictions in light of Hindu thought.

A few notations from Lehman reflect further his encounter with Hindu thought or practice:

•   Dr. Page (MC) noticed that when a Hindu patient was about to die, relatives brought a calf to the bedside and put its tail into the patient's hand. Because of Hindu belief in the cow as sacred, the intent with the tail is to assure a safe transition of the person's soul into a higher caste. So also one who repeats an oath after a judge in court might hold onto a cow's tail. (20)

- Motivation for Hindu work focuses on personal merit gained or assistance for holy beggars. Some pondered how white foreigners gave aid to famine sufferers, those overlooked by Brahman priests. The few rich Hindus in villages, from which orphans went to food distribution places assisted by missioners, seemed far less concerned with the fate of such children, Lehman suggests. (39)
- Thousands of Hindus might gather for a *mela* (religious fair) at a famous temple on the Mahanadi River bank near Dhamtari Lehman observed. After performing a ceremonial bath they entered the temple to give rice or offerings to different gods, hoping for good crops or protection from problems in return. On most occasions Hindus worshipped more privately at a temple or in one room of their homes reserved for an idol and worship segments. Colored paint might be used for putting a caste mark on the person's forehead. That Christians worshiped as a *group*, as early on in a grove of mango trees, seemed a novelty to Hindus who observed, Lehman says. (30-31, 36)
- He also notes changes in Hindu perceptions. Whereas on hearing early mission speakers, Hindus might judge the gospel as preached "not *true*," that phrase shifted to "not *new*" when educated Hindus realized that principles in their own *Shastra* (scriptures) were similar. Then on learning about western cultural wealth or lack of care for the poor, they shifted to a third slogan: "Christianity is not *you*." (110-11)

Missionaries. (MC) "Experiences" in *Building on The Rock*. First Quarter Century Mission Work of American Mennonite Mission, Dhamtari, C.P. India 1899-1924. (Scottdale, PA: Mennonite Publ House 1926), 154-73.

Moyer, S. T. (GC) *They Heard the Call*. (Newton, KS: Faith and Life Pr, 1970).This resource honors twelve missioners. The collection of Samuel Tyson Moyer and Metta (Habegger) Moyer materials appear as MLA.MS 105 in 6 boxes at Mennonite Library and Archives, Bethel College, North Newton, KS.

The Moyers served as GC missioners in India from 1920-1956. Several anecdotes related to Hinduism from this resource follow.

P. A. Penner met a high-caste Brahman law student who needed treatment for leprosy. On learning that no conditions were required for staying at the Leprosy Home, except permission from staff to leave the patient area to go into the village of Champa, the man joined others who had the disease. He cooked his own food. Having never missed a church service, the Brahman died without choosing to follow Christ "but having heard the gospel frequently" Moyer adds. (21)

When Penners left India from Calcutta to retire in 1949 they visited the famous Kali temple dedicated to the goddess of destruction. Walking through the temple grounds they heard "Mamaji! Mamaji! Don't you know me?" Running to meet Penners, an ash-daubed, dirty *sadhu* reported being a former *Tahsildar* (top revenue officer of the civil division) of Janjgir where Penners then lived. Having become weary of the world he had become a *sadhu*. . . ."You have truly shown the love of the true God. Every Indian [whom you met] was your child," he said as they parted. (71)

Moyer reports that when looking for an area to locate a mission program, missioner C. H. Suckau either inadvertently struck with a cane or spoke against the powerlessness of a particular idol. In that act he so desecrated the image that a nearby priest pronounced a curse upon him. When he became deathly sick with a severe case of tropical fever, Hindus considered his condition hopeless. Newly aware of satanic powers permitted by God, even toward death, Suckau developed a new trust for a text from Job: "Only spare his life." He declared that never again would he "flaunt the powers of darkness." (76)

Moyer, S. T. (GC) *With Christ on the Edge of the Jungles*. (Berne, IN: The Mennonite Book Concern, 1941).

Again, Moyer includes numerous anecdotes to convey his story. Again also this resource draws on Hindu-related episodes or thought.

"I saw the power of Christ on the edge of those jungles" confesses Moyer. Examples of superstition, often due to ignorance, occur in Indian village settings, Moyer reports. For example, a pregnant woman who died during her pregnancy was not to be buried within village borders. Her soul, taking the form of an evil spirit, might continue to torment all activity in the village. (77)

Cholera and death inevitably followed monsoon rains that washed unhealthy materials from the countryside into village reservoirs. People might presume that a village witch or wizard had cast a spell on their village, causing gods or goddesses to bring a scourge. (11)

After praying for months for a son, a villager named Kongalu feared intensely when his two-month old son Yohun became sick with smallpox, Moyer explains. Village Hindus believed that since the great goddess Mata was displeased, smallpox cases occurred in the village. They suggested getting milk from a herdsman in which to wash the baby's feet before praying to Mata for mercy. They resented that Christians no longer gave offerings to Mata or other gods; that Kongalu prayed to Jesus the Christ angered them. Two days later, when

Kongalu's son recovered with no pox marks on his skin, fearful Hindus said, "Your God is most wonderful; even goddess Mata fears you Christians." (76-77)

A Hindu couple had waited ten years for a child; they grew fearful when their first son became ill. Who would release the parents from "purgatory" at the time of their deaths if he died? Guniya, a man known to combine native medicines and poisons with belief in evil spirits, applied a 'remedy.' A few hours later a funeral was held. (53-54)

Moyer offered a ride to a high-caste man carrying a baby. Soon Moyer offered a low-caste Christian a ride in the front seat with him. At that point the man in the back seat left the vehicle; the "untouchable" rider would defile him. (53)

Nothing reflects Christian faith to Hindu neighbors like an Easter morning celebration. Christians gather in hope, at sunrise, near where a family member had been buried. They sing resurrection hymns and read the resurrection text from the Bible. Hindus are surprised to learn that "Christians expect to meet those who have died beyond the grave." (79)

A new convert, when building a new house, chose not to install a window. Caste Hindus might persecute him for presuming "to get uppish," for thinking himself of worth like they, he told Moyer. (84)

Moyer includes a lengthy account of having learned to avoid robbing local police of their honor, their "izzit." He had openly withstood them in the process of defending a poor, homeless, Christian girl who had been physically abused. (118-25)

Nafziger, Florence. (MC) "Temples I Have Visited in India," *The Youth's Christian Companion*, (July 31, 1949) 658, 664. Annotations then follow from Nafziger's archival materials, HM I-175, Mennonite Church Archives, Goshen, IN.

Missioner nurse and educator Nafziger characterizes the sights—open shops along the road, coolies carrying heavy loads, and dirty children playing in the dust—of the ancient city of Calcutta as "magic." Inside its outer wall next to well-laid-out walkways stood the Jain temple with three towers. Going to the largest of three temples Nafziger removed her shoes before ascending wide, white marble stairs. Inside the temple's center sat the goddess form surrounded with a fence. Near her feet lay money; above her hung a huge, glittering cut-glass chandelier. Nothing mystical seemed to mark the sophisticated city folk who thronged the garden and temples. Near a pink lotus pool was a little gate into an area noted for a small brick building with a large "fat-bellied (sign of prosperity) idol with the head of an elephant and superhuman four hands." This Ganesh form, "ugly" in Nafziger's view, is thought by adherents to bring success by removing all obstacles. A legend surrounds the form: One day when god Shiva was away on a hunting trip his wife created a small boy form out of mud to sit on guard near the door of their house. Since that form refused to let Shiva enter on his return, Shiva struck off its head. To appease his wife, Shiva ordered a messenger to "bring the head of the first living thing seen." Clapping an elephant's head onto the boy's body, Shiva restored its life before returning him to his wife, Nafziger learned.

Behind a tea stall and bazaar in a garden near the edge of Dhamtari's watering tank, where people might wash themselves and clothes or animals, stood a small, whitewashed, two-roomed temple surrounded by an iron fence. Inside Nafziger and friend saw pictures of god and goddess forms on the walls and a large, ancient-looking cobra god form carved into the stone floor. That cobra form reminded her of ancient religion. When walking in the grassy garden they met an old caretaker working with flowers, no doubt out of fear or love for the god. He scolded them for not having removed their shoes.

Having located in the village of Ghatula with other missioners Nafziger climbed a hill behind their bungalow to see the plains beyond. Nearby were two watering tanks and a whitewashed temple with courtyard. Waiting for a priest to come from his house beside the temple to permit them to enter, they removed their shoes. Inside the oriental styled temple with an open front they saw seated in a small niche in the wall forms of king Ram, revered by many in the area, his faithful wife Sita, and Lakshmi. Nearby was a two-foot-long bed with a quilt. The priest explained the bed as the place where the gods are put to sleep each night. Temple bells are rung and a conch shell blown each evening at bedtime and each morning to awaken the gods. Nafziger wonders whom the adherents depend on to protect them during the night. She left thinking about their simple yet sincere devotion, within what she considered "deluded faith."

In Nafziger's archival materials appear brief references to Hindu thought or practice. Her autobiography titled "My Walk with God" (1999) reflects on her years (1946-1984) as a missioner nurse and educator in India's cultural context. She notes having visited the Kali Temple and Mother Teresa's original home for the dying in Calcutta and having ridden the narrow-gauge train between Dhamtari and Raipur—a trip that took five hours to go the fifty miles. She recalls a sign that she saw inside the train car: "If the wind blows strongly, please open the windows so the cars don't upset."

Nafziger writes in detail. She discusses the Hindu view of sacred cows with her first *pandit*—Hindi language teacher—a member of upper-caste barbers. He commended her for doing such good work among the poor: "In her next life she might possibly be born into the Hindu caste system." "Deliver me from that," she wrote. She notes the area's "endless Hindu shrines with their numerous idols," the end of the

Diwali season to celebrate the victory of light over darkness, or good over evil, and the god form Krishna being "all decked out" for a drama. She kept a diary in a small notebook with a photo of Krishna and his consort Radha on the front cover. Having observed religious plurality, she notes "seeing all kinds of things in the bible not seen before."

From medical practice Nafziger observes: "Never a day without abscess to open.". . . Some patients fear taking medicine from a foreigner. . . . Most patients were Hindus, Muslims, or Sikhs. . . . Student nurses—who studied for three-years with an option for a further year for midwifery or compounding (pharmacy)—often didn't at first know how to read well. . . . Nafziger's first meal in a Hindu home followed her delivery of a son to the family. . . . Her years in India after 1973 were given to teaching in a school for graduate nurses at Indore, India.

Peters, Gerhard Wilhelm. (MB) I. "The Telugu Field of South India," in *The Growth of Foreign Missions in the Mennonite Brethren Church.* (Hillsboro, KS: Board of Foreign Missions, MB, 1947) 134-207.

While Peters explains the broader "mission minded" nature of MB people and identifies tasks accomplished by numerous individuals, annotations here turn to his discussion of Hindu influence in the south India state of Andhra Pradesh where the Telegu language dominates.[8]

Peters believes that astute readers can grow in respect for as well as benefit from the spiritual outlook of Indian philosophy and religious literature as found in the Rig Veda and Upanishads. He understands Hinduism among Telugu people in a broad sense; it combines southern, ancient Dravidian with northern Aryan aspects. While some worship Ganesha the elephant-headed god form of Wisdom or Hanuman the monkey-god, more Telugus give attention to local deities of Dravidian heritage, Peters explains. Each village may designate its own god with practices linked to nature, animal, ancestor, demon, or spirit worship. Support for the great temples, where Brahmanic priests serve Aryan gods born in "the abode of the gods," are visited mostly for festival days or by those loyal to Krishna, an incarnation of the Aryan Vishnu. Peters also explains god Siva's influence through lofty philosophy, *bhakti* (more theistic devotion), and his consort Kali, whose "revolting look" is meant to inspire fear. (143-46)

In addition to a vital god-concept among Telugu folk, Peters explains other religious concepts within Hinduism. He expresses empathy and appreciation for religious Telugu people despite their fears and superstition, their perhaps "twisted" concepts of deity. (147-49)
Important terms to know:
Vedas – sacred writings divided between *Sruti* (revelations) and *Smriti* (traditions). While outcaste folk are excluded from hearing them,

caste members can receive merit from simply listening to these texts.

Brahman – the all-pervading, absolute, supreme cosmic principle or god that is manifest in all things.

Atman – the physical, psychic principle that pervades man (a person).

Maya – Whereas reality is Brahman, the material world is illusory, Peters notes from the Upanishads.

Samsara – Fully linked with *karma* (each good or evil action) and transmigration of the soul, a person's soul "wanders eternally," depending on merit or failure from one form of existence to another.

Moksha – Having longed for salvation, release from the *karmic* cycle and being absorbed into the All or Brahman explains *moksha*.

Margas – These are *paths* to release of the soul with Brahman:

karmamarga (action path as through rituals, sacrifice, penance, or pilgrimage);

jnanamarga (knowledge path or mental realization); and

bhaktimarga (devotion path; faith or submission to a personal god).

Peters details extensive efforts by John E. Clough a missioner who preceded Russian and American MBs in Andhra Pradesh with mass revival movements among Telugu Madigas and Mala caste folk. He also notes effects by some Brahmins to prejudice Hindus against Christians through spreading false reports. For example, when Christians disinfected wells as a precaution against plague, they were charged with intent to poison the people. (188) But missioners, before they left the land, persisted in assisting nationals to reach, instruct, and shepherd India's people through indigenous (rooted) churches.

Ressler, J. A. and **Lina Z.** (MC) *Lights and Shades from Hindu Land.* (Smithville, OH, January 1910).

This resource from early Mennonite missioners in India has a photo from observation on the right hand page with a paragraph about it on the left—a useful way to introduce westerners to India. Scattered comments about Hinduism appear (no page numbers).

- Resslers report that more than two-thirds of India's population claimed the Hindu religion. . . . Their worship is some form of idolatry. . . .It is difficult to imagine the trials and difficulties of those who have lived in idolatry. . . with their heads bowed down to images of wood and stone. . . . The depths of degradation from which converts from idolatry have come can hardly be imagined by those who have not seen it, they add.
- The large school building and chapel shown in the center . . . is made sacred by use. . . The natives would be apt to think of it in the same way as they do their temples—a place where the pulpit or stand is worshiped in place of the idol.

- A group of representative men of Dhamtari in front of one of the most frequented Hindu temples in Dhamtari.
- The Hindu priest has come to the rich man's house with his sacred "puran" (religious historical book). Listening to the reading of this book constitutes the man's worship. We see here the sacred *tulsi* plant in the presence of which the reading becomes more sacred. The lamp with seven branches stands on the other side of the priest. An offering of fruit is on the plate in front. "The head of the house satisfies the longings of his soul with such meaningless forms and ceremonies," Resslers judge.
- Here is another Hindu worship ceremony. The idols are displayed in the center. The offerings are in front. . . . The rich man and his son, who pay for this *"puja"* or worship, are seated to our left. The worship in this case consists mostly of "music" of a weird character chanted by the priest or the paid musician to the accompaniment of the "rude banjo" he holds in one hand.

Ressler, Jacob Andrew (MC) *Stories from India*. (Scottdale, PA: Herald Pr, 1916).
This book Ressler dedicates to his wife Lina. Bits of information about Hinduism are repeated from the above source in addition to further insight. Ressler confesses "How little I knew the workings of the Indian mind." (73) Yet he willingly learns: that Hindus felt that each person needs a priest through whom to approach a god. Even Brahmins looked to the Gosain caste to serve as priests for them. . . . Ressler also understood Hindus to believe that at the point of dying a person's soul passes into another newly-born person or an animal, either with a soul. To kill an animal therefore prompts fear of killing an ancestor. (130) . . . A Christian convert has generations of previous habits to process. Ressler knew one Hindu mother who bitterly opposed missioners for helping her son Bisrampuri understand and practice his new faith. (99)

Sell, Blanche (MC) HM I – 183 Papers, circa 1930-2001, Box 2, folder 12 Mennonite Church USA Archives, Goshen, IN,
Not a published writer, Sell's content was primarily shared in personal letters written to family or friends. Her pattern was to write paragraphs, keeping the same to add more for a month or more before sending them. Segments that refer to Hinduism appear here and within the *Anecdotes* chapter.[9]

An April 22 letter of Sell's written from the Delhi Railroad Station platform (year unknown but when traveling for early Hindi language study) describes an experience with woman coolies (likely of Hindu or tribal connection). Sell hated both to bicker with them for payment and to see their being burdened with her luggage. From days spent in Agra, Sell notes having seen the Taj Mahal, the tomb that Mohammad Shah Jahan had built for his wife who had requested that he not remarry. The nearby fort where Shah Jahan had been imprisoned also impressed Sell. While there, she engaged conversation with a woman of the Bahai religion—those "who think heaven and hell are now on earth," Sell explains.

From 1946 Blanche reports walking with missioner, nurse friend Florence Nafziger (MC) up the Mount of St. Thomas (disciple of Jesus') located in Madras, South India. They read "the stations of the cross" en route. Their Hindu taxi driver, walking along, "was quite moved as we read each meditation. . . Our essential call is to follow Christ" she added.

February 11, 1951 – On seeing a "devilish, Satanic sight with eerie music and a grotesque idol," Sell wrote that "we must know, see, and understand such 'religious' ceremonies in order to teach intelligently." . . . Divali, the festival of lights, honors Lakshmi, goddess of wealth. Little oil lamp flames mark houses and each shop along streets. When walking with several missioners among the crowds Fyrne Yoder (MC) greeted a Muslim woman friend. "We then entered the inner, gold-bejeweled women's quarters "to discuss the Hindu holiday."

Sell reports from a village where cows were dying. Each villager was asked to give eight *annas* (small coin) per cow owned as part of worship. The Christian village owner (*malgazor*) refused to donate for other than his "true God." The owner's servants were asked by other villagers to quit working for him. Seventy cows belonging to idol worshippers died. When none of the *malgazor's* cows died young Christians judged the contrast as a sign of lack of help from others' gods.

On March 3 (year unknown) Sell writes of stopping in Benaras, the holiest Hindu city, when traveling toward Bihar State. In the near-darkness of narrow streets and alleys between temples, Sell sees "hideous idols on every side." Devout pilgrims, their faces marked with expressions of longing for forgiveness of sins, bowed prostrate. They kissed the image and offered flowers and rupees. "Our unholy feet were not permitted to walk inside the 'most sacred' spots," Sell adds. Many *sadhus* (holy men) half draped in saffron colored cloths mingled with the pilgrims. Very ancient temples leaned or had fallen; Sell describes some sculptures as "revolting." Women tried to sell her a small lamp—a tiny clay bowl with a wick in oil on a mat—to float on the Ganges. The longer a lamp stayed lighted the greater a god's favor, she learns. Blanche also learns that Hindus vary in worship patterns and religious fervor: some drink the holy water; some worshippers believe that a person whose ashes are sprinkled into "Mother Ganga" goes directly to heaven; some are too poor to buy wood for burning (cremation).

Requests might come to Sell via letter too; on 21st April 1964 she received the following from a Hindu acquaintance:

My Holy Mother!

I am your child, mother . . . I am proud of you, mother, my holy mother. I will not hide anything from you. I have written some letters to _____ in which I requested her to pray before the Lord for the success of my examination, nothing else . . . I am born for success; the condition is if you too will pray . . .Keep my remembrance in your mind to the bitter end of your life.   With best regards, your child,

Ramakant Chandrakar

The Shah family, distinctly loyal to the Jain religion that broke from Hinduism while retaining some of its features, remained long-time, close friends with Blanche. Lakshmi (Kaki Bai) the mother was called "Ma" by hundreds of friends. Of her children Modi and Dinesh, Dinesh was like a son to Sell. In a letter of 12-3-60 Sell refers to Dinesh Shah's uncertainly in belief. To see him involved in idol worship was heartbreaking for her. . . When engaged to be married, Dinesh told Dina to read the New English *Bible* that Sell and Marie Moyer (MC) gave her "because his one mother (Blanche) is Christian." Eclectic, Dinesh "reads the bible, prays, and knows God as guide but sees no need for Jesus Christ as Savior," Sell explains. On Good Friday of 1966 Dinesh visited Sell. When expressing her desire that his marriage be Christian, "all seemed so confusing for him, with many ways to believe in God."

When Lakshmi had a stroke, nurses Blanche and <u>Florence Nafziger</u> rode with her by ambulance to the Mennonite hospital in Dhamtari. En route Lakshmi asked the driver to stop for her to make a small offering to the idol in a Hindu temple; Blanche reports feeling devastated. She knows that "Ma Lakshmi" had said that she believes in and prays to Jesus. Her peacemaker friend fails to know "true peace," Sell concludes. The ailing mother requested her sons to read Jain scripture to her, asking for and being granted forgiveness. The prayer "Paras Ram" soon accompanied Kaki Bai's dying breath—that woman "so full of love, of doing loving deeds, though not a Christian," Sell adds.

Sell's letter of 5-16-1971 reveals that Dinesh "can't understand why God's Will would be shown only through Jesus." Sell concludes that a missioner's task is to "sow the seed" and let God take care of the harvest. "This is the Spirit's work," she says. A letter to Blanche of 23-9-73 with letterhead: "Dr. Dinesh K. Shah, Shah Nursing Home, Raipur, M.P." tells of his newly established medical place. He requests her to get information about medical supplies for him; his signature followed: "With prayers, yours always, Dinesh"

Conviction of Sell's approach with non-Christians recurs in her writing: "I cannot judge others about my view that Christ is the only way to salvation." . . . "I cannot hold a grudge." . . . "I cannot withhold forgiveness or force other people to do what I think is right." . . . "I cannot manipulate others' lives—no matter how much salvation for the Shah family, for example, may be God's will." . . . "Will not the judge of all the earth do right?" . . . "I do not need to defend myself but be ready to forgive and ask forgiveness."

---

[1] Western Christians often negate sacred Hindu images or god forms as mere *idols*. They may in turn overlook their own "idols" (replacements for God). To negate diverse forms and names of Hindu images may prompt critics to fail to understand that whereas illiterate village folk may indeed worship an object before them, educated Hindus understand their diverse images to represent the One Universal Being.

[2] As described by Ruth Unrau in "The One and Only Martha Burkhalter (1889-1964)" in *Full Circle Stories of Mennonite Women* Mary Lou Cummings, ed. (Newton, KS: Faith and Life Pr, 1978) 66.

[3] Not about Hinduism *per se*, Independence was of distinct significance for missioners to share with the people of India where the Hindu religion dominates.

[4] Mussoorie is also the location for Woodstock International School where children of missioners of diverse denomination, including some Mennonites, attend boarding school with students and staff from India and elsewhere.

[5] See further reference to Dr. Ella Bauman's (GC) assistance in Hindu refugee camps during Partition.

[6] Jantzens' report of missioners' encounter with Partition death appears directly above and on pages 107-11 here.

[7] What Hindus signify with such rituals appears elsewhere in this resource.

[8] The writer values Peters' attention to single women missioners within this story of growth.

[9] Decades later the writer video-taped Sell, along with missioner nurses Florence Nafziger, Lena Graber, and Katherine Yutzy, in lively conversation about their medical experiences at Dhamtari Christian Hospital.

Middle Era - 1950s-1980s

Arnold, P. B. (MB) "Witnessing Discipleship in Asia," *Mission Focus: Annual Review* (14, no. 4, December 1986) 49-52.

Arnold, a physician and MB Indian leader for several decades, is a fourth generation Christian on his mother's side and third generation on his father's side. An ancestor of his had sculpted deities for a Hindu temple. At one point when his father was gone to preach, their lower-caste hut was burned, presumably by someone who opposed Christianity. Having become a Christian at a young age, Arnold thought that missioners were "sent by God from heaven." Comments from this article reflect insight deeper than that perception. He notes the importance of approaching Asian cultures and religions with genuine love and empathy.

How people *live their lives* attracts others to Christ more than does argument over doctrines, Arnold says. The worthy witness truly loves rather than judges, shares insight without argument, and patiently listens to another's point of view, he adds. As disciples imitate their *guru* (teacher), new followers grow in divine grace. Arnold expects disciples to present the gospel in "an appropriate manner"—in mutually enriching dialogue—assured that Jesus' Spirit is ever with them. (49)

To reject or devalue Asian religious systems or cultural and historical meanings hinders rapport. Arnold values the disciple (or missioner) in Asia who approaches Asia's cultures and religions with genuine love and empathy, appreciates all that is "good and genuine" within them, and enables new believers to see how Christ makes even more noble their already noble longings. Anti-Hindu, anti-Buddhist, anti-Confucius, even anti-Indian attitudes of western Christians mar their message. Ancient Asia's religious life, rooted in a deep inner instinct for worship of God, prompts genuine searching for the sacred, Arnold says. Christian converts retain such religious identity and simply renounce what is not Christ-like from within prior meanings, he explains. The Hindu heritage encourages a posture of complete surrender through striving toward absorption into God which, for Hindus, means being freed from rebirth. Instead of being a small minority, Christianity would be "at home" in India had missioners of all groups appreciated the good already there. Arnold values Hans Staffner for having made that observation in 1985. (49-50)

The missioner witnesses from current experience to help a new disciple build a present that enriches the good of the past. Not a mere object of evangelism, the new person is to be befriended, not seen as "a trophy to be won," Arnold states with conviction. Problems of social change become the new challenges—to loosen caste or tribal bonds, decrease severe poverty, make assets more equitable, counter violence done to women and other weak sections of society. Preaching alone is not enough. Being an exclusive or closed community often fails to address Indian national issues. Rather than be intent to preserve itself, the church will give itself away as it enables people. Arnold calls the Indian church, within India's religious pluralism dominated by a Hindu ethos, to rethink and discover its identity through basic human rights. He sees no place within Christianity for arrogahce or separation excused as being inferior. The Hindu pattern for tolerance might welcome Christianity or Islam if those religions were not tied to colonial conquest or marked as "foreign," he adds. (50-51)

To be the church is to be the "whole people of God." An authentic, international church will bridge each nation's own historic and socio-cultural context, Arnold believes. Gaps between clergy and laity need to be narrowed. Why youth critique or leave the church needs to be scrutinized. Whereas churches often pattern the west in separating religion from politics, Hinduism, Islam and Sikhism do not, Arnold notes. In India that distinction limits benefits for Christian and Muslim untouchables; they are restricted from being Scheduled Caste folk who receive such benefits. Further, some Christians are being drawn back to claim Hinduism in order to gain privileges. To 'win' without serving people has limits. Arnold quotes a great Indian evangelist Bakht Singh (1978): "We must know what our responsibility is: not only to preach but to take the people deep into the foundation truths of the faith." (51-52)

Beachy, John E. (MC) *"Pastoral Counseling: Counseling the Christian, former Animist, in Crisis Experience."* Paper written for a course Associated Mennonite Biblical Seminary, January 11, 1968, 21 pp. Located in General / Student Papers, AMBS Library,
John and <u>Miriam (Weaver) Beachy</u> were missioners in Bihar State in India for twenty-three years (1948-71.) Within the broader Hindu context within the state, missioners served more with tribal peoples; several tribal languages in addition to Hindi were spoken. John supervised the building of missioner homes and the Nav Jiwan Hospital and Miriam, in addition to being "surrogate mother to students who came to the area to study" established an annual women's retreat. Both were involved with training pastors and a major famine relief effort.

Missioner Beachy wrote the paper about pastoral counseling when on furlough after having lived in India several years. He explains that Bihar Mennonite Church members are primarily from aboriginal tribes called Oraon or Munda. They were part of very early migrations into India; about one-fifth of such animist folk are Christian. Most converted when they realized that *guru* (teacher or mentor) Jesus was greater than the spirits. Animists believe in a hierarchy of spirit beings alongside one Supreme Being, the creator of spiritual force and the universe. While no image portrays the Supreme Being, all of life owes it loyalty, not necessarily called worship, Beachy explains. For Oraon and Munda folk, worship is motivated by fear—with intent to appease evil or hostile deities. At the time of death, which is always considered a mystery, the soul or spirit leaves a body to return to its former home while the dead one is thought to pass into a deity or spirit that inhabits the person's dwelling. It hovers over the family that then serves it. (3-4)

Beachy understands that animists may expect spirits to bring misfortune like crop failure if they are displeased. Such spirits, thought by most Christians to be of Satan, also rebel against Jesus and the kingdom of God. Since most of the tribal folk are first generation Christians, former religious practices, rituals, and ceremonial activity persist, not far removed. When an animist faces a crisis, religious expressions that had been memorized or patterns of response may re-surface, Beachy explains. Former priests, figures thought to have evil powers, or medicine men may be called on to assist. Presumed to have powers to control evil, they might discover which spirit needs to be appeased or which witch with supernatural power was responsible for the crisis. (6-7) As a pastor, missioner Beachy hoped to learn more about counseling—about relieving fear and anxiety, about death within tribal cultures, about enabling confidence among young Christians, about dependence on Holy Spirit leading.

Burkhalter, Sheryl (Gupta) (GC heritage) "India's Women within Ancient Tradition," Student paper at Goshen College (1980), 6 pp.
Having grown up in India as a daughter of missioners, Burkhalter took a break from study in the US to return there for a year of further language study. During those months she lived in a totally Indian context with a family where the father had recently died, a family with a daughter who anticipated her arranged marriage. While patterns have changed during the past thirty-five years, this paper examines traditional aspects of Hindu society. Burkhalter knew then of the limited place for a single woman in society. A female depends on others to protect her: parents when a girl, husband when an adult, or son if she becomes a widow.

Burkhalter finds truth in some stereotypes. Hindu tradition wishes to pass on tradition unchanged, without individual innovation or progress. The occasion of birth can prompt different responses: celebration for a son and tears for a daughter. Sons can expect to receive more formal education; a young bride can anticipate becoming a servant for her mother-in-law. (1) Mythical figures from religious texts shape the Hindu ideal of womanhood, Burkhalter explains. For example, the mythical Savitri lives out a wife's duty to be subservient to her husband: to venerate him like a god in life and follow him even in death. From early Vedic Hinduism Burkhalter learns how a wife acquires religious merit through her husband. A later devotional aspect (*bhakti*) of Hinduism offers salvation for women through their own devotion to a divine form. As a wife serves meals to her husband before eating, so she partakes of the morsels already given to and blessed by the god at a temple. Tradition also expects a husband to esteem his wife, in part for his own benefit or merit. (3)

Social dimensions also shape attitudes toward a Hindu woman. From an anthropologist's study of village India, Burkhalter notes the disadvantage for a young bride. Required to move, often some distance, to her in-laws' home she, because of being of the lowest status, works hard for the mother, is strictly obedient to her husband, and remains veiled whenever near men older than she. Restricted from social circles, a widow wears a white sari, removes all jewelry, eats a daily simple meal, and rarely remarries. Known to cause bad luck for festivities, a widow is to keep herself pure. Burkhalter observes that the widow with whom she lived gave up possessions, cut off three feet of her hair, and wore old, simple saris. (Her daughter urged her not to buy traditional white ones). (4) Within a year, also contrary to Hindu tradition, the widow accepted a job outside the home. Burkhalter describes the mother's change in bearing that followed as "beautiful to see."

The daughter named Sarla both followed and countered traditional features in preparing for her marriage. Aware of the financial burden for her mother, she refused to have a dowry be given on her behalf, requested that fewer than usual saris and jewelry be given to relatives, and reduced meal catering expenses. She also boldly informed her future in-laws that she did not expect to do their household work alone and that she expected to get an M.A. degree in Sanskrit rather than become a doctor. Burkhalter realizes both how a transaction could become a business deal and how Sarla's personal identity can either expand beyond or retain the traditional. Further, Burkhalter observes that Sarla and her mother continued to fast on Fridays in honor of their Hindu husband and father. (5)

Whereas traditional social patterns persist more in rural areas, urban and middle class women ever-produce changes due to further education, women's organizations like Mahila Mandals, and increased income generation. Burkhalter concludes, however, by wondering: when a single woman will be seen as a "person in her own right."

Duerksen, Christena. (GC) "Was It Fate?" *Mennonite Life*, (January 1966) 36, 48. Christena (Harder) and Jacob Duerksen (GC) papers are located in MLA.MS.117 – 9 boxes in Mennonite Library and Archives, Bethel College, North Newton, KS.

Duerksens went to India in 1926. C. Duerksen notes a distinct cultural feature to begin her account: whereas westerners knock before entering someone else's home, a common Indian way is to either discreetly cough or clear the throat when just outside the door, to indicate interest in meeting or entering.

An anxious, Hindu Indian merchant stood greeting "Namaste" (meaning "I honor the god within you.") at the Duerksen door. He pled with Jacob to drive his pregnant wife who was deep into a complicated birthing labor to the Mennonite hospital at Champa. The jeep could extend to hold a full-length bed; several women sat near to comfort the woman during her uncomfortable ride. When the doctor reported to the new father that a son was born, he was delighted; the couple's earlier infants had not survived. When the father told Duerksen that because he had been willing to assist with the trip to the hospital, "You are god to me," Duerksen credited the true God's help instead. The growing son spent hours in his father's shop. Later when Duerksen stopped by the merchant's shop, he noticed the father's sad face. "He's gone. We did not know that he was so ill or realize that he had typhoid," said the grieved father. Christena concludes her article by asking, "Had they offended the gods or was it just *fate* that they must [live] without a son to administer the last rites when it came their turn to die?"

Dyck, Paul I. (GC) *Emergence of New Castes in India*. Master of Arts Thesis, University of Manitoba, (June 1970).
After serving as a mission hospital administrator in India from 1962-1968, Dyck wrote a Master's thesis on new castes among tribal people in India. His academic study of social, political, and economic factors reflects his interest to know what conditions exist or changes transpire when groups emerge as new caste groups. Dyck found Indian caste to be "one of the most highly elaborated systems of social stratification in the world." Its bases are multiple: labor specialization, distance between segments of society, and views of purity and pollution. Dyck's writing centers on tribal peoples—Gonds, a dominant political force, and Santals, known for an 1855 rebellion—from 1850 to 1950 in the Chhattisgarh region of India (then called Madhya Pradesh State).

Assorted insights emerge from Dyck's study of caste.
- Tribes that shift into castes rarely give up all their cultural traits.
- *Culture* refers to "dynamic responses to particular circumstances." (iii)
- Cultural features of caste groups that bear a common name: birth (as ascribed), special labor categories, and strata— whether above or below others.
- Higher caste people see *karma* (rebirth) as a valid reason for why lower-castes do not share their privilege.

- Dyck uses the word Sanskritize to explain "becoming more Hindu." Sanskrit is the sacred, literary language of ancient, medieval India. It developed through stages of bringing belief and ritual practice closer to the Bramanical.
- As *Brahman* or *Sikh* can be designated caste names, so also might *Christian* with its sub-groups.
- While converts retain their caste status, they may take on newly emerging occupations. In fact, in the Champa area best known to Dyck, converts all took on new occupations; they also absorbed ritual changes, he reports.

Esau, Mrs. H. T. (MB) "The American Mennonite Brethren Mission in India," in *First Sixty Years of M. B. Missions.* (Hillsboro, KS: Mennonite Brethren Publishing House, 1954) 68-209.

Toward mid-nineteenth century women of the Ladies Missionary Society of the Herwana Chapter of Mennonite Brethren in Kansas studied MB mission efforts throughout the world. The secretary of that chapter, Mrs. H. T. Esau, wrote this report of a ten-year study; numerous photos are included.

Esau's fourth chapter focuses on India. It includes multiple references to Hinduism, the complexity of which is "likely not understood by the western mind," Esau admits. (72) She names three Hindu stages—Vedism (time of Rigvedic hymns up to 900 BCE), Brahmanism (with emphasis on the priestly caste and ritualism), and Hinduism (mainstream religion in India)[1]—and the triad of gods— Brahma (creator of all), Vishnu (preserver of the universe known through incarnations like Rama and Krishna), and Siva (destroyer of all). Lower class Indians may not be informed of such categories. Esau understands that while some Hindus compare Krishna with Jesus, the idea of a suffering or dying God is offensive to them. (77) Already with "millions of idols" available, more spirits and god or goddess forms can be added to Hindu worship.

The Hindu caste system, based on *varna* (color), remains the social foundation of Hindu experience. Esau writes: "For twenty-five centuries Hindu people have had every detail concerning occupation, kind of food, type of dress, mark of caste, home and marriage decided for them by rules of the caste to which they belong." Esau views the caste system as "the greatest obstacle to the spread of Christianity among Hindus." (73-74) People who openly become Christian may be disowned or deprived from using a well with Hindus. Different caste groups live in separate village sections; the *pallem* section for outcaste folk might be removed from a village or located next to unhealthy conditions like public latrines. Low-caste women work hard and, in addition to being subservient to husbands, are kept ignorant. Esau explains that Hindus consider the cow and its products (milk, butter, buttermilk, urine, and dung) to be holy. Such products can be useful for ceremonies that forgive *sin due to* breaking caste rules. Or, devout Hindus might take long pilgrimages to sacred rivers to be released from sin, Esau adds. Castes prominent where MB missionaries live are named Madigas, leather workers who make straps for sandals or buckets for drawing water, and Mala who weave coarse cloth. (73, 76-77, 82)

Marriage and death issues within Hinduism, as practiced near MB efforts in India, are explained by Esau. On birthing a girl child parents may be deeply distraught. Because plans need to be made before a girl reaches puberty, child marriage can be common. For the future couple to be members of the same caste matters most. If a husband then dies, for which death a wife can be blamed or "cursed by the gods," being a widow is difficult, marked by disdain. A widow may be stripped of parent-gifted jewelry (dowry) and become a "slave" to her mother-in-law. Only a son can carry out Hindu death rites for his father—"to deliver him from a negative rebirth." Esau often contrasts Hindu with Christian practice: a 'heathen' home may show little "love, respect, or purity," she judges. Hindu mothers are "hard to win"; they cling to traditional religion despite fear of a god's wrath. But a Christian widow may gain honor, Esau suggests, by working in a medical setting or by joining Bible Women who, with women missionaries, share biblical stories and songs in village homes. (79-80, 83, 86-7)

Esau admits that mass movements toward conversion, though with inherent risks, seem to "better reach" India's caste-oriented people. Since Hindu wives tend to be shy due to their subjection to husbands; they rarely meet where men gather. Esau explains that among Telegu language folk, where MB missionaries interact, more men turn to Christianity; they then need to influence their wives and children. Baptism can lead to separation. Christian men no longer 'wear' Hindu forehead markings; they participate in fewer Hindu festivals. Renewal within Hinduism can also follow new strengths of Christian revival, Esau notes. Then too, compromise might combine "Christian truth and Hindu tradition." (88-89, 170-72)

Fast, Peter. (MB) Review of *The Christian Message in the Non-Christian World* by Hendrik Kraemer. (Grand Rapids, MI: Kregel Publ.), *Mission Focus: Annual Review* (8, no. 3, September 1979) 54-55.
Fast explains that Kraemer's book was written for the International Missionary Council as it prepared to hold the Third World Missionary Conference in Tambaram/Madras, India, in 1938. Prior to 1920 Kraemer had misjudged the Eastern world as disintegrating; he presumed that Christianity would then fill the vacuum that was likely to follow. Instead, a strong sense of national religions transpired in the East

Fast explains Kraemer's limited division of two religions—Christian and non-Christian—instead of plural religions. Kraemer faulted non-Christian religions, such as Hinduism, as individuals in revolt against God, as desperate, with human apprehensions misdirected. By contrast, the individual in Christian faith surrenders to God and Jesus Christ is revealed, he presumed. Fast defines Kraemer's approach to people of other faiths as marked by "confrontation, conflict, and revolutionary contrast." Since Kraemer presented the Christian faith as absolute, he failed to see or value Christianity's potential to adapt; he made it "exclusive and brittle, less flexible," Fast notes. Whereas missioner voices in the 1930s revealed western, centuries-long, Christian traditions, Fast in the late 1970s credits non-western people with backgrounds shaped by multiple traditions beyond the Christian one.

Fast, Peter. (MB) Review of *The Unknown Christ of Hindus: Towards an Ecumenical Christophony* by Raimundo Panikkar. (Maryknoll, NY: Orbis Books, 1981) *Mission Focus: Annual Review* (10, no.4, December 1982).

Panikkar's book was first published in 1964; this review is of the second, revised and enlarged reprint. Professor Fast sees Panikkar's effort to broaden an "ecumenical ecumenism" within intrareligious dialogue. Fast knows that one of Panikkar's parents was Hindu while the other was Christian. Not opposites, Panikkar sees both Hinduism and Christianity involved in conversion. To imply that Christianity is superior is not adequate he believes; to suggest that Christianity fulfills another religion like Hinduism denies the Hindu a place in God's economy; syncretism obscures both. Fast understands Panikkar to retain clear differences between the two religions. Panikkar realizes that the symbol of the mystery of Christ "can be so expanded and deepened that the Christian can already find Christ in Hinduism." Fast understands that responses to Panikkar will differ: while some will find him too Christian, others will question his brand of Christianity, and others will wonder if Panikkar can remain a Christian.

Good, Mary M. (MC) "Suresh and Sushila visit relatives" *Christian Living*, (December 1954) 14-15, 38-39.

Good tells of two Dhamtari friends who return to their former village. Having left that village during the famine, Suresh had never returned the ten rugged miles. A cousin surprised him one day when he came to Dhamtari to invite him and a missioner to share the gospel in Danitola. Together the cousins went to the missioner's home to make plans. Though offered chairs, the shy Hindu cousin chose to sit on the floor where Suresh joined him. So the missioner sat on the floor too.

They decided that Danitola would be the first location for "touring." Good describes in detail the preparation needed for "touring" to villages during winter months. Several Indian evangelists, Bible women, and a missioner or two go together. Suresh along with Sushila and her family would go along for the first week-end; Sushila's husband's "people" also lived in Danitola, Good explains. The carts were laden with tents, implements, folding furniture, reading materials to sell, cooking vessels, bedding, and basic food—washed rice and dal. Several rode part way in a tonga before walking the last three miles.

On arriving, the missioner and cousin met the Hindu *malguzar* (village owner) to arrange where the crowd of several hundred from nearby villages might gather after late evening meal time to sing *bhajans* and hear scripture stories. Aware of how futile would be a foreigner's effort to "make the Way of Salvation plain to illiterate villagers" (some had never before seen an American), an Indian Christian simplified the story of Jesus. Good notes that even the *malguzar* responded on occasion with "*Ha, Ha*" (Yes, yes) or "*Sach bat hai*" (It is true). Before Suresh shared with those gathered how the missioner had taught him, another Indian evangelist informed the village Hindus of the meaning of talking with God. He then prayed before welcoming all to return the next night, Good concludes.

Hamm, Peter M. (MB) "A Reappraisal of Christianity's Confrontation
   with Other Religions," in *The Church in Mission*. A. J. Klassen, ed.
   (Fresno, CA: MB Board of Christian Literature, 1967) 222-50.
As ancient Israel challenged Baal worship during Old Testament times, so the MB church has confronted world religions since the latter half of the modern missionary era Hamm says. His repeated call in this article from fifty years ago is for "renewed dedication to the exclusive message of Christianity." (223) The resurgence of Hinduism among world religions was marked in 1893 when Swami Vivekananda appeared at the World Parliament of Religions in Chicago. Hamm writes that Hindu philosopher-statesman Sarvepelli Radhakrishnam found his religion to be superior due to its patterns of tolerance. For him, "all roads lead to the summit"; to make exclusive claims reflects sin, he suggests.

After introducing resurgence in Buddhism and Islam, Hamm turns to *syncretism*, "the merging or reconciliation of differing beliefs in religion." Hindus assume that all religions are relative (limited). Each religion only approximates truth for "truth is essentially unknowable." Universalism is another religious aspect about which Christians need to be guarded, according to Hamm. Whereas Hindus affirm that all paths lead to the one summit, Christians insist "on the universal presence of the universally active Christ," Hamm declares. Secularism also shapes religion. Noted Indian Christian P. D. Devanandan saw in Hindu secularism a critical attitude toward religion in general alongside traditional Hindu thought in particular. Cautious about subtle differences among foes, Hamm wishes for MB churches to present exclusive claims of Christ's teachings to non-Christians. (227-30)

Within these selective annotations Hamm names four attitudes that missioners might exhibit in confronting other religions. First, if little or nothing is seen as valuable in the other, the Gospel *displaces* or destroys that other. Second, those who present Christianity as absolute or perfect presume that it *fulfills* whatever may be good or true in another faith (as does the evangelical J. N. Farquhar). Third, some like W. E. Hocking choose to *synthesize* or assimilate the valuable essence of each religion, not insisting that only one is unique. The fourth approach *discontinues* one from another as might missiologist Hendrick Kraemer. For example, outside of biblical revelation, rational arguments are not seen as valid, Hamm hears Kraemer suggest. (232-33)

Religious dialogue or conversation becomes an issue. Whereas Hamm sees theologian Tillich call for dialogue, not exactly conversion, Hamm expects evangelical missioners to listen to as well as present faith through exchange that confronts. For him, a Hindu partner is to be brought to a crisis that calls for decision about an exclusive solution. Or the partner comes to "a commitment to the person of Jesus Christ." While dialogue requires airing the best in each religion, Hamm justifies "exposing the Hindu view" through comparison that shows "the effectiveness of Christianity's claims." (234-37)

Hamm offers three basic presuppositions for MB witness with a non-Christian friend. The first sees revelation as a historical, written fact of "self-disclosure of God in Jesus Christ." To pursue that idea the missioner explains the existence of Hinduism, exposes its errors, and judges its adequacy. Further, Hamm emphasizes Christ's superior revelation as: final, universal, and unsurpassable." Not seeing those descriptors as arrogant, Hamm justifies them as scriptural. The MB's witness is centered in evangelical thought, he says. (237-38)

In the final section Hamm explains an encounter with Hinduism through the Christian focus of certain doctrines: God, Humanity and Sin, and Salvation. A few annotations regarding *God* follow. Whereas Christians have a monotheistic, Hebrew view of a personal God, philosophical Hinduism experiences two levels of the divine: "*absolute*, a-cosmic or transcendental level or *relative*, a cosmic or phenomenal" level. With the former God is known as Ultimate Reality or Brahman: without attributes and a "non-dualistic, unconditioned *It*," Hamm adds. He cautions readers about comparing the Christian Trinity alongside the Hindu Triad of Creator (Brahma), Preserver (Vishnu), and Destroyer (Siva) without close attention to distinct differences. (239-44)

Hamm concludes with four implications for MB missioners in doing the sacred task of meeting non-Christians such as Hindus with challenges. First, missioners need to repeatedly examine themselves to keep focused the person and message of Christ. Second, MBs will reinforce Anabaptist concepts of discipleship and practical living along with New Testament insight for the culture that is being addressed. Third, the missioner will be open to changes in technique for the missional task, whether on location or in North America, and fourth, she or he will expect and welcome being challenged—in order to give account for personal hope within. (1 Peter 3:5) (245)

Hiebert, Frances F. (MB) "Doing Mission with a Universal Gospel and Cultural Diversity," *Direction* (Spring 1988, 17, no. 1) 81-86.
A summary statement of Hiebert's here is: "We must learn to affirm pluralism of all kinds." (81) Pluralism is not new; the need remains for openness to it along with preserving distinctions of cultures and religions. In a statement of how her understanding of mission developed, Hiebert, who always felt a stranger to India's culture, chose to see her identity in God's kingdom as the means through which she listened to understandings of culture and religion among Indian folk.

Hiebert, Paul G. (MB) "A Sacrifice to the Goddess of Smallpox," in *Case Studies in Missions*. **Paul G. and Frances F. Hiebert.** (Grand Rapids: Baker House, 1987) 126-28. See also **P. Hiebert's** discussion of smallpox in Wiebes' (MB) *In Another Day of the Lord*, p. 126 and Christina Duerksen's (GC) account of appeasing Indra, god of thunder, in her *Come with Me: 19 Children's Stories* (Newton, KS: Faith and Life, 1971).
Anthropologist Hiebert reports worship related to the goddess of smallpox Misamma. A Christian father, on feeling his daughter's fevered forehead and seeing increased, red spots on her body, struggled with whether to give even one *paisa* (small coin) to satisfy the angered goddess. Pressure from Hindu brothers and the village mounted. Hiebert writes that when the village diviner concluded that the local godling or spirit, Misamma, was angered by the village folk, donations were gathered from every household to sacrifice a water buffalo on the village's behalf. High-caste elders resent Christian claims that loyalty to the God of the Bible makes impossible such donations; to disobey the village elder can be unforgiveable. Hiebert knows also that noncooperation can lead to banning the Christian from the common well or access to irrigation, or from being free to work in his field.

Hiebert, Paul. (MB) "The Category 'Christian' in the Mission Task," *International Review of Missions*. (72, no. 287 July 1983) 422-27.

Hiebert, Paul. (MB) "Conversion in Cross-Cultural Perspective," in *Conversion: Doorway to Discipleship*.Henry J. Schmidt, ed. (Hillsboro, KS: Board of Christian Literature Mennonite Brethren Churches, 1980) 88-98.

Hiebert asks in several writings whether a Hindu, Telugu language speaker named Papayya becomes "a Christian" after one exposure to the gospel. Papayya worships Vishnu, one of the main Hindu god names and forms. He heard a stranger, circuit preacher say that there is one God whose Son appeared among people. Talking with the stranger about his message, Papayya by impulse prays to "God." He may recall a few songs that were sung. Will he continue to go to his temple to pray as he stays with his caste job? How will he learn more about the one named Jesus since he cannot read the papers left by the stranger; he knows no other 'believers' either.

The Hindu Telugu-speaking man refers to *devudu* which has a different meaning from *God* as used by a westerner. Hiebert realizes that Papayya will more likely use familiar terms like: *ishvarudu*, *bhagavanthudu*, *parameshvara*. Telugu speakers think that all forms of life manifest a single vital force, that Hindu gods manifest a cosmic energy field. While English speakers separate natural beings from supernatural ones, giving a distinct meaning to the term *incarnation*, Telugus understand that gods repeatedly come to earth as *avatars* (translated "incarnations") to help people.

Whereas God understands the human heart, people observe what others say or do. People may include or exclude, seeing conversion as a process. If requirements for being a Christian, like following doctrines, are 'too high to attain,' Papayya may fail to understand. If his behavior indicates change—slowly toward or away from—Jesus as goal, does that mean that Papayya is *Christian*? Hiebert concludes that what matters for Papayya is "not what he knows" but "Does he seek to follow Christ and to know him more fully?" (97)

Hiebert, Paul. (MB) "Indian and American World Views: A Study in Contrasts," in *Religion in Modern India*. Giri Raj Gupta, ed. (New Delhi: Vikas Pub., 1983) 399-413.

Hiebert, Paul. (MB) "Missions and the Understanding of Culture," in *The Church in Mission*, A. J. Klassen, ed. (Board of Christian Literature, Mennonite Brethren Church, 1967) 251-65.

Two of the issues that Hiebert raises in this article are: How best is the basic word "God" to be translated? For, village folk "see gods as part of the present illusory universe" or know "only gods who share in the weaknesses, rivalries, and sins of the rest of creation." Further, since

Indian villagers know little of a role such as "missioner"—their options being landlord or ranked, superior policeman—Hiebert asks: How will we be "brothers" with national church leaders? (256, 259-60)

Hiebert, Paul G. and **Frances F. Hiebert.** (MB) *Case Studies in Missions.* Part 2 "Women and Men": chap. 37 "A Group Conversion"; chap. 38 "Conversion or Social Convention?" (Grand Rapids: Baker House, 1987) 43-47, 126-28, 158-63.

Juhnke, James C. (GC) "India, 1900-1947" in *A People of Mission History of the General Conference Mennonite Overseas Mission,* (Newton, KS: Faith and Life Pr, 1979) 20-42.

Reports regarding missioner ties with Hindu traditions often start, as does Juhnke, with caste. More people living in GC locations in India were of the low Chamar group, leatherworkers who skinned and processed products made from dead animals. Such activity was seen by most Hindus to pollute. Juhnke learns from a 1970 occupation survey that in 1970 eighteen different castes and three tribal groups were members of the Champa Mennonite community; three-fourths of them were of low-caste origin. (36) While early missioner J. F. Kroeker, who at one time hired 500 nationals, gained rapport with some higher caste Hindus, none of them changed religious loyalty. Juhnke notes the Hindu reformer and religious prophet Ghasi Das. [2] Exchange between missioners and Hindu priests of the Brahman caste often led to argument. As Hindu priests might vilify Christians who value Virgin Mary or presume parenthood for God (through the title *Father*), early missioner P. A. Penner (GC) could willingly try to shame Brahmans through naming "gross sins of Hindoo deities," Juhnke notes. (25)

Juhnke mentions issues of politics and reform. In India some political authorities saw missioners as intruders; delays with transactions or outright opposition could follow. (39) MC work in the area of Dhamtari was under direct British control. Distinctly different, GC missioners engaged a local landowner king in Champa to secure land. They also "paid formal respects" when appropriate, as on the occasion of marriage in the royal family. Often unpleasant relations developed between GC missioners and members of the Hindu reform group called *Arya Samaj.* Reforms included belief in one God and rejection of idol worship while claiming the Vedas as revealed scripture. Juhnke explains that *Arya Samajists* strongly opposed missioners and faulted them for using situations of famine, orphans, and ignorance to prompt people to convert to Christianity.

Juhnke, James C. (GC) and **Robert Kreider** (GC), eds. "India." *Mennonite Life* (June 1980) 10-14.

North American historians Juhnke and Kreider introduce types of experience within Hinduism that missioners encountered in India. They observe that P. A. Penner never distinguished between the "high" and "low" aspects of Hindu religion. Penner failed to see how religion that presumed to build on exalted ethical teachings, helpful gods, or ancient, noteworthy texts ("high" Hinduism) could lead to superstition. He also might have benefited from realizing how "low" Hindu religion—without scripture and marked by erratic, local deities or role reversal rituals that marked a festival like *holi*—might degrade common folk.

The authors discuss learnings encountered by either missioners or new Christians. Distinct aspects for missioners to face include: believers new to Christianity within the dominant Hindu setting; the broader church in India alongside the small mission effort of GC missioners; and issues that surfaced in their churches where one caste group dominated compared to locations with people of multi-caste origin. (11) Writers also report dilemmas that new believers faced: the need to overcome being seen as inferior and out-of-caste and being charged with converting from Hindu roots in order to gain social status.

Kaufman, James Norman. (MC) *Walks and Talks in Hindustan*. (Goshen, IN: Self-published, 1963). Content for this book first appeared serially in the *Mennonite Weekly Review*, 1963.

Arriving in India in 1905 Kaufman failed to understand the pattern of worship that workers at a Bombay factory went through until his escort explained. Each worker, on entering, briefly paused at the gatepost to gesture toward a quantity of vermilion mixed with oil. The oil-colored symbol represented the Hindu pantheon. . . . Wherever one looks, you see people in an act of worship, Kaufman concludes.

Then, before leaving India from Calcutta in 1948 Kaufman watched a woman perform *puja* (worship) from the balcony of her home. Facing the morning sun, she sprinkled water—perhaps holy Ganges water—in the direction of the sun totally focused despite the street traffic below. Kaufman recalls missioner J. A. Ressler having said: "They eat religiously, bathe religiously, even sin religiously." (13-15)

Kaufman's memories of religious and cultural features recur. Chapter two titled "In Recognition of the Gods" proves "how intensely religious the people of India are." En route from Dhamtari to his village of Rudri by bicycle, Kaufman met a Brahman (high-caste) friend who scolded him for being out in the hot sun before offering a drink of water in his brass *lota*. When Kaufman handed the empty container back, the Brahman asked him to set it on the ground; Kaufman's touch had polluted the *lota*. The Brahman's servant would restore its purity by "scouring it with cow dung" after which he could again use it. (8)

Kaufman describes activity along the Holy Mother Ganges (*Ganga Mata*) River especially near the sacred city of Benares (called *Kashi Ji*). From its source in the Himalayas to its delta that pours muddy waters into the Bay of Bengal, the Ganges is considered holy. Its banks in Benares are lined with bathing ghats (steps leading into the river used for religious purposes) and temples (often gifted to gain merit by wealthy Hindus or *rajas* (kings). Set on uneven foundations some temples have partially sunk. A superstitious mother who wishes to do homage to the sacred river might toss her tiny infant into the crocodile-infested river, Kaufman explains.

Kaufman hired a boatman to be his guide along the shore. At the burning ghats he saw wood piled several feet high before placing a dead body on it after which more wood was added. Then the eldest son or a near relative circles the pyre a certain number of times before torching the wood. When totally burned, the ashes are cast into the river; merit for the family follows. Many Hindus who live elsewhere wish to have their ashes, kept in an urn after cremation until a family member makes pilgrimage, cast into the Ganges at Benares. Kaufman also walked through the area of narrow passageways and dark, intricate corridors of the temple area of the city. He notes the area filth; the leers he met from "vile and sensuous looking priests"; a central, deep, most holy well from which water is drawn by a windlass. Pilgrims understand that to drink that water "brings the blessings of the gods upon their unworthy souls." (17-19)

On a business trip to Calcutta, then India's largest city and located on the banks of the Hoogly River, Kaufman stopped to see the important Hindu religious center of Kalighat, a temple shrine dedicated to the goddess Kali. There too worshippers gain merit by offering animal (goat or young buffalo) sacrifices to Kali, who welcomes their warm blood. Or they might bathe in the river to wash away sin. An English-speaking priest offered to be Kaufman's guide. Kaufman gives extensive detail of the gory process of sacrifice and his encounter with the large, clay goddess form inside the temple. The experience provided him "quite enough food for meditation." (19-22)

Kaufman provides a dozen informative pages about Hindu (and a few Muslim) festivals with their "continual boom-boom of the tom-toms." *Dashera* festival crowds gather in October for procession, drumming, and festivities; Kaufman observed this event in 1910 with MC visitor J. S. Hartzler. For weeks baskets of rice had been rooted and kept damp, later to be carried in procession on women's heads, Kaufman describes. People also gather around individuals whose increasingly frenzied dancing is "inspired." One in each procession group carries a Hindu trident symbol—a tapered, three-foot long iron rod about pencil thin at its thickest with an attached crosspiece of three curved ends. At a "supreme moment" the gods will choose someone to be honored by having the trident lubricated with a lemon piece before being thrust through his tongue or cheek, Kaufman says. Performed in the name of the gods, no harm is done, he is told. Then all process to a nearby pond into which the sprouted grain is thrown. (22-23)

Legends mark Hindu festivals. Kaufman knows legend origins for Holi to be from a disease called *holika* that affected children. Those who celebrate the three-day event clean house, fast, keep a fire burning through the night, sprinkle colors (wet or dried) on each other, and use filthy, obscene language. Only men practice the profane aspect as they visit shops, expecting permanent colors to be showered on them.

A Hindu festival for men only called Ganesha Chaturthi honors the elephant-headed god named Ganesha's September birthday. Legend holds that on a visit to heaven Ganesha fell. When the moon-god laughed to insult Ganesha, he cursed the god causing anyone who looked at it to receive a black face. Through prayer and fasting, other gods asked Brahma the Creator, and Brahmans to wipe out the black stain; the moon-god complied. Those engaged fast for a day (up to ten) before worshiping Ganesha's image and eating, Kaufman states. (24-25)

Kaufman credits an aspect of the Hindu festival Dewali as beautiful—the many, small, lighted lamps outside newly-cleaned homes and along streets. He explains a legend behind the autumn event that involves the god Vishnu, a demon, Ramachandra's return from Sri Lanka, and a gambling family named Mahadeo initially cursed by goddess Parvati. That she later cancelled the curse led to people's using the occasion to worship their wealth and to close their financial accounts in readiness for a new year. Kaufman fails to mention that most Hindus associate this festival with Lakshmi, goddess of wealth.

Kaufman later notes goddess Lakshmi as represented by cattle. He reports having bought a pair of oxen to pull their *tonga* (wheeled cart). Not too long after the team was broken in, he was returning from Dhamtari to his village of Rudri when one of the team 'stubbed' his right front hoof. On discovering that the leg was broken, Kaufman left it for care with a Hindu friend. Since Hindus worship cattle, they neither kill cows nor eat beef. The Hindu friend fed and gave the ox some native remedies for three months before returning it to Kaufman. Kaufman nearly offended the good friend on offering to pay him, for he "had been well rewarded by the goodness of Lakshmi." The bullock, thought by Hindus to be sacred, served the missioner well for more years. Pious Hindus make large donations to cattle asylums (*Pinjarapol*) where any crippled or old animal is fed until its "natural" death. Such gifts are known as *Lakshmi puja,* Kaufman explains. (25, 29-31)

A surgeon friend of Kaufman's, a high-caste Brahman, disclosed more Hindu thought. He told of his close attention to what the gods required of him. He, like many intelligent Hindus, approached the Deity directly rather than with the aid of idols. Some Hindus felt that idols provide help for more ignorant folk. He also told Kaufman about his plan to finish working with the government to qualify for his pension before practicing medicine for three years in Raipur where his family lives. With savings set aside for his wife and children he then explained, with tears rolling, his plan to "go alone to the Himalaya Mountains to spend the rest of his days as a *Rishi* (recluse) in meditation and prayer." Kaufman felt "inexpressibly sad" on hearing the sincere plan. (31)

Kaufman also describes transmigration of the soul and efforts done to determine a person's next life. Through an unknown number of rebirths based on good deeds during each life time, a person might eventually be reborn a demigod before being absorbed into Brahma, the supreme being. Had a man been known for ever-wrongful deeds he could be reborn into a lower caste or then a jackal or snake prior to being reborn a woman, Kaufman explains. Motivation for gaining personal merit enables public causes—assisting the poor, donating toward a new temple, providing for sick cows.

One day as Kaufman walked through the mango grove near the MC church he met a *sadhu* (religious mendicant) with his arm raised high above his head. Asked why he did such an uncomfortable thing, the *sadhu* explained his vow to please the gods by doing that feat for twelve years; he had succeeded for eight years. Kaufman could tell from the man's rigid shoulder and elbow positions plus atrophied arm muscles that the man would never, however, be able to lower his arm. (31-32)

In a chapter titled "Terror of the Unknown" Kaufman explains in detail an ancient myth about the Vedas, a Hindu sacred text. The account includes gods and their promises, demons, and mysterious powers—whether to churn the ocean depth or provide immortality. This belief was recalled on August 21, 1933 on the occasion of an almost total eclipse of the sun near Dhamtari. The eclipse that started at 9 a.m. had but a crescent fringe left by 10:30. After the moon passed between earth and sun the crescent started again to grow until by 12-noon the sun again shone full-orbed. Many folk have scientific explanations for such occurrences. A period of eclipse is defiling for Hindus; pious Hindus need to bathe in order to wash away the experience of such pollution.

Movements of heavenly bodies like planets and accurate sundials have inspired people for centuries. Fascinating for Kaufman was his visit to an old observatory in north India built by the Moguls more than two hundred years earlier. Kaufman had also watched the movements of Haley's comet in 1910 from Naini Tal (at seven thousand food altitude) in the Himalaya Mountains. Kaufman understands that superstitions reflect fear of the unknown—as from a yawn, a child's colic pain, black mixture for eyelids, or devil-inspired witch. (36-41)

Lapp, John Allen. (MC). *The Mennonite Church in India 1897-1962* (Scottdale, PA: Herald Pr, 1972).
Not primarily reflecting Lapp's experience, this dissertation reports missioner activity and views along with insight into Indian Mennonite experience. Annotations provide information related only to Hinduism. Lapp describes missioners as genuinely caring but limited in knowing how to make the gospel relevant in a predominantly Hindu land. They regarded Hinduism as pagan ("heathen"). A century ago they thought that religion was unlikely to enrich people's literacy or moral living.

Lapp also reveals insight into views of Mennonites "back home"; some reflected less-than-openness to crossing cultures. Missioner M. C. Lehman met resistance when he informed westerners that Christian fellows had played a soccer match with non-Christians. While the Christians won that match, Lehman acknowledged that prayers to begin the game had been addressed to God, Allah, and Ram. Lapp explains that Lehman was faulted for more emphasis on broad education than evangelism (to inform and invite belief). Lehman also approved Indian Christian men's wearing mustaches. Then too he endorsed missioner ecumenical relations with other denominational mission groups active in India. (60-2, 97-8)

Academic Lapp commends several missioners who studied Hindu thought and practice. He notes that J. A. Ressler left his study titled "In Hindu Land" unfinished, that George J. Lapp reported more strengths than weaknesses of Hinduism. George's study informed colleagues about important Hindu deities, systems of devotion, sin and superstition, festivals, and deeds of merit. He called the epic Ramayana "a wonderful piece of literature" and commended the Upanishads (scripture) for noting the "influence of scattered Jews located in India during the fifth century BCE." The younger Lapp notes weaknesses for which the elder Lapp faulted Hinduism: shortness of life due to early marriage, regressive medicine, promotion of poverty, denial of education for the masses, and tyranny through certain customs. (81)

John Lapp provides other details of interest. He explains M. C. Lehman's survey of village life, including the process whereby villagers paid a local priest, with their harvested rice, for protecting village idols. (80-81 within chapter 9 titled "The Missionary View of India.") Lapp credits missioners for coming to understand caste issues and distinctions between cultic village Hinduism and reform movements of intellectual Hinduism. But they commented little about Indian personalities other than Gandhi, he said. J. N. Kaufman's thought about Gandhi's effort for *swaraj* (self rule) is noted elsewhere.

Lapp's ideas about Hinduism useful to discuss are annotated.

- Hinduism claimed a strong hold on people's lives in the Dhamtari area. That fact affected missioner efforts to attempt to evangelize, to invite people who experience all of life as religious to consider belief in and commitment to Jesus Christ.
- Lapp names J. D. Graber's "The Conquest of Fear" as the "finest type of Christian apologetic in the Hindu context." (157-58) Public scrutiny by efforts of strong, resurgent Hindu groups like RSS and *Arya Samaj* restricted enthusiasm among Indian Christians for the task of evangelizing.
- Lapp reports schoolmaster Stephen Solomon's questioning why Hindus were offended by the Christian claim for salvation only through Jesus. Hindu scripture similarly suggests that without Ram or repeating Ram's name, salvation fails, he said.
- Both fear and faith were further prompted by an anti-mission riot in October 1957 at Raipur, fifty miles from Dhamtari, when the Christian Gass Memorial Center was burned down. (197-99)

Loewen, Jacob A. (MB) "The Christian Encounter with Culture," *World Vision International.* (Monrovia, CA, January, February, March 1967) 25 pp.

Jacob A. Loewen, trained anthropologist and missioner, understands cultural dimensions at a profound level. His global experience focused more in Columbia, South America and several areas of Africa than Asia.[3] Academic teaching experience enriched Loewen's explanation of how peoples develop, interrelate, and worship.

Loewen observes that most resistance to the gospel occurs when messengers who go to regions ignore basic principles of culture such as a universal concern due to belief in evil spirits. Whereas folk may keep their yards clean in order to avoid spirits hiding in refuse, such motivation for cleanness may lessen when the fear of spirits is removed due to a new view of God's care. (10) Missioners also need to be cautious in preaching a message that anticipates *individual* response within a culture that depends upon *group solidarity*. Honest assessment of a missioner's own culture matters too—being alert to how it may impose a particular view of scripture or way to worship that denies the fact that God meets people in diverse ways in cultures. (20-21)

Loewen, Jacob A. "Which God Do Missionaries Preach?" (*Missiology: An International Review,* (xiv, no. 1, January 1986) 3-19.

Loewen's awareness of how God-concept matters for peoples around the globe and within different religions appears in this article. Most tribal or peasant societies experience their deities through tribal, geographic or specialized functions. They reflect questions: Is a deity thought of as universal or distinct, as limited, as "high" or more spirit or fetish-oriented? (3-4) Loewen refers to biblical texts that reflect cultural issues: Genesis 1 with all races being from one stock; prophetic concerns for multiple nations as Isaiah (56:3-7): "My Temple is to be called a house of prayer for all people of all nations"; and "high" references, to God (Elohim) or places (Yahweh of the hills). He also welcomes awareness of shortcomings that may surround God-concept.

Malagar, P. J. (MC) "A Memorandum on Building an Indigenous Church in India" Paper written when attending Goshen Biblical Seminary (May 4, 1950) 42 pp.

Malagar alerts the reader to varied issues that deserve attention.

- He notes how difficult the task is to keep an indigenous church from repeating centuries-old habits or degrading features from a Hindu past—superstition, witchcraft, or enchantments. Missioners did not always discern that Hindu performance of every act in the name of religion did not always transition into a healthy Christian body. Some new church members confused conversion with mission employment, for example.
- The Hindi word for church—*mandli*—resembles a Hindu caste name of those who worship a common deity and gather for *puja* or family festivities.
- A 1935 survey by missioner A. C. Brunk of one thousand villages in the Dhamtari area noted its division into seventy different castes—Hindu, Aboriginal, and Untouchable.
- Mission physician C. D. Esch noted that East Indians feel that "missioners often don't understand them"; they rely too much on western ideas.
- Malagar calls for missioners to enable an indigenous church to better understand its Hindu context.
- He also repeatedly credits work accomplished by Indians, noting that only rarely are Indians given equal status with missioners.

Malagar, Pyarelal J. (MC) "The Meaning of Discipleship Sadhu Sundar Singh, A Saint," *The Youth's Christian Companion* (July 31, 1949) 661-62.

Malagar, the first MC Indian bishop, identifies Sadhu Sundar Singh who was born in 1889 to wealthy Sikh parents. Sundar Singh often attended worship at a Sikh *gurdwara* or temple with his godly mother. He practiced yoga (to become enlightened) and, at an early age, had memorized large portions of the Hindu *Gita* and Muslim *Koran*. Malagar tells of Sundar's attending a Presbyterian mission school where he disliked Bible classes (especially those that countered his Hindu/Sikh heritage) and, in response, caused disorder in the classroom.

Sundar Singh's mother died when he was fourteen causing him a deep sense of loss. Longing for peace and intent to find God, he prayed one night: "Oh God, if there be a God, reveal Thyself and guide me in the right way." He reports seeing the face of Jesus in a great light that filled his room while he meditated. His family tried hard to dissuade him a Sikh (of the lion race) from disgracing them by becoming a Christian (a dog). Leaving his house because disowned, he went by train to a Christian minister's home where the fact that he had been poisoned was soon discovered. A doctor declared him "beyond recovery." When Sundar awoke the next day "full of life and joy" the first of many miracles in his life had occurred.

Malagar reports Sundar's baptism by an Anglican clergy (1904), his renouncing the world to live in deliberate poverty and celibacy, his walking throughout India and Tibet with a blanket, saffron robe, and Persian-Urdu New Testament to "preach his new-found faith." Eventually he, like Muslim Sufi mystics, fasted on occasion and traveled a great deal including to other Asian countries. Reformer Keshab Chandra Sen said: "Behold Christ come to us in the garb of an Asiatic."[4]

Malagar, P. J. (MC) *The Mennonite Church in India.* (Nagpur, India: National Council of Churches in India, 1981).[5] A review of Malagar's book by H. S. Wilson appears in the Indian journal *Religion and Society*, (29, no. 2, June 1982) 88-89.

Wilson explains that this book is the first of "the churches in India series" intended to inform Indians of the history and ministry of different denominations located in India. Not about diverse Mennonite groups, it reviews the American Mennonite (MC) mission work from 1899 to 1980. While it provides useful statistical information and a chronology of events, it fails to interpret those events, Wilson says. It fails to convey a denominational point of view via, for example, "the impact of Indian socio-economic culture on Christianity." If the series is to enhance unity among Indian Christians, separate books should reflect integration of Indian theology on topics such as discipleship, Church and State relations, the suffering church, and the sacraments, Wilson says.

Mosher, Arthur. (GC) "This is India" sections: "The Land and Its People," "The Hindus," and "The Village." *Mennonite Life*, July 1950.

Neufeldt, R. W. (MB)"The Response of the Ramakrishna Mission," and "The Sikh Response" in *Modern Indian Responses to Religious Pluralism.* Harold G. Coward, ed. (Albany: SUNY, 1987) 65-83, 269-89.

Neufeldt, Ronald W. (MB) "The Study of Other Religions: Its Necessity and Problems," *Direction* (12, no. 2, Apr 1983) 28-33 and http://www.directionjournal.org/article/470; 8 pp.

Neufeldt here explains to a Mennonite Brethren readership how he as a historian of religions with particular beliefs and perceptions interacts with ideas valued by other, often called non-Christian, religious traditions. He expects to understand what beliefs, such as personal destiny, others find meaningful, how they shape daily living within today's world, and how they have changed through time. Two questions surface: Why be concerned to understand others? and What questions emerge for an Anabaptist who learns to know traditions of others? (1)

Neufeldt is aware of western patterns. Response to non-western religious traditions can be hostile or bigoted. Our world has 'shrunk' in the sense of increased travel and communication. The number of people living in the west and loyal to religions other than Christian has increased. He observes how Christians have overlooked the fact that all people are by nature "deeply religious" because linked with God. Created in God's image all people witness to and are confronted by God within history. While Christians claim Christ as revealed by God, others also live in God's presence. All people perceive things partially; without ultimate or final truth, all will both teach and learn from others, Neufeldt believes. Mennonites, within the Believers' church tradition, claim voluntary confession of faith alongside religious liberty and pluralism. Therefore, an exclusivist, evangelical Christian stance will be questioned, in part, because the universalistic message of the Bible needs to be owned, not ignored. Further, being realistic and honest about both differences and similarities between religions will matter. Neufeldt also encourages admitting uncertainties about others, assessing implications of how others have been approached in the past, and learning through interfaith relationships, events, and formal studies in order to broaden personal faith.

Nyce, Dorothy Yoder. (MC) "Strands of the Sacred" and "Indian Women Speak for Themselves." in *Strength, Struggle and Solidarity: India's Women*. Dorothy Yoder Nyce (Goshen, IN: Pinchpenny Pr, 1989) 7-24, 70-85.

Yoder Nyce's experience with a five-week, Fulbright study tour focused on "Women, the Family, and Social Change in India" led to this C. Henry Smith Peace Lectureship in 1989. Her personal quest for the sacred combines with attention to the sacred that permeates life in India, through scripture, Hindu deities, or festivals. Through experience and tenets or from temples, forehead symbols, and priests, insight accumulated. Yoder Nyce briefly notes the history of Hinduism and its reform movements. She gives attention to Hindu women's experience—

fertility, the "ideal" woman, laws, and their poetry. Noted saints Mira Bai, Lalla, and Andal introduce further sacred strands.

Over a hundred Indian women, some of whom were Hindu, responded to a questionnaire of one hundred items that Yoder Nyce created and analyzed. While cultural aspects dominate the information that was gathered, religious aspects also appear—lighting the evening *puja* room lamp, praying, and festivals. Important Indian Hindu women appear too—Sarojini Naidu, C. S. Lakshmi, and Kasturba Gandhi. Among books annotated were those about Hindu family and marriage, inequality and caste, women saints, and goddesses.

Rao, R. R. Sundara *Theology in the Telugu Hymnal* (Madras: Christian Literature Society, 1983). Mennonite Brethren are located primarily in the Telugu language area.

This helpful resource by Rao, who is not a Mennonite but well-known among MBs in India, reveals how the idea of complete surrender to the *istadevata* (favored God) was adopted from Hindu culture for Christian purposes. Rao suggests that two-thirds of Indians today look to *bhakti*, a phenomenon known for twenty-five centuries, for spiritual redemption.

When Stanley Friesen (MC) reflected with the writer[6] on Mennonite perceptions of Hindu thought or practice, a memory from his missioner father, John A. Friesen (MC), linked *bhakti* (word for Hindu devotion) with *bhajans* (hymns) sung by Christians. Both express *devotion to the Divine*; both express longing to be near or desire to be faithful to the One God. *Bhakti* is one of three key Hindu *marga* (ways) toward salvation, the other two: *jnana* (knowledge) and *karma* (action).

That Indian Christians—literate or illiterate—sing faith or express *bhakti* through *bhajans* is equally clear, Rao explains. Aware of ancestral composers brought up with intense *bhakti* in Hindu temples, Christian *bhajan* writers glorify the Son of God through names like Giver of Life and Personification of Light, Rao adds. The first Protestant Telugu hymn was written by Purushotham Choudhury on the occasion of his baptism in 1833. Of his additional 130 hymns, twenty appear in present Mennonite Brethren hymnals. Through such *bhajans* Christians witness to a desire for stability in life, the Lord's divine presence, and the Spirit's guidance from darkness to light. (7, 12, 77, 80, 100]

Paul Wiebe (MB) in correspondence with the writer[7] reports his recent conversation in India with E. D. Solomon (MB) who recently completed his PhD on the life and times, therefore contributions, of Purushotham Choudhury. Solomon explains that Choudhury was Hindu Brahmin in background from two centuries ago. He was "wonderfully poetic and profoundly attuned with classical Indian traditions in music in his melodies" prior to and since being baptized into the Church. Throughout Mennonite Brethren communities that speak Telugu, members sing Choudhury's devotional hymns. Wiebe finds Choudhury's blend of Telugu with Sanskrit roots to reflect an India-wide philosophy combined with fully, Christ-centered *bhakti* to be profoundly part of Mennonite worship experience. Wiebe also mentions R. R. K. Murthy, who, like Choudhury from Brahmin background, was baptized into the MB Church. He saw Christ as the 'fulfillment' toward which the *bhakti marga* could and does lead a committed follower of Christ. Wiebe—through Solomon's insight into Choudhury's religious depth, plus through his own and his missioner father John Wiebe's (MB) acquaintance with Murthy—realizes anew that Indians and missioners alike "from the beginning saw all that comprises the 'stuff' of *Bhakti*—the 'love of God'—within their own worship."

Yoder, **John Howard**. (MC) "Other Faiths: Fragments" from John H. Yoder: "The Christian View of Other Religions" 2-5 and "The Finality of Jesus Christ and other Faiths" 6-33. (Notes for course "Theology of a Christian World Mission" at Eastern Mennonite College and Seminary summer 1964. It became a chapel talk at Goshen College, 1973, and part of "Ecclesiology in Missional Perspective" at Associated Mennonite Biblical Seminary, Fall 1983.) Both appear in General Papers Files, AMBS Library.[8]

Yoder, **Jonathan G**. (MC) *Jungle Surgeon* (Self-published, 1989) A serialized version of this appeared in *Mennonite Weekly Review*. Missioner John A. Friesen (MC) drew the sketches that accompany stories.

Jonathan G. and **Fyrne** (Miller) Yoder lived in India from 1937-1945, and 1947-1953, returning five more times, twice to India and three times to Nepal, each time for one to three-year assignments.

When tigers, leopards or snakes killed village animals or people, Yoder was often called, with his helper Bisamber, to kill the villains. The stories themselves captivate. Dangerous snakes appear often in India's jungles; their bites seldom allow a victim time to reach a doctor. Village Hindus consider snakes to be demons; to kill one is feared. The unknown can prompt terror in either powerless or powerful people. When called to a village where a woman had been bitten hours before, Yoder found six men lined up three on a side holding the woman on their laps while ritually blowing long, deep breaths over the body to exorcise the evil spirit. They explained their uncertainty of whether she was dead until he declared such reality. Ever-grateful for "divine kinship" in India among Christian denominations, Yoder learned from a Lutheran physician that Indians believe that a snakebite victim "goes through a twilight stage of suspended life"; full life might return. (36)

Of several things Yoder is certain: that a Hindu who blindly accepts fate as due to past sins or a Christian who claims merit for past blessings are both wrong. Hindu patients respond in different ways to Dhamtari Christian Hospital's scheme for payment and care, for body or soul. While many poor folk paid nothing for the medical assistance that Yoder provided, others may have paid four to eight cents. The grateful poor of the charity ward provided fulfilling thrills. "Truly the poor were my best patients; the Lord paid their bills," Yoder confesses. (80)

Yoder tells of his varied patients. Raja Ram arrived with a case of advanced tuberculosis. Of the highest (Brahmin) caste, known as Hindu spiritual leaders or teachers, Raja Ram came to know Jesus as surely as earlier he had claimed Hindu answers. Another patient, a low-caste Hindu, arrived with a massive skin problem in the genital region. Manu had been abandoned by his relatives and former friends. After slow healing occurred, he confessed interest in baptism. On the occasion of that worship service, three members of a political party intolerant of anything religious other than Hinduism appeared. Asked if Manu wished to be baptized and have his *chuti* removed (small strand of hair worn in the back of a Hindu man's head), he replied, "Cut it off." That act done, the three visitors followed Manu to his hospital room before escorting him to the front gate. When asked there if he was "leaving of his own free will," he answered that he was. Yoder's confident conclusion to the story is: "The kingdom of heaven is sure to prevail." (86)

Other events with religious meaning drew Yoder's attention. After seeing the sacrificial slaughter of a buffalo in Nepal, he observed blood from the animal being applied to a wayside image before the devotee took the carcass home. Yoder also knows of nearby Gond tribal people's worship of Mata Dai (goddess of smallpox); he knows of their wish to be freed from fear expressed at Kali Temples.

Yoder often talked and joked with neighborhood children. When smallpox 'visited' the tribal folk around Dhamtari, several hospital workers went to vaccinate them. Having been gone for "hot season vacation" Yoder then asks some boys, "How did you get rid of the Mata? I don't hear about it anymore." "We got rid of the witches" the boys replied. "Witches," Yoder asks, "Who were they? And what do witches do?" Certain, the boys named different mothers who "make dead people get alive again before eating them." "Really, Jethu," Yoder asks one fellow, "Didn't your mother always take good care of you? Surely she was not a witch." Jethu explained that "the witches just got frightened and ran away." Yoder ponders a long time before writing about how "Kali," fear, and Hindu escapism continue for some folk. Thinking then of 'hunts' in Salem, Massachusetts Yoder contemplates American myths too. (90-92)

Yoder also writes about Hindu-Muslim conflict. During early years in India, Yoders noticed at train stops how venders shouted "Hindu Pani" (water) or "Musselman Pani" or Muslim or Hindu "Chai" (tea). While colonial England may have benefited from such divisions, it hoped to leave India united on leaving. But the problem runs deep; bloody riots may on occasion erupt between people of the two religions. Living in Bihar State during ugly riots in that state's city of Ranchi led Yoders to fear getting out onto main roads. They were reminded of similar problems during the time of Partition or after Gandhi's death. "Wars that are fought in the name of religion are always the worst wars. Even Christians have not understood our Prince of Peace," Yoder laments. (111-15)

Soon after arriving in India, Yoders had learned about issues surrounding death and fatalism, learned in part through a firm Hindu language teacher of Hindi. For a Hindu to touch a dead animal or person prompts disdain. Yoder describes a funeral pyre scene—the soberness, sadness, and solemnity. Along with preference for cremation of the dead, Hindus hope that ashes enter flowing water. Practices regarding reincarnation and Nirvana then follow. (116-20) Yoder also knows Hindus who claim that fate, rather than choice or responsibility, determines outcomes. Rather than admit that he dropped the broken cup, a cook might explain, "From my hand it broke." Or a person with leprosy might say, "Leprosy met with me." When Yoder strained to extract a tough tooth (not a dentist, he nevertheless encountered that role), the patient mumbled, "I must have been a great sinner in some previous life that I now have to suffer all this pain." (124)

Yoder's accounts convey a distinct time period in which a deep gulf between "haves" and "have-nots" persists; for that situation he expresses regret. (134)

Yoder, Sanford Calvin (MC). *Eastward to the Sun*. (Scottdale, PA: Herald Pr, 1953).
Having been Secretary of Mennonite Church Missions and Charities, S. C. was invited to attend the celebration of 50 years of missioner involvement in Dhamtari, India. He reports several Hindu dimensions.

Yoder experienced Indian Hindu people as beautiful and deeply religious, with profound respect for things "holy." For example, he learns that their reason for dealing kindly with monkeys centers in their mythic story of Sita wife of Ram, King of Ayodhya. When being kidnapped from a forest retreat by the ruler of Island Kingdom toward the southeast, she drops pearls along the way including into a cluster of monkeys seated on a hilltop; they later come to her aid. (120-2)] And from the northern border Yoder learns of ancient, thrifty Aryan invaders described in the Vedas (hymns) with deep concern for the hereafter or

things beyond this world. Among others they worshipped "bright gods."
From the *Rig Veda* scripture Yoder highlights:

Many tinted Dawn, the immortal daughter of heaven . . .
Darkly shining Dusk, thy sister has sought her abiding.
Dusk and Dawn bring birth! O sisters! Your path is unending.
Bright luminous Dawn . . . Wide-expanded Dawn!
Open the gates of the morning. (130-31)

Yoder verifies that for a person to know India, to know how its villages and ancient faith convey basic Hindu ways of life is essential. Most of India's population at the time of early missioners lived in villages where needs as for sanitation pervaded. All institutions begun and served by Mennonites—education, industrial, medical, and charitable—arose out of people's needs. (139, 182) . . . Of ancient Goddesses, Yoder observes that Swami Dayanand Saraswati was a leader based in the Vedas; practices like caste, polytheism, and idolatry did not then exist. He understands the yearning that people had for times past when hymns expressed hunger as no more prominent for poor than for rich folk. . . . Yoder also senses the antagonism felt by masses toward those who might lead Hindu nationals away from their faith. And he perceives the ascetic, fasting Gandhi's dependence on spiritual resources, his reliance on council table rather than battle field.

Yoder also confesses how close God seemed when he met with missioners near the Mahanadi River to pray for wisdom and grace—for the "tangled skein" of their circumstances to be "unwound and woven into a pattern that fits into the design set by the Man of Galilee." (195, 190, 193, 207)

---

[1] Stage definitions named are enhanced by the writer from Karel Werner's *A Popular Dictionary of Hinduism*, (Surrey, UK: Curzon Pr, 1997).

[2] Chad Bauman (MC) introduces in more detail the Satnamis who followed Das.

[3] But this writer believes that it applies directly to religious aspects of Hindu culture.

[4] Readers who are interested in learning more about Sundar Singh might value: *Wisdom of the Sadhu Teachings of Sundar Singh*, compiled and edited by Kim Comer, (Farmington, Pa: Plough Publ House, 2000).

[5] Not about Hinduism, the writer wishes by noting this resource to credit Indian Mennonites, noting Malagar's having been invited to write for this series.

[6] Personal conversation in Elkhart, IN, August 26, 2014.

[7] October 24, 2014.

[8] Yoder sent these "Fragments" to the writer on 25 July 1995; her lengthy response to him (as requested) followed on February 20, 1996.

Mahatma Gandhi

A number of Mennonites have written about the noted, Hindu Indian personality Mohandas K. Gandhi (Mahatma or "Great Soul" in Sanskrit): peace advocate, social reformer, implementer of *satyagraha*, and leader of masses of people. Some commented from North America, others from locations in India.

From India's Bihar State S. J. Hostetler (MC) wrote to the Mennonite Board of Missions Elkhart, Indiana, office several weeks after Gandhi's death: ". . . having been invited to the local 'immersion day,' I joined a procession to the river where I read Matthew 5:1-14 and gave a little tribute to Gandhi. That I could do with an honest heart," he said.

S. T. Moyer (GC) called Gandhi's negation of British rule "satanic"; by promoting *swarag* (home rule) he did "all that he could to break down their rule." Others judged Gandhi "blind to the evils" of caste and Hindu Brahman money-lending patterns. Hardly surprising, Moyer's solution would have been for Gandhi to accept Jesus' and his nonviolent way.

Views about Gandhi ever-differ. In India for a Fulbright lectureship year in 1960 and after later, short MCC (Mennonite Central Committee) assignments there, life-long peace advocate Atlee Beechy (MC) quotes Gandhi who served as his mentor: "Nonviolence succeeds only when we have a real living faith in God."

John A .Lapp's (MC) 1972 study of Mennonites in India reflects missioner awareness of Gandhi's conviction against conversion between religions; to prompt others to join your religion is arrogant, he had said. Lapp reports that some missioners questioned Gandhi's nonviolent techniques, describing them as "rabid, stubborn, revolutionary, and belligerent." Their critiques, however, combined with a growing defense of or love for India and Indians.

Duane Friesen (GC) notes that Gandhi's Hinduism did not "stand in the way" of most Mennonites viewing positively his position. The final chapter of Friesen's *Christian Peacemaking and International Conflict: A Realist Pacifist Perspective* discusses Gandhi's idea of *satyagraha* within Christian peace theology.

Leah Sonwani (GC), an Indian attending the Mennonite seminary in Elkhart, Indiana, at the time of Gandhi's death wrote of him as "the brightest star of the Indian skies." She was aware of both British lust for power and Indian weakness; the latter had been defeated by this honest, determined man, she thought.

Griselda Gehman Shelly (GC) shares a human interest account of Gandhi the man with her father. [1] Of Mennonite background, 34 year old Gilbert Gehman, with keen interest in peace and nonresistance, wrote in appreciation to Gandhi after he (Gehman) preached on peace. He addressed his letter simply to "London, England." Gandhi's response, sent from Port Said on 17th Dec. '31:   Dear Friend,

> I must thank you for your letter of 15th Nov. last. I am glad that your congregation appreciates the non-violent means we are adopting to regain our lost liberty.
> Yours Sincerely,   M. K. Gandhi.

Rather than bring what Mennonites have written about Gandhi together within a narrative format focused on particular themes, this section annotates material from specific authors' insight or experience. Distinctions become obvious. Not in alphabetical order with others, a short article by **Orlando Waltner** (GC)—"Mahatma Gandhi and World Peace," *Mennonite Life*, (17, no. 2, April 1962) 55-58—reviews life details about Gandhi; it serves here as an introduction to the man:

- born October 2, 1869 . . . married Kasturba when he was thirteen and she eleven. . . studied law in London;
- invited by a Muslim firm in South Africa to be a legal advisor; he refused to submit to "second-class citizenship" . . . formed the Natal Indian Congress; used weapons of pen and type, spades and shovels, along with *satyagraha* . . . started a nonviolent movement: to oppose the South African 1906 requirement that all Indians register (like criminals) and to protest an action taken in 1913 that marriage of Muslims with Hindus was illegal;
- having returned to India, launched by 1919 a nationwide resistance to the Rowlatt Bill that permitted the British to keep people in prison without trial or through secret trial . . . started a non-cooperation program with symbols of spinning wheel and homespun cloth . . . promoted local manufacture of salt after a two-hundred-mile march to the sea that proved the right of access to salt rather than pay a British salt tax . . . Ninety thousand were imprisoned for this act of non-cooperation.
- pursued first fast unto death that resulted in permission for "untouchable" Indians to vote . . . fasted at age 79, fearing partition to come, until on the sixth day a peace pact to restore Hindu-Muslim relations was signed . . . died thirteen days later (30 January, 1948) from a bullet shot by a radical Hindu. (55-56) "Ram, Ram" was his dying expression.

Waltner quotes eight lines of a Gujarati hymn that shaped Gandhi's meaning of *satyagraha* or "soul force." This hymn combined with Jesus' teaching in the Sermon on the Mount fixed in Gandhi's heart awareness that Truth cannot be destroyed. *"Satya,"* the fact of truth, and *ahimsa* (nonviolence or non-killing), the method for applying the fact, came together.

> For a bowl of water give a goodly meal;
> For a kindly greeting bow down with zeal;
> For a simple penny pay thou back with gold;
> If thy life be rescued, life do not withhold.
> Thus the words and actions of the wise regard;
> For every little service tenfold they reward.
> But the truly noble know all men as one;
> And return with gladness good for evil done. (56)

Waltner also finds Gandhi to believe that the Indian mind and heart can practice using these weapons:

- We will match our capacity to suffer against your capacity to inflict the suffering.
- We will match our soul force against your physical force. We will not hate you but we will not obey you. Do what you like and we will wear you down by our capacity to suffer. And in the winning of our freedom we will so appeal to your hearts and consciences that we will win you. So ours will be a double victory. We will win our freedom and our captors in the process. (57)

With the sword of *satyagraha* being love, Gandhi refused government protection when going directly to where Partition needed his message of love and peace. The division of India (Partition) led to mass killings between Muslims and Hindus along with Sikhs. But fasting, after due spiritual preparation, became the major moral force for him, Waltner explains. Gandhi compared his redemptive 'conversion' known through fasting with the 'coercion' practiced by Jesus from the cross. Each made others good by taking on suffering himself. Convinced that his objective and method were correct, Gandhi set out eight points needed for agreement between Hindus and Muslims, points that favored the minority group. Then he "left the consequences to God."

Gandhi's *satyagraha* can prompt bias. Some Christians question whether *satyagraha* was by itself effective since it was used against British people who believe in God and human rights. Further, some fanatic Hindu folk reflect bias when they negate Gandhi because he credited people other than Hindus. "Things that make for peace" lie in the *atma*, the Hindi word for *eternal spirit*. The Hindu power that Gandhi reflected was *atma*. Waltner summarizes Gandhi's universal principle this way:

No individual group or nation needs to submit to wrongs or injustices nor need they go to war to right that wrong. There is a third way, the way of nonviolence. If nonviolent resistance is organized in a thorough and disciplined way, then the individual, group, or nation need not be forever vulnerable. Gandhi would insist that his method will conquer any and all enemies. (58)

Groff, Weyburn W. (MC) titled his 1963 PhD dissertation "*Satyagraha* and nonresistance A comparative study of Gandhian and Mennonite nonviolence." Originally submitted at Princeton Theological Seminary, this doctoral work was not in print until 2009. Groff was, while studying Gandhi, a missioner faculty member at Union Biblical Seminary in Yeotmal (Yavatmal) located in the state of Maharashtra. He often took seminary students and guests, through the 1950s, the forty miles to Gandhi's Sevagram Ashram. Aware of Gandhi's hopes for "freedom for all faiths," Groff counsels Mennonites to understand that Christian faithfulness emerges in the context of multiple faiths, not in isolation. He hopes that readers of his study will gain "insight into the many efforts being made to find nonviolent ways to resolve conflicts and bring peace with justice." (2009 Preface xvii)

Groff explores "Gandhian nonviolence: *Satyagraha*" in his third chapter. Intent to bring together teaching from the Hindu religious text, the *Bhagavad Gita*, and Jesus' Sermon on the Mount, Gandhi views complete renunciation as the "highest form of religion." (52) The battle within the Hindu *Gita* story symbolizes a person's struggle between good and evil; the battlefield represents the human soul, Groff explains. Krishna, depicting the divine "dweller within," whispers counsel in response to Arjuna's inner struggle, his duel between evil and good. Krishna recommends faithfulness to the Divine within. (78)

Gandhi's nonviolent direct action called *satyagraha*, his principle of social action for a situation of conflict, is known as "truth-force," "love force," or soul-force." It insists on Truth. For him, to realize Truth is to realize God; to realize God is to realize Truth. Through a half century Gandhi's creed became "Truth is God." Truth for him meant "what the voice within tells you." Faith expresses the "living, wide-awake consciousness of God within." (67)[2] Either Truth or God transpires through reason as well as living faith. Groff explains that methods of *satyagraha* may then involve any of multiple steps of civil disobedience like negotiation, strike, demonstration, self-purification, fasting, or economic or tax noncooperation. (77, 81, 86-94)

"Mennonite nonviolence: Nonresistance" is the title of Groff's fourth chapter. The Anabaptist-Mennonite term *nonresistance* means "belief that the will of God requires the renunciation of warfare and

other compulsive means for the furtherance of personal or social ends."
(2, 125)[3] Chapter 4 highlights important writings, events, and names
through Anabaptist-Mennonite history on the theme of nonresistance:
from the *Schleitheim Confession of 1527* to Menno Simon's *Fundament-
Boek of 1539-40* (emphasis on truth in the scriptures) to the *Dordtrecht
Confession of 1632* (Articles XIII and XIV) to a cluster of writings and
meetings in 1946, 1950, 1951, and 1961. Shapers of North American
Mennonite nonresistance named are: Guy F. Hershberger, Gordon
Kaufman, Edward Yoder, John Howard Yoder, and J. Lawrence
Burkholder.[4]

Several of Groff's informative statements about Gandhi include:

- In contrast to his father, Gandhi's mother Putiba lived a very
  devout life: keeping fast days, regularly visiting temples,
  teaching the Indian maxim "There is nothing higher than Truth."
  . . . Admitting a deep childhood fear of ghosts, Gandhi's servant
  Rhambha suggested a remedy for him—to repeat the holy
  name *Ramanama*. It became a lifetime devotional habit. (46)
- Gandhi liked Hindu flexibility, tolerance, space for self-
  expression, respect for and freedom to draw from all religions.
  Born a Hindu he felt responsible to remain one. (59)
- Spiritually independent, Gandhi's ideas emerged through
  reading—Jesus' Sermon on the Mount and Tolstoy's *Kingdom of
  God is Within You, The*—actions, and inner resources. (54)
- Gandhi said of his 1909 book, *Hind Swaraj (Indian Home Rule)*: It
  teaches the gospel of love in place of hatred, replaces violence
  with self-sacrifice, and pits soul force against brute force. (59)
- Gandhi insisted that his leadership in India's "freedom struggle"
  enhanced uplift for the masses and preparation for nationhood,
  rather than to be rid of the British government. (60)
- Gandhi's devotion to Truth led him into the field of politics. (65)
- Familiar with many terms or names for God perceived through
  faith, none seemed to Gandhi more appropriate than *Truth*. (66)
- Cardinal virtues of Hindu thought and practice include:
  harmlessness (*ahimsa*), truthfulness (*satya*), non-stealing
  (*asteya*), chastity (*brahmacharya*), non-possession of
  unnecessary things (*aparigraha*), and fearlessness (*abhaya*). For
  a*himsa,* the greatest force includes from Jain thought non-injury
  to all creatures. Without *ahimsa*—despite an opponent's
  goodness—truth is impossible to find, Gandhi suggests. (48, 71-
  2, 82)

Groff's final, short (151-59) chapter identifies a few ways that
satyagraha and nonresistance differ and are similar.[5]
Similarities:

- *Satyagraha* and nonresistance both see continuity between religion and morality.
- Nonresistance and *satyagraha* are essential to wholeness of life.

Differences:

- Whereas *satyagraha* evolved over decades in a setting of political and social activity, nonresistance reflects religious, not political, reform. However, Groff admits that Gandhi was "essentially religious" in his political and social activity. (151)
- Whereas *satyagraha* as a technique was conceived pragmatically, nonresistance came into being through dogma.
- Whereas Hinduism and Gandhi claim that Ultimate Reality (with many names like Truth or God, and incarnations) is indefinable, Mennonites know with certainty through history and scripture something of God's nature and that God exists. (152-53)
- Whereas *satyagraha* credits humanity as good, Mennonite belief sees natural humankind as essentially evil; it becomes good and responsive to good only by God's gracious act.
- Whereas Gandhi's *satyagraha* is based in reason, nonresistance finds sanction in scripture. (153)
- Whereas Groff sees motivation for self-suffering in *satyagraha's* appeal to justice and empathy, to move an opponent, suffering naturally follows from identity with Jesus. (155)

Hiebert, Paul G. (MB) "Conversion in Hinduism and Buddhism" in *Handbook of Religious Conversion*, H. Newton Malony & Samuel Southard, eds. (Birmingham, AL: Religious Education Press, 1992) 9-21.

Hiebert's article includes a brief section about Gandhi. Gandhi understands *conversion* as a change of behavior within a way of life, not a change of creed, action or conduct. As Margaret Chatterjee writes in *Gandhi's Religious Thought*, the goal within the *satyagrahi's* search for truth is to improve relations, Hiebert says. Not a matter of changing one's label or turning against former traditions, *conversion* improves how Hindus and Muslims or caste Hindus and untouchables behave with each other. Not to defeat or win over another, the other's nonviolent conduct leads a person to transform personal action and understanding.

Jantzen, Luben W. (GC) "Has Gandhi Gone to Heaven?" *India Calling*, (GC Missioner Newsletter, (10, no. 3, Autumn 1948).

This report follows Jantzen's hearing lectures on Hinduism by A. C. Chakravarti, a former Hindu Brahmin who worked among Hindu priests and ascetics in holy places like Vrindaban and Benares. Jantzen heard Chakravarti at the Landour Language School, Mussoorie, U.P., India.

Jantzen repeats Chakravati's reasons why Hindus answer the question raised by the title in the negative. *First*, a person consists of three parts: 1. Gross body made up of five physical elements; 2. Subtle body (desire or the mind, intellect and ego; 3. *Atma* or eternal spirit.

When Gandhi was shot on January 30, 1948 at 5:00 p.m., his spirit entered directly into another gross body determined by the seat of desire (no. 2). Gandhi clearly continued to desire either the full realization of India's freedom from a foreign controller or that Hindus and Muslims be united in a New India. As long as desire persists, further existence (rebirth) is required, Jantzen learns from Chakravarti. Salvation, that follows innumerable re-incarnations, means that desire no longer exists. At that point the spirit returns to the Great Atma (or Heaven) along with the absence of desire.

Second, the lecturer informed listeners like Jantzen that Gandhi could not have gone to the Hindu understanding of Heaven. He was not born a Brahman, the highest caste in the Hindu social system—those who perform religious rites and ceremonies. Only Brahmans might escape rebirths because of the merit that they achieve through performing religious observances. Even so, a born Brahman also knows *karma*, consequences positive or negative for how life is lived.

Jantzen then turns to the Christian view of Heaven. Some Christians might presume that following Gandhi's physical death he, because of his good quality of life, would have entered Heaven. Others would deny Heaven to Gandhi. Between those two options many would choose not to decide, leaving the matter to God. Jantzen expects literal, traditional interpretations of biblical scriptures to answer his question: from John's gospel: 3:36, 8:24b, 14:6; Acts 4:12, and II Corinthians 5:17. "Apart from Christ, there is no other Savior for man's soul," he believes. For the "Christian, heaven is to be with Christ eternally, after death."

Jantzen's final paragraph notes three clues from Gandhi that might prompt readers to draw a conclusion to the question in the title:
I cannot give Jesus Christ a solitary throne.
I place Ram, Krishna, and Jesus Christ on one level.
His last words on being shot: "Ah, Ram."
He fell asleep in Ram, not Jesus Christ, Jantzen concludes.

Kaufman, James Norman (MC) "Political Matters" in *Walks and Talks in Hindustan*. (Self-published: Goshen, IN, 1963) 103-10.[6]
Kaufman describes the agonies, imprisonments, and riots en route to India's independence. He credits Gandhi's double role—political and religious leader—in the struggle for swaraj (self-rule). Political neutrality led to varied decisions. The account of Kaufman's receiving a postcard from Gandhi on 30-6-47 appears elsewhere.

Kaufman reports how Dhamtari area missioners felt cowardly after having obeyed a British official's command to gather one night from their scattered locations to the medical station in Dhamtari in case riots would follow from a plan to arrest Gandhi. Their cooperation prompted the group's decision to "stick to our duties and take the consequences" should a future such "emergency" arise. . . . On another occasion Kaufman turned down a government offer to be an honorary magistrate. Such a mix of church work with government affairs would counter a resolution forged already in 1921 by missioners. . . . With his wife Lillian, Kaufman attended a tea party with Dhamtari lawyers on Independence Day (15-8-47). Officials were pleased to find a flag unfurled that day in the Mennonite school yard he reports.

Krahn, Henry G. (MB) Review of *A Gandian Theology of Liberation*, Ignatius Jesudasan (Maryknoll, NY: Orbis, 1984) in *Mission Focus*, 13-14.

Krahn credit's Jesudasan for interweaving Gandhi's liberation theology, life experiences, and link with India's history. He sees the theology of "*Swaraj*" as central. Rather than clarify that term to mean "self-rule," he describes it as a "universal concept upheld by most living religions . . . built on the broader ground of culture, religion, and civilization." From Jesudanan, Krahn understands Gandhi's foundation for *swaraj* as religious—his opposition to any godless civilization, and his belief in "no autonomy apart from God-realization." Krahn observes Gandhi's challenge to Christianity as a whole, to "the lordship of the church" through tension with exclusive and universal views of Christ.

Kunjam, Shantkumar (MC) *An Exploratory Examination of the Ethics of Gandhiji in the Light of Biblical Teachings.* Thesis for a Master's in Peace Studies, (Associated Mennonite Biblical Seminaries, Elkhart, IN, May 1982).

To ponder an Indian Mennonite's view of distinct themes relevant for understanding Gandhiji matters. He identifies Hindu Gandhi's personal characteristics as sincerity, disciplined determination, self-less service, identification with the masses, untiring energy, harmlessness, honesty, truthfulness, and openness in personal life. Kunjam further observes that: Gandhi claimed no personal perfection. A firm believer in God, rebirth, and salvation, Gandhi longed to know God face to face. (26, 41, 56, 72) Other main themes of Kunjam's study appear.

- *Ahimsa* and *Satyagraha* – Kunjam values not only features of nonviolence; he commends the positive aspect of *ahimsa*—love toward all including the non-human. For Gandhi *satyagraha* searches for, insists on, holds to, and applies Truth (God) or soul force. To so pursue Truth also explains *bhakti* (devotion).

Neither God nor *ahimsa* can be fully described, Kunjam learns from Gandhi. (1, 22-23)

- *God* – Kunjam understands Gandhi to know God or Truth through varied terms: all-pervading Spirit, transcendent or beyond proof, detached yet not to be evaded, conscience within, and Cosmic Moral Law. (20-21) Through service especially to underprivileged, common people, Gandhi's sole longing or purpose was to meet or merge with God face to face—his understanding of *prayer*. (20, 21, 24, 26, 28, 41)
- *Gita* - For Gandhi this Hindu text—"The Song Celestial"— provides satisfaction for his soul or full solace through Krishna's revelation of divine qualities, Kunjam states. The Gita is his "book par excellence" for seeking and knowing Truth, for experiencing renunciation as "the highest form of religion." Kunjam notes Gandhi's belief in all Hindu texts like the Upanishads and Vedas. (10, 17, 31)
- *Duty* and *salvation* – From birth on, each person is assigned duties devoid of reward. *Spiritual duty* (*dharma*) or action is one way to attain salvation (*moksha*), to realize Truth. Duty for Gandhi could be expressed through cooperation with a just government and non-cooperative opposition to unjust governing. Kunjam credits Gandhi's belief in a moral principle for humanity. (22, 26, 41, 83)
- *View toward Christianity* – Having grown up with a very saintly mother and a father who showed love for all religions, Gandhi at an early age disliked hearing Christian preachers critique Hindu practice. Intent to worship Truth (God) and live morally, he resented Christians in England who displayed a "single purpose of winning him to Christianity." Christians never convinced him of their singular claim for Christ's uniqueness. He valued the moral teaching of Leo Tolstoy and John Ruskin's writing. (8, 13) Kunjam notes that Gandhi never "tried to understand the Christian faith from the standpoint of its followers." He presumes that although Gandhi never openly accepted Christianity, he was "Christian in heart."(56, 82)[7]

Lehman, M. C. (MC) "Gandhi's Program of Non-violence—A Critical Estimate from a Christian Point of View," *Goshen College Bulletin*, Alumni Newsletter, (xxx, no. 5, May 1936) 1-4, 11.

From direct conversation with Gandhi at his ashram in 1929 Lehman learned that Gandhi's belief in nonviolence stems from Hindu scripture rather than being purely politically motivated. The Sanskrit term *ahimsa*—to avoid doing harm of any kind to any person or living thing— offers a religious context for Gandhi's belief. (1) Mentioned in the early

Vedic literature this concept gains prominence in the sacred Hindu text called Bhagavad Gita. Gandhi expressed personally to Lehman how the Gita and Laws of Manu formulated his ethics. Lehman encourages readers to read a good English translation of the Gita to understand that Gandhi's non-violent stance stemmed from Hindu scripture, despite some inconsistencies.

Lehman describes two major cases that illustrate Gandhi's non-violent resistance. After a year of legal practice in India, Gandhi was called to South Africa to advise Indians who lived there regarding unfair laws. Miners and farmers worked in Natal while thousands crossed the border (against the law without permission) to settle in Transvaal. Offensive laws affected registration, marriage, property, and personal worth; they attacked religion, national honor, and racial self-respect. Gandhi organized mass meetings, mine picketing, and strikes. Four thousand joined the march, going great distances each day, continuing their non-violent pattern even after Gandhi was arrested and jailed—until General Smuts yielded.

A second case that Lehman reports transpired in Bombay in June of 1930. Warned "If you come as far as the corner, we will shoot!" the silent crowd moved "relentlessly, proudly" forward. The English fired as promised. With leading ranks fallen, the next in rank moved, stepping over the dying, toward the guns. As more fell, more women and men replaced them ready to die until a young English lieutenant asked that the guns be moved to the next corner. The crowd continued to march on. The Indian leader broke the silence:

"So long as you point your guns at us, we will march. Rescind your order against our meeting, take away your guns . . . and we will disperse!"
"But that would be to surrender!" came the reply.
"Very well then; we will march until every one of these thousands is dead!"

When the guns were removed, "the crowd melted away like magic, lifting up the wounded and burying the dead." Gandhi's process of nonviolent protest, designed to exhaust, caused the powerful to see tax, legislation, and strength in a new light, Lehman explains.

Loewen, Jacob A. (MB) "My Personal Pilgrimage toward Peace, *Mennonite Life*, (September 1993) 11-14.
Loewen's article includes the brief section "What Gandhi Taught Me." Although Loewen had been warned by an MB minister not to use Gandhi's life as an example for acceptable protest, because "Gandhi was not a Christian," Loewen proceeds to name Gandhi his "best example of what a Christ-like life of renouncing force and depending only on the moral force of love and self-giving looks like." (13) Feeling

that orthodox Christianity distorts Jesus' message, Gandhi turned to the Sermon on the Mount, to engage with his Hindu Gita.

Obedience to non-use of force appears in Gandhi's protest efforts, as in South Africa against passbook laws, Loewen explains. When protestors wished to blockade the passbook office, Gandhi countered: they had no right to inconvenience either passersby or those with legitimate reason to enter that office. Instead, protesters gathered in a park across the street. Loewen also tells that before striking with textile workers in southern India, Gandhi studied what wage increases the mill owners could in fact manage. Although workers wished for more advantage, Gandhi proposed a just solution, fair for all involved. He nudged protestors to be neither arrogant nor subservient. Gandhi also learned in the process: that some workers simply needed to return to work in order to survive; that although he had food available at his ashram, going on a hunger strike was appropriate for him as moral leader; that to "suffer without flinching empowers the sufferer." (13)

From Gandhi, Loewen further learns that Anabaptist efforts of nonviolence dare not violate the dignity of another. Also, verbal aggression to disrupt, block traffic, or shame others can be questionable reflection of moral power. (14)

Neufeldt, Ronald (MB) "The Hindu Mahasabha and Gandhi" in *Indian Critiques of Gandhi*, Harold Coward, ed. (Albany: State University of New York Pr, 2003), 131-51.

Here Neufeldt provides a distinct (among Mennonites) view of Gandhi; a reader encounters key terms or names:

- Mahasabha—the loyal organization begun in 1915, during an all-India Hindu conference at Hardwar, through which comes strong Hindu nationalism, Neufeldt explains.
- V. D. Savarkar was president of the Mahasabha between 1937 and 1942, years when Gandhi worked zealously among the masses to gain India's independence.
- *Hindutva*—foundation for the ideology of Hindu Mahasabha— refers to Hindu consciousness or "Hindu-ness," being "real Hindu." Such traditions are based on the Vedas.[8]
- *Suddhi*—reconversion or "rite of purification" of former Hindu loyalists who return to claiming that religion.
- *Arya Samaj*—Hindu reform movement founded in 1875 by Dayananda with the motto "Back to the Vedas"; it emphasized *suddhi*. *Arya* means noble.[9]

Although the Mahasabha and Gandhi agreed on several points—against religious conversion and for nationalism—their approach to counter the former and achieve the latter differed.

Believing in religion as a "heart-process known only to God," Gandhi saw no reason to change loyalty. Neufeldt explains how Gandhi opposed efforts to proselytize and urged each individual to become a better, more faithful person of whatever religion in the pursuit for Truth. The Mahasabha credited only Hindu being for Indians. (140, 147)

While the Hindu Mahasabha saw violence, Vedic martial heritage, and male machismo as necessary for nation building, Gandhi called for a nonviolent strategy. Mahasabha reacted intensely toward Gandhi's "rabid," senseless principle; he described their tactics as "vicious." Neufeldt saw how Sarvarkar glorified martial aspects and teaching for *himsa* (violence) in the Gita and Ramayana epic as directives for the fight for independence. Gandhi understood the Gita as allegorical; he explained the battle therein as an internal struggle between good and evil. (134, 147-48)

Neufeldt explains Savarkar's view of *nationalism* as a whole way of life, being intentional to defend the Fatherland as Holyland, with no plan for minorities. He saw *suddhi* not only as reconversion to Hindu practice but as removing all that had become impure from having been loyal to another religion. For him, a person could not be loyal to India as a country if not loyal to its indigenous religion. Savarkar judged Muslims as intent to turn India into a Muslim state. In contrast to Muslims, he presumed that Parsees, Buddhists, Sikhs, and Jains were all Hindu in a cultural sense. For a true Hindu defends Hindu, not foreign, culture. By contrast, Gandhi expected India to be open to people of any religion; he himself valued and drew from diverse scriptures. (138, 145-46) Neufeldt suggests a stark conclusion: "Gandhi believed in breaking down barriers; Savarkar and Mahasabha were intent to set up barriers." (149)

Pankratz, James (MB) "Gandhi and Mennonites in India," *Conrad Grebel Review* (30, no. 2, Spring 2012) 136-61. Presented for the 2012 Benjamin Eby Lectureship at Conrad Grebel University, Waterloo, Ontario.

Eby, a leading shaper of Mennonite culture in Upper Canada during the 1830s, believed that "motivation to learn is a response to the Christian Gospel." (161) Pankratz did doctoral research in India on 19th century religious debates between Hindu society and European Christianity and served three years in Bangladesh, India, and Nepal with Mennonite Central Committee.[10]

Pankratz explains Mennonite and Gandhi interpretations of their religions via several pages of history about each. Direct encounters between Gandhi and Mennonites were rare. In addition to M. C. Lehman, Pankratz includes an anecdote from Leoda Buckwalter's writing about Amos Dick, a Brethren in Christ missioner located in north Bihar State.[11] When Gandhi planned to visit a nearby town, Dick prepared to provide goat milk for Gandhi's entourage. Looking forward to ask personal questions from having read Gandhi's speeches, Dick was disappointed to learn that because the day was a Monday, Gandhi's weekly day of silence, to converse with him was impossible. Sitting six feet from Gandhi all day, all he heard was the click of a spinning wheel. Then when Gandhi addressed the crowds on Tuesday, no occasion for Dick to engage the guest occurred.

While early missioners knew little about India or the Hindu religion on arrival, they gradually formed assumptions and attitudes through experience, Pankratz says. Some letters and reports provide personal insight into Hindu teachings, scriptures, and deity forms or names. Without providing direct sources, Pankratz observes: that a North American and European framework and cultural assumptions shaped missioner comparisons; that they described Hindu shrines and worship; that they met opposition; that their overall evaluation of popular Hinduism "was strongly negative. Further, he said that "more than a dozen" focused advanced academic degrees over seven decades on aspects of Hindu thought or practice. (5)[12] For example, George J. Lapp noticed that worship of images may be symbolic or literal, depending on a practitioner's depth of understanding.

Language used both shapes and reflects perspective. While missioners often used the term *heathen*, to suggest that people were inferior or spiritually misguided, common public discourse also used it. Pankratz' answer to his own question: "What did Mennonites find offensive in Hinduism?" can be summarized as: 1. polytheism— universal or local god forms with stories; 2. sensuous, popular worship—priests and processions, temples and sacrifices, devotees encountering god forms; 3. diverse scriptures along with diverse levels of literacy; and 4. social identity through the caste system, seen by missioners as degrading for the majority with whom they worked. (7-8)

Pankratz also explores how Gandhi interpreted and practiced Hinduism. Having grown up in a vegetarian family that honored the god form Vishnu, he had friends known for "philosophical-occult" thought. Theosophists influenced his life-long claim to accounts from and Truth in the *Bhagavad Gita*. Religious practices of meditation and prayer and scripture texts from diverse religions came to be vital for Gandhi. As is characteristic of most people of faith, Gandhi was selective about Hinduism. (8) Some features he praised, others, like support for the label *untouchable*, he questioned. Pankratz explains that while Gandhi was not a literalist with scripture, he rejected what was inconsistent with key terms of *satya* (truth) and *ahimsa* (nonviolence). He interpreted the *Gita's* key battle as symbolic of a person's inner conflict between good and evil. As is true for honest people of any religion, Gandhi did not defend social ills viewed in texts or acted out by co-religionists. With no intent to change religious loyalty, Gandhi could critique the Hindu caste system and avoid offending common people who relied more than he on certain rituals. He was intent, Pankratz says, "to work within Hinduism as it was." (9)

Bypassing Pankratz' non-Hindu section titled "Mennonites and Christianity," several comments deserve annotation from pages focused on "Gandhi and Christianity." On reading a copy of the Bible from a friend in England, Gandhi said: "While chapters following the book of Genesis invariably sent me to sleep," the Sermon on the Mount "went straight to my heart." (11) He thereafter brought together teaching from the *Gita*, the Buddhist *Light of Asia*, Jesus' Sermon, and Tolstoy's *The Kingdom of God is within You*. While he valued Christian hymns like "Lead Kindly Light," he seriously objected to Christian thought about human beings being inherently sinful or vile, Pankratz explains. Viewing each person as responsible for sin, he did not accept the idea of Jesus' atonement for others' sins. Valuing Jesus as one of the greatest, but not perfect, teachers led Gandhi to see him as belonging to all people. (12)

Pankratz also notes critiques of Christianity named by the Hindu Gandhi, some of which Mennonites would share. He opposed Constantine's claim of Christianity; he strongly countered conversion (except "in the sense of self-purification, self-realization"). All religions are resourceful; none is arbiter for others or the "only path to spiritual fulfillment." To add enriching aspects from other faiths to a person's being a better Hindu, Buddhist, or Christian is the goal for Gandhi, not to replace another's faith, Pankratz explains. Gandhi was irked when former Hindus became Europeanized (as with clothes) and was truly offended by Christian' use of abusive language to describe Hinduism. (13) When massive political agitation called for *swaraj* (self-rule), new Indian Christians who no longer used their "mother tongue" could be charged for ceasing to be Indian. What he really scorned was Christian blessing of war through prayers of military chaplains who blessed wartime murder. (14)

While Gandhi and Mennonites agreed on non-violence being based in spiritual being, they differed in detail. Pankratz describes Mennonite nonviolence as "obedience to God and a symbol of separation from the world." He might glorify Mennonite nonresistance when describing it as "direct obedience to God" symbolic of their separation from the world. Gandhi was convinced that nonviolence relied on God (Truth) rather than a religion and that human nature is basically good. Mennonites thought of human nature as inclined to sin and violence, as needing a radical conversion to God through encounter with Jesus Christ. Pankratz notes both the disfavor toward Gandhi of some Mennonites who lived in India prior to independence in 1947—his confrontational noncooperation with Britain—and Gandhi's dislike for Christian clergy who "blessed killing" on battlefields.

According to Pankratz, Mennonites countered Gandhi's "Quit India" approach that could make use of arms or nonviolent force like non-cooperation. (15) They faulted his civil disobedience for being provocative or coercive with intent to retaliate. But, for Gandhi, passive resistance was negative. His intent with *satyagraha*, an active principle, was to lift up or move the adversary's conscience on meeting an opponent willing to suffer. Pankratz makes but an endnote of Gandhi's insistence that "nonviolent, suffering-resistant discipline was rooted in reliance on God." (23, note 63) Whereas violence tried to crush an opponent, nonviolence worked to gain a partner, Gandhi said. (16-17)

Pankratz' final section notes further attention to Gandhi from Mennonites. Correspondence between Gandhi plus several Indian leaders and MC leaders J. N. Kaufman and P. J. Malagar transpired in 1947. (17-18) A couple months prior to India's Independence Kaufman and Malagar wrote to him asking that provision be made in the new Constitution for Mennonites whose conscience opposes "militarism in general and war in particular." Assuring that their intent was to be responsible citizens, Mennonites expressed willingness to give public service instead of participate in war, if that ever occurred.

Gandhi replied via a handwritten postcard dated 30.6.47:

Dear Friend,   Your letter.
Why worry! I am in the same boat with you.
Yours sincerely,   M. K. Gandhi.

Pankratz presumes that Gandhi meant to assure Mennonites of receiving the same treatment since they agreed on the issue. He notes that no provision for conscientious objection appears in the Constitution but that "freedom of religion" is expressed. Further, since an all-volunteer army has functioned during India's three wars since then, the "same boat" could reflect, Pankratz says, that "religious identity and convictions are not factors." (18)

According to Pankratz, Mennonites also noted Gandhi's assassination that occurred on 30 January 1948. Aldine and Eva Brunk's (MC) records include a torn copy of the two-page clipping that appeared in the Goshen, Indiana newspaper, *The News-Democrat*, the day of Gandhi's death. Pankratz notes that within missioners J. D. and Minnie Graber's (MC) files is a copy of the Memorial Service held on February 1, 1948 at the New York City Community Church; honoring Gandhi, Graber reflects ecumenical openness. Graber's *Gospel Herald* (MC) column a week later reflected on the fact that "Gandhi is dead." He credits the Hindu's worthy example, his love for principles based on Jesus' Sermon on the Mount. While not crediting Gandhi's devotion to the Gita and writings from other religions, Pankratz notes that Graber concludes: "Gandhi, the Hindu, helping Mennonites to be better Christians." That statement would have pleased Gandhi, Pankratz says. (19)

John Howard Yoder (MC) "The Religious Origins of *AHIMSA*: a Twentieth-Century Distillation" links with Gandhi, 5 pp.[13]
Theologian Yoder is known for extensive teaching and writing about nonviolence along with Anabaptist-Mennonite mission history. He discusses a quote from M. Gandhi that appeared in *Indian Opinion* April 6, 1921 that makes public the ancient "law of self-sacrifice, the law of suffering." He refers to the *Rishis* (legendary Hindu scholars behind the *Rig Veda*) who discovered the law of non-violence. "Non-violence is the law of our species as violence is the law of the brute." Such non-violence Gandhi wished Indians to practice. Yoder's commentary affirms the rootedness of nonviolence and the place for suffering in ancient Hindu religion; he shows how Gandhi modernized that legacy.

Yoder explains that with more publicity given to Gandhi by the 1930s, an Indian author Krishnalal Shridarani (*War without Violence*, 1939) spent several years in the Gandhian movement and Tagore's school near Calcutta. He made public "the spiritual and cosmological roots of the notion of 'the power of suffering." (1) Yoder details Shridarani's outline of stages through which nonviolence emerges, beginning with the Vedas. There *Yajna* (ritual sacrifice) was natural law; sacrifice or suffering produced a reward from the gods. After sacrifice became a discipline to refine the self, noted in the Upanishads, Jainism made *ahimsa* (non-harming) the very core of religion through legends of those who conquered via non-violent force.

Next, Yoder reports through Shridarani, that Buddha used *ahimsa* to get rid of the cause of suffering. In turn, he was followed by the ruler Asoka who shifted *ahimsa* from a focus on spiritual qualities to its daily cultural dynamic. With the Muslim takeover came a return, as through poetry, to *ahimsa's* being "spiritual resistance for people without political power." (2) Shridarani notes legends and songs that promoted nonviolence. Gandhi then linked this Hindu heritage of stages with his own exposure to Hebrew, Christian and western views of suffering to shape his expression of *ahimsa*. Yoder also mentions an even earlier level, pre-Vedic (but not earlier than tenth century BCE) *ahimsa,* with an ascetic vision through Unto Tahtinen's 1976 overview.

Such extensive history of a concept based in Hindu and more broad religious practice, while also important to Mennonites, can prompt their (our) being more humble about the example and practice of presumed distinctiveness of Christian nonviolence.

Yoder Nyce writes: Based on content discussed in this study of Gandhian influence, this writer observes that Mennonites agree with Gandhi about *religion* as the foundation of life and *nonviolence* as the preferred approach to occasions of conflict. Not all of these writers show freedom to credit what Gandhi valued within his Hinduism. Some might notice Gandhi's positive gestures toward Christianity but not reciprocate. The writer wonders why this imbalance exists and how it determines what we fully learn from this religious world figure, or what overall rapport we expect with Hindu people.

---

[1] *Mennonite Life* (June 1983) 27.

[2] Groff does not always follow Gandhi's pattern to capitalize *Truth*.

[3] Groff briefly admits that "nonviolent resistance" might be a more accurate or adequate term than *nonresistance*. (156)

[4] The writer would prefer if Groff had given more attention to comparing Mennonite nonresistance with the Hindu Gandhi's *Satyagraha* rather than provide such extensive Mennonite history, especially since an earlier chapter had focused on *pacifism*.

[5] Groff's seeming bias for nonresistance may at times glorify it.

[6] Leonard Gross lifts much from Kaufman's chapter into two pages of the April 1983 issue of *Mennonite Historical Bulletin*.

[7] The writer wonders to what extent Mennonites seriously understand Hinduism from the view of its loyalists.

[8] See Neufeldt's article "Hindutva and the Rhetoric of Violence. . ." below. This ideology gains prominence again with RSS (Rashtriya Swayam Sevak Sangh) pressure on the current Prime Minister Modi.

[9] Several GC Mennonite missioners report opposition from this group in their central India area.

[10] The writer's page numbers refer to a 23-page, Xerox copy of Pankratz' lecture; a few of her comments appear with annotations.

[11] *Silhouette: Colonial India as We Lived It*. 108-09; note no. 13, p 20.

[12] Pankratz mentions four of those studies in a note; one is quoted.

[13] This chapter appears in the *History of Religiously Rooted NonViolence: A Series of Working Papers of the Joan B. Kroc Institute for International Peace Studies*. Retrieved on 6/4/00 as http://www.nd.edu/-theo/jhy/writings/history/ahimsa.html Yoder had sent the writer a private printout of this "archive piece" on 12/28/95, two years before his death, then titled: "A twentieth-century distillation of the origins of **ahimsa**."

Later Era - 1990 Onward

Asheervadam, I. P. "The Dalit Character of Indian Churches," *Mission Focus: Annual Review* (vol. 19, 2011) 125-30.

Asheervadam explains something of the vastness of Dalit (formerly known as "Untouchables") history. About 70-75 percent of Christians in India were of these oppressed or "broken" people; within the state of Andhra Pradesh, 59 subgroups of Dalits exist. The Hindu caste system, based on purity and pollution, judged Untouchables as inferior, to be exploited. With their identity being destroyed by higher caste people, groups of Dalits converted to diverse religions—Sikhism, Jainism, Buddhism, Islam, and Christianity. Conversion was "the only way to escape continual discrimination and disgrace," Asheervadam explains. An "Untouchable" Madiga, when touched by a white man on being baptized asked, "Now is this body like a Brahmin, like a Reddy (noted name in AP State) that can now touch everything and everyone?" The missioner replied, "Of course; for Christ nobody is untouchable." (126-27) Dalits have begun to affirm their humanity, to expect equal rights; they also retain sub-caste categories. Madiga and Mala reflect Dalit origin; Christian or Mennonite terms reflect faith and religion. (129)

Asheervadam, I. P. (MB) "The Mennonite and Brethren in Christ Churches of India," in *Churches Engage Asian Traditions*. Global Mennonite History Series: Asia, John A. Lapp, and C. Arnold Snyder, Gen. eds. (Intercourse, PA: Good Books, 2011) 125-219.

"Asian people feel deep connection and unity with the cosmos around them." Mennonite missioners, influenced by a western duality between human beings and nature, arrived in India with love for people and concern to "save souls." Dutch Mennonite Alle Hoekema observes that early sending boards and missioners to India "did not consider theological education to be important either for missionaries or indigenous believers." Nor did they emphasize Anabaptist identity. (18)[1] Japanese Mennonite writer of this book's Conclusion, Takanobu Tojo, states: "All along Christianity has failed to seriously dialogue with Islam, Hinduism, Buddhism or Confucianism in Asian nations." (5, 340) Readers can hope that Asheervadam the Indian writer of this chapter felt free to disclose an indigenous view of the story told here. Hindu or Indian tribal content will be the focus of these annotations whereas Mennonite and church content remains central to the informative chapter.

What is today called Hinduism has gradually grown over five thousand years' time in Asia and India, Asheervadam notes. As religions engage each other they absorb characteristics from each other.

Asheervadam knows that Hinduism includes monotheism, polytheism, and pantheism. He knows about worship of the great Shiva and Vishnu god forms with their female counterparts, village deities, and spirits of trees and rocks. Not surprising is the Hindu view that many paths lead to the same goal. Starting with Vedic scripture dated between 1500 and 500 BCE, Asheervadam explains how Hindu beliefs have shifted—the the transmigration of souls as award or lack of it for current action, and the caste system that determines social arrangement. (129-30)

Asheervadam credits the hierarchy of four major caste groups, along with hundreds of *jati* (sub-castes), as clear cause for inequality. A person's birth shapes identity and dignity; it determines occupation and position within the local scheme. Main groups are: *Brahmins* (priests or teachers), *Ksyatriyas* (rulers or soldiers), *Vaisyas* (merchants or traders) and *Shudras* (laborers or artisans). (129) Most women experience secondary roles. A woman of the highest Brahmin caste is best assured of salvation through serving and honoring her husband. All outside the *varna* or caste scheme, those designated for tasks that defile or pollute (called "untouchables" or Children of God), long for new identity. They prefer to be called *Dalits*. They and as many as 400 tribal groups (together about a quarter of India's population) have been largely oppressed by caste groups—like being refused temple entry. A high percentage of Mennonites have tribal or Dalit heritage. Asheervadam notes that following Independence in 1947 a five-fold increase of Christians from tribal regions took place. (131-33)

Along with Christian growth, strong religious movements emerged in independent India. Hindus responded with "Missies Bharat Chodo" ("missionaries leave India") from 1954-56. Some Dalits chose to have a distinct *jati* identity in addition to being Christian. Noted Indian theologian M. M. Thomas sought to bridge some Hindu philosophy with Christian theology toward an Indian Christian consciousness. "Christian values of sacrifice, charity, and commitment to others all intertwined in this profound understanding of solidarity." (153-54)

Appropriately, Asheervadam credits Indian Christians. Through decades MB Indian leaders have carried the main work of evangelism via organizations of Church Extension Workers and Interfaith Ministries. They went from village to village to preach. They knew sacrifice, selfless service, and tribulations within their own communities. (140-41)[2]

Asheervadam describes MC national leaders like Stephen and Phoebe (Sheela) Solomon who were active with established programs. They grew up in mission hostels and later both were graduated from universities. Stephen became a prolific writer, musician, ordained pastor, and translator with the Bible Society of India. Phoebe, an ordained deacon, became a notable teacher. (159)

From Bharatiya (India) General Conference Mennonite Kallisiya (Church) experience, Asheervadam includes several anecdotes. 1. A senior pastor Ibrahim Nand tells of his grandfather's conversion from the worship of Krishna to the Baptist denomination; GC Mennonites were later accountable for that Baptist area. 2. Although the BGCMK had not engaged much with India's move toward independence, they planned an event for Hindu, Christian and people loyal to other religions to join in Jagdeeshpur on the initial Independence Day August 15, 1947. Indian Samuel Stephen and missioner John Thiessen raised the first flag before all sat together to eat, a rare interreligious happening.

From UMN (United Mission to Nepal founded in 1954) with which numerous Mennonites served comes Asheervadam's account: In the Hindu nation of Nepal where conversion was at the time prohibited, a national pastor was about to baptize a new believer in a nearby river on a Hindu festival day. During Hindu festivals people often go to the river for a sacred dip. When police arrived, all attending the Christian event ran except for the pastor and the one to be baptized. Asked what he was doing the pastor said, "As Hindus do, we are doing a ceremony." "OK, go ahead," the police responded. (173-74, 202)

Bauman, Chad M. *Christian Identity and* Dalit *Religion in Hindu India, 1868-1947* (Grand Rapids, MI: Eerdmans, 2008).

This dissertation is further annotated in the *Academic* chapter. This notes Bauman's account of "blind Simon" from India's Chhattisgarh region where Mennonites are located. Whereas Hindus might link Simon's blindness to *karma* (some previous negative action), Christian Simon openly praises God through it. He links his musical skills to *bhajans* about healing. He conveys biblical stories and expresses devotion to Jesus. As Hindu scriptures often appear in poetic form, Simon creates Christian lyrics. Bauman reports that Hindus familiar with their major epics know stories similar to blind Simon's accounts from Hebrew scripture. His 250 *bhajans* are sung in church settings—some with music from Hindu folk songs, others of Christian doctrine. (200-09)

Bauman, Chad M. "Singing of Satnam: Blind Simon Patros, Dalit Religious Identity, and Satnami-Christian Music in Chhattisgarh, India." *Journal of Hindu-Christian Studies* (2006), 27-35. Available at http://digitalcommonsbutler.edu/facsh_papers/13. See reference above to "Simon Drastahin (Simon the Sightless)" in Bauman's *Christian Identity and* Dalit *Religion,* 200-12.

Early on, Christians in the Chhattisgarh area of India embraced Blind Simon's lyrics that claimed their Satnami roots. As Satnami-Christians later gained more education and social respect through agriculture, they downplayed his content that claimed their lower-caste, Chamar status.

Chamars, the largest *dalit* caste in India, was known for work with tanning, leather goods, and dead animals. Ghasidas, the Satnami founder, had, according to Satnami-Christians, through a vision predicted that a "white-faced man with a book under his arm" would come to them. Bauman explains that Satnami-Christians credit that reference to the coming of missioners but that reformed Hindu Satnamis leave it out of their accounts about Ghasidas. (28)

Blind Simon's songs and musical innovations were welcomed by both Christians and Hindus, Bauman explains. Blindness had kept him from attending school as a child. Juvenile antics that he picked up from unruly playmates, combined with his mythic imagination. Some Hindu observers recalled their stories—like the god form named Krishna's being known for stealing butter when with a cluster of maids. Bauman notes that Simon taught himself to play multiple musical instruments— the *tabla* (drum), *dafali* (small tambourine), *chikara* (stringed, bowed instrument of the *sarangi* family), *tambura* (long-necked, four-stringed instrument made from a gourd and used to accompany a singer), and later the harmonium. At his first formal concert, a Christian *mela* (celebration), he combined the biblical story of the prodigal son with a tune and well-known Indian folk song about two brothers. (29-31)

For some stories, like Paul's conversion, Simon sang a *kirtan*, a chorus with verses. Bauman reports that the *kirtan* is "the most common form of devotional song among Hindus in village India." (31) Large, outdoor crowds of people from all castes gathered to hear Simon. His devotion for Jesus and skill to evoke emotions through stories as of Samson and Delilah drew support as did his performance of Hindu *kirtans* alongside recitations from the *Ramayana* epic. Blind Simon's *kirtan* story songs might follow a Hindi poetic meter or provide a local, indigenous flavor while telling a Christian story. For example, the father in the prodigal son story became a great *malguzar* (landlord), and friends advised the son to spend his inheritance on buying a village!

Bauman adds that blind Simon composed 250 *bhajans*, songs with simple devotional tunes used in church settings. He was graduated from a seminary in the Chhattisgarh city of Raipur in 1923, married, and settled in a nearby town to work in a leprosarium. His *bhajans* might teach themes of Christian doctrines like salvation or follow the Hindu *bhakti* tradition to express his devotion for Jesus his *guru* (teacher). In light of his own handicap, Simon's *bhajans* might deal with the theme of healing in which God would wash wounds. Or he could base a *bhajan* on a regional harvest song or a Hindu wedding segment. Simon's songbook, *Chhattisgarhi Christian Bhajans*, was reprinted nearly every year between 1937 and the late 1940s, Bauman reports. Nearly fifty thousand copies were sold in a region "where fewer than fifteen thousand Christians lived, where less than ten percent of the population could read," Bauman adds. (31-33)

Of further interest is Bauman's report about Simon's parents, converts to Christianity from the local Satnami group. Simon questioned whether his blindness caused them to love him less than his siblings. He also realized their not having fully given up some pre-Christian religious practices. They continued to secretly honor Hindu deities like the smallpox goddess Mata or god Nishana, consulted for auspicious occasions. After hearing an account at church of the Hebrew prophet Gideon who destroyed his father's altar to Baal (Judges 6:25ff), Simon and his brother vowed to get rid of their parents' image of Nishana. That plan scared them, however. They knew that their father Patros (birth name Vishnath) felt that his own father and brother had died after their deity forms were destroyed. Bauman notes how courage and prayer led Simon to succeed in pulling the basket-covered form from the ground before throwing it into the village brook. (29-30)

Annotations here conclude with reference to an interview that Bauman held with a woman who knew some of Simon's songs. Their conversation took place near where Simon first performed a century earlier. Bauman notes: "as the Satnami-Christian story demonstrates, the pre-Christian past . . . remains a live issue." The creative, cultural-based Simon is an example of "hybrid religious expression." (34-35)

Bauman, Chad and Jennifer B. Saunders. "Out of India: Immigrant Hindus and South Asian Hinduism in the USA," *Religion Compass* (3, no. 1, 2009) 116-35.
This chapter by Bauman and Saunders explains some religious shifts that Hindu immigrants to the US have made since the Immigration and Nationality Act of 1965 opened the way for South Asians to settle here. [3] Rather than reflect personal data gained themselves, the authors share insight from other authors. Many first generation Indian immigrants were called "model minorities" because they came as well-educated professionals. Not intent to change their Indian cultural identity or religious affiliation, Hindus in America have become "more religious." They gather together to worship more regularly than they had in India, mostly on weekends (as do their neighbors). They wish to teach their children Hindu traditions and rituals. In India individuals would worship at temples or home altars; there, Hindus would practice the sixteen life-cycle rituals more often too, Bauman and Saunders report. (119)

Hindu Americans also may be more ecumenical, generic, or 'homogenized,' as they bridge between varied deities, rituals, and sacred texts. With access to fewer temples in which to affirm and preserve cultural features, loyalists practice core, distinct expressions of being Hindu without conveying superstition or fanatical patterns.

Bauman and Saunders draw from V. Narayanan four assertions that Hindus in the U.S.A. wish to convey: that Hinduism is a way of life more than religion; that it is tolerant; that while the divine is one with multiple, symbolic representations, it too has a *trimurti*—Brahma, Vishnu, and Shiva; that Hindu rituals convey an "inner meaning" that often promote good health and a safe context. (121)

Through multiple sources Bauman and Saunders credit immigrant Hindus who "look to India for authority and 'tradition.'" Whereas in India Hindus more likely stress purity laws and caste regulations, Gandhi and *Bhagavad Gita* teaching have gained importance in the west. (120-21, 123) American Hindu views vary also regarding the conservative focus among some Indian nationalists about *Hindutva*—'Hindu-ness.' Bauman and Saunders convey from author Prema Kurien that while *Hindutva* defends Hinduism such an ideology can also be destructive. In discussing *transnationalism* they draw from Peggy Levitt's argument that while religious people, practices, and institutions are rooted in particular places, they also cross and transcend such borders. (129) American Hindus, therefore, contribute to a broader Hinduism, Bauman and Saunders conclude.

Finger, Thomas. (MC) "How shall we speak with people of other faiths?" *Gospel Herald*, (January 11, 1994) 1-3.
Finger's subtitle both confesses and questions:
- "Jesus is Lord" is a Christian confession of absolute allegiance.
- Are there ways we can share this confession without oppressing others with our culture?"

Finger's sole reference to Hinduism cautions that media permits "dedicated Muslim or Hindu groups" to wield great influence in our world. He concludes: "Real dialogue cannot be facilitated by attempting to renounce absolutes. It is possible only among those committed to some absolute."

Groff, Weyburn W. (MC) "Hinduism." *Global Anabaptist Mennonite Encyclopedia Online.* (Web. 17 December 2010). http://www.gameo.org/encyclopedia/contents/H563.html; (retrieved 12/17/2012) 2 pp.

Groff notes that early Mennonite encounters with Hinduism involved primarily missioners in India, of whom he was one. They noted superficial aspects like superstition and oppression, observed practices in homes or temples, read books about culture, and attended conferences. A few missioners engaged with the National Christian Council of India or linked with other Protestant denominations. Twentieth century Mennonite contacts with Hinduism have occurred more as Hindu immigrants come to North America and through academic courses. Groff quotes scholar Sarvepalli Radhakrishnan's description of Hinduism as: "not a definite dogmatic creed, but a vast, complex, but subtly unified mass of spiritual thought and realization." Hinduism is expressed through philosophy, festivals and rituals, caste regulations, and images or visual representation of gods, as well as through arts of sculpture, drama and literature. Groff includes MB Peter Hamm's reference (resource elsewhere) to how Christians may approach other religions: through displacement, fulfillment, cooperation (synthesis), or discontinuity. Rather than anticipate broad engagement, Groff concludes with the missioner's task: not to locate points of contact or contrast, they confront Hindus with God's message of redemption in Christ Jesus and invite their response. He notes two related doctoral studies: his own about Gandhi and M. C. Lehman's about a noted Hindu, Indian poet named Harischandra.

Hiebert, Frances. F. (MB) "The Accord Factor in Missions," *Direction* (Spring, 1994, 23, no. 1) 91-100.
Missioner, theologian, and writer Frances Hiebert raises the key dilemma or 'virus' of Christian division into Protestant denominations in settings of multiple religions (like Hinduism). She desires Christian unity, better known as *accord,* in the ecumenical spirit. She highlights a "most potent and effective meaning of witness": when "oneness of disciples" appears, "so that the world may believe." (John 17:21b)

Hiebert, Paul. (MB) *Anthropological Reflections on Missiological Issues.* (Grand Rapids: Baker House, 1994) 72-3, 106-7, 134-5, 144-5, 152-55.
Anthropologist and missioner Paul Hiebert notes diverse situations that are posed when crossing cultures or world views. For example, Hindus may give offerings in church settings or ask Christ to heal their child. Then too, Indians might prefer not to designate a specific number for church membership rolls, to note those who "belong." Village people may range from being "casually interested" to those who are baptized. Counting the latter but not former might discourage those "interested" from continuing to explore. Also, whereas mission-controlled church elections involve only member votes, Indian village Christian candidates for a position may recruit Hindu relatives or friends to attend church on a certain election day in order to vote for them, Hiebert explains. (135)

Non-western societies may focus right relationships while westerners may emphasize order—being on time, straight walls, or cleanliness—and fear chaos. Westerners feel uncomfortable with disorder during church services, ambiguity, or loss of control. Hiebert stresses that people who cross cultures need to understand world views—their own and that of those they encounter. Issues of identity also surface with crossing cultures—what features to borrow, adopt, or reject from others. "We can suppress, but never kill the culture into which we are enculturated as children" he says.

Hiebert, Paul. (MB) "Beyond Anti-Colonialism to Globalism," *Missiology* (19, no. 3, July 1991) 263-81.
Here Hiebert raises concerns that arose during the colonial era and that have been changing within more modern times. Such ideas need attention by anyone meeting people of diverse religions—Hinduism in particular. For example:

- The view that Christianity is true while other religions are false can prompt failure to study another religion, if not worse—intent to replace it. (265)
- In colonial time, those with more power seldom take other cultures and religions seriously or truly perceive the colonized as they understand themselves, Hiebert says. The assumption pervades that those with power are inherently superior. (267) To take others seriously involves taking their beliefs seriously.
- Serious interfaith encounter can prompt people to lessen confrontation and displacement while turning toward dialogue. Hiebert notes John Stott's view: interfaith dialogue involves humility and sensitivity, critique and challenge. To accept other religions as valid systems of belief with internal logic and understandings of truth is part of an anti-colonial stance. (268)
- "Communication must be measured not by what the sender means but by what the receptor understands." (270)
- The anti-colonial reaction "called into question western cultural arrogance and forced western Christians to differentiate between the gospel and their culture." (271)
- Hiebert notes that whereas Christian leaders emphasize *biblical texts* during colonial times and *contexts* during anti-colonial times, a global perspective notes scriptural meanings in many human contexts changed by the message. (276)

Hiebert, Paul. (MB) "Christian Response to Hinduism," in *The Missiology for the 21st Century: South Asian Perspectives*, R. E. Hedlund and Paul Joshua Bhakiarag, eds. (Delhi: ISPCK 2004) 324-35.

Hiebert, Paul G. (MB), R. Daniel Shaw, Tite Tienou. *Understanding Folk Religion A Christian Response to Popular Beliefs and Practices.* (Grand Rapids: Baker Books, 1999).
An important insight here: After living several decades in south-central India, anthropologist Hiebert wrote that villagers' religion might have less to do with formal Hinduism and more with local spirits living in

trees, rivers, or hills. Christian converts might no longer go to Hindu temples, but they continue to struggle with realities of spirits, magic, or ancestors. Therefore, Hiebert nudges missioners to understand village beliefs and practices along with the study of formal Hinduism. (9).

Kaufman, Gordon D. (GC) "Imagining Peace in a Religiously Plural World." MCC Peace Theology Colloquium held at Messiah College, Grantham, PA (18 June 1994) 25 pp. Also published in *The Conrad Grebel Review* (14, no. 1, Winter 1996) 33-47.

Affirming the Mennonite view of Christian *faith* as being *how life is lived*, Kaufman urges hearers to view others as also faithful in doing pacifism. Rather than presume to possess *the* truth, Kaufman wishes hearers and readers to realize that since truth belongs to God alone, they will approach their partial truth with a "non-defensive openness" toward others who have significantly different views. Doing peace theology then involves both claiming Christian insights and keeping alert through imaginative construction to where or how those insights need to be modified, Kaufman says. Rather than primarily through hermeneutics (biblical interpretation), new ways to orient life are useful in developing an ethic of peace theology (ethical thinking about God). Our pluralistic world, including Hinduism, invites our disciplined imagination to welcome those who know different ways to be human—to live—beyond our own parochial stance. Kaufman encourages a profoundly moral Christian faith that is "open to insights, criticism, and correction from other points of view"—other religious or secular worldviews as well as differing views among Christian. To acknowledge God means to admit sin for claiming absolute truth or normative rightness for Christian moral practices that fails to credit truth and worthy practice among others. To value the Christ-event shows both what being human can be and what God is doing. To be about peacemaking, to be about reconstructing our world involves full, imaginative "loving our neighbors as ourselves" (even enemies), Kaufman concludes.

Koontz, Gayle Gerber. (GC) "Speaking prophetically," *Canadian Mennonite* (January 25, 2010) 6-7. This brief response followed discussion of a 4-page paper titled "Confessing Jesus Christ in a religiously pluralistic world" among GC Mennonites held at Winnipeg (July 7-8, 2008).

The paper being discussed acknowledged: current need to "display greater tolerance and acceptance of those who believe differently than we do"; God's universal sovereignty and particular expressions; the need for respectful dialogue—deep humility, careful listening, and honest confessing—with those who profess a spiritual way different from ours; and questions about commitment to the truth of one faith alongside claims for universal truth. Readers will apply specific religions, like Hinduism and Christianity, to general comments from Gerber Koontz like: convictions or practices of any religion can distort truth, harm others, or reflect idolatry. Rather than speak prophetically, Gerber Koontz would prefer to reflect on issues raised by the theme through "a more comprehensive and generous approach" via biblical phrases like "tend the fruits of the Spirit," "walk as children of light," or "give account for your hope."

Koontz, Gayle Gerber (GC) **& Alexis-Baker**. Ch. 21 "Christianity and other Faiths," in *Theology of Mission A Believer's Church Perspective*. (eBook Collection) 362-74, printed 7/30/14.
Ideas of the authors hardly meet this resource's main emphasis. But Mennonite writing about "other faiths," as applied to Hinduism, will need to pay attention to aspects raised by the authors: (365-68)
- cultural relativity (that every culture is limited due to dependence on its own past);
- apologetics (to argue for one's own religious superiority based on personal criteria);
- selective reception (to observe the ideal of personal faith while noting vices of other faiths);
- syncretism (to mix side-by-side elements from two different religions);
- preparation and fulfillment (like to suggest that Christianity fulfills Hindu expectations).

Authors recognize the eastern view that affirms both sides of a wide reality in learning from other faiths. They also refer to Gandhi's approach of learning via Tolstoy about Jesus' way of nonviolence. He in turn adapted his preferred Hindu heritage. (370)[4] Useful interfaith ideas applicable to relating with Hindus include: the principle of never approaching people of another culture saying that your faith fulfils theirs; the freedom to recognize on occasions superiority of other religions; and avoiding the presumption that Hindu religionists represent or endorse all prime aspects of Hinduism. (See John Howard Yoder's material in Koontz's dissertation in *Academic* chapter.)

Koop, Karl. (GC) "God's work extends beyond our worldview," *Canadian Mennonite*. (January 25, 2010) 4-6.
In this article Koop responds to the assembly held in Saskatoon referred to with the Gerber Koontz article above titled "Speaking prophetically." He reminds readers of God's presence in the world before Christianity emerged. The rainbow symbol promised in the First Testament Noah's

story was intended for "every living creature" (Genesis 9:12-17). Titles like Messiah, Savior, Son of Man, Wisdom and Word were all known before Jesus the Christ's time, Koop states. God is not to be limited to one people's story, spirituality, or culture; God's wisdom, pattern for peace efforts, and desire for human community stretches beyond Christianity.[5]

Krantz, Miriam. (MC) Archives of the United Mission to Nepal, Record Group No. 212. Special Collections, Yale Divinity School Library.
With Krantz, a brief introduction to UMN seems appropriate. She has served with UMN since 1963. Archival materials about the Christian NGO (non-government organization) named UMN are now held in the library at Yale Divinity School, New Haven, Connecticut.[6] Materials are noted here "Yale/Box #."

Krantz is not only noted for creating 'Super Flour" (Sarbottam Pito). That basic product uses cleaned, finely-ground and sifted grains (wheat, corn, and soyabeans), perhaps mixed with soft, green vegetables of the Kathmandu Valley. Krantz encourages grassroots involvement, specialization, innovation, first-hand knowledge, and self-help patterns. She calls for wise use of land resources, experimentation and modeling what people can pattern. (Krantz letter of January 7, 1979, Yale/81-8)

Krantz's major contribution as a nutrition consultant testifies to her living, religious faith through care for peoples' food intake— whether Hindu, Buddhist, or Christian. She encourages people to reinforce faith in traditional foods; she corresponds with global colleagues in her discipline from her desk at Headquarters in Kathmandu. "What do we say to a hungry world?" she also asks in a short article in the Mennonite journal *Gospel Herald*.[7]

Krantz's long-term experience in Nepal qualified her for an active role with a seven-year "Coordinating Committee of UMN to Study Culture and Religion" during the 1970s. For that study she gathered a Lending Library for UMNers located beyond the capital with diverse projects as engineers and educators, or for medical, development and agricultural needs. [Yale/42-9] Resources focused on: "The Song Celestial" (*Bhagavad Gita*), Buddha, family, culture, Christian approach to Hindus, indigenous Christianity, conversion, syncretism, persecution, sin, dialogue, goddess Kali and sacrifice, missioner mistakes, and trust. She helped plan for guest speakers who presented Hindu and Buddhist insight—about morality, sacrifice, water, purity, Truth and ways to it, *karma* and salvation, caste, *bhakti,* yoga and more.

Krantz, Miriam. (MC) "Finding the Sacred in Nepal—Janaki Devi, Rashmira Maharjah" in *To See Each Other's Good*, Dorothy Yoder Nyce, ed. (Newton, KS: Wordsworth, 1996) 24-28.

Krantz here introduces two Nepali friends. Raised a devout Hindu then widowed and childless, Janaki Devi made long pilgrimage through India and visited multiple Hindu holy places in Nepal to gain merit and find peace. When nearly run down on a busy road but saved by a stranger's pulling her aside, she talked with her Nepali rescuer. Invited to share worship she has since joined others each Saturday for prayer, song, and sacred truth. She in turn inspires others to claim God's grace.

Rashmira, from an orthodox Hindu-*cum*-Buddhist town of Nepal, was first taught by a Christian physician when her mother was hospitalized, before dying. The persecution that followed after Rashmira expressed faith in Christ was severe, Krantz says, but her determination led to training as an auxiliary nurse midwife. Christian friends arranged her marriage when twenty-six; her first child, who weighed a little over four pounds at birth, survived on her mother's milk followed by "super flour" porridge.

Kraus, C. Norman (MC). "A Christian Spirituality for Intervention Ministries," and "Relating to People of Other Faiths," in *An Intrusive Gospel? Christian Mission in the Postmodern World.* (Downers Grove, IL: InterVarsity Pr, 1998) 80-91, 111-32.

While Kraus writes very little about Hinduism in these two chapters, several comments apply from the context of spirituality, and Hinduism is understood to be one of the religions among whom *relating* matters, referred to in the later chapter.

Kraus notes different spiritual systems each with a distinct style: mysticism, humanism, and personal theism. While Hindu and Christian mysticism have similarities, the more ancient Hindu type contains a deeper mystical unity of divine with human along with less attention to history and social ethics. Kraus draws a parallel between Buddhist intent to reform aspects of Hinduism as did Protestant with Roman Catholic patterns. (81-82)

Kraus identifies seven features of Anabaptist-Mennonite spirituality useful for ministry among religions: grace, compassion, discipleship (to the nonviolent Jesus), praxis or action (being obedient), service (mutual and reciprocal), community (social and political), and love (*agape*). (84-86) He encourages a missioner's spirituality to be dialogical in relation It will include deep respect for people who and cultural values that differ, such as within Hindu practice. (89)

Kraus commends New Testament Paul's example of relating with non-Jewish people. Clearly a Jew himself he did not draw people to Judaism, to Jewish circumcision or purity laws, for example. Aware of the context of those he met, Paul did not condemn their religious ways. He commended worthy values within their systems and emphasized that *God saves*. An authentic, true source that makes God known is Jesus the Christ who nudges all within distinct cultures to be transformed through active love. Kraus notes how crucial several of Paul's texts in Romans are: 2:4-7, 3:28-30. Faith matters for all; so does desiring to do God's will. Since all people have access to God's light, as Christians have through Jesus the Christ, the need to respect *God's image within each human being* helps one to avoid sin, Kraus explains. The grace or goodness of the One True God enables all people within each religion and culture to choose to do the right. While Jesus the "Christ is normative for Christians but not for Hindus, Buddhists or other cultural religious groups," people of each religion need to reexamine their meanings, strategy, priorities, and goals, Kraus suggests. (115-19)

Kraus notes implications of six theological theses that follow for Christians when relating with people of other faiths. 1. One loving God exists, "has spoken in many and various ways," (Heb. 1:2-3) and makes universal salvation available for all humanity. 2. Salvation is healing— social and personal, from ethical and spiritual disorders. Not through rites carried out or beliefs lived, the process and goal of holistic salvation centers in new life, in peace and justice, Kraus notes. 3. Salvation transpires not through practice of a particular religion but as a gift, out of goodwill, through love. While cultural religious observances may reflect sincere faith, they do not in themselves save. 4. Religions are limited human responses to God's light. Not the privilege of a single religion or something over which to compete, God's light or Spirit is available to all religions. 5. Judgment follows when light is refused, not when it is unknown. 6. Divine covenants with all of humanity have occurred since the beginning of time. Already engaged with every culture, God persists in meeting people as when the message of Jesus is shared. (119-27)

Kraus explains that since "religion is part of each person's cultural identity" a Christian fails to relate with integrity with a Hindu if the Hindu religion is not taken seriously. To "take seriously" involves being informed, understanding the other's meanings, avoiding prejudicial judgment, and presuming that Hindu culture is able to carry "good news," Kraus says. Missioners will critique (be self-aware) and convey the gospel from within their own religious culture. At the same time they validate the Hindu's religious culture as receptive to exchange, with potential to change lives or society. Not prone to alienate another, the motive is to enable people to "achieve their highest God-given destiny as revealed in Christ." Kraus confesses that "Jesus did not require Jews to become non-Jews but to enter [God's] kingdom in the context of their own religious culture." (132, 129)

During 1966 Kraus traveled in India. When visiting Mahatma Gandhi's former home in the village of Sevagram, he noticed a painting of Jesus Christ hanging on the wall with the words "He is our Peace." From the Hindu side, Kraus reports: (131-32)

> Gandhi had been graced to see beyond the façade of Christendom to the Christ who is our peace, even though he did not claim to be Christian. It is our task from the Christian side to authentically represent this Christ in word and deed.

Edgar Metzler (MC), in a review of Kraus' book (*Mission Focus Annual Review*, (vol. 7, 1999) 91 states that while the final, biblical chapter "Relating to People of Other Faiths" "may be a stretch for some readers" he found it helpful for relating with varied religions in Asia.

Kunjam, Shant. (MC) "Christian Challenges and Readiness: Mennonite Church of India Mission Centenary Celebration (1899-1999)," *Mission Focus: Annual Review*, (vol. 7, 1999) 21-24.

In reference to violent incidents against Christianity in India during the prior year, Kunjam suggests that believers need to expect such persecution from non-Christians. In the process he encourages Christians to "keep looking to Jesus" as they discover anew God's grace. They are to grow in love as they prepare for opposition without in turn being corrupted by the world. (22-23)

Annotations of Kunjam's study of Gandhiji's ethics appear in the *Gandhi* chapter above.

Lemuel, R. S. (MB) "Salvation According to Hinduism" *Direction* (vol. 23, no. 1, Spring 1994) 22-26.

Lemuel was executive director of the Mennonite Brethren Board of Evangelism in India when his article appeared in *Direction*, an MB journal published in the west. The oldest (3500 BCE) of all living religions and the one with most adherents in India (near eighty percent), Hinduism builds on the system of caste and salvation options in its move toward "*Sanathan Dharma*" (Eternal Religion). Lemuel discusses salvation through distinct periods: early, popular, and modern Hinduism.

Several time brackets shaped the early period: Pre-Vedic 3500-2000 BCE, Vedic 2000-1000 BCE, Brahmanic 600-250 BCE, and Devotional 250 BCE – 250 CE. During the polytheistic focus of worship of trees, animals, and forms of Pre-Vedic gods/goddess, no way of salvation is clearly named. Lemuel suggests that Hinduism began along with sacred Vedic scriptures, the most important being Rig-Veda. To prompt forgiveness of sins people gave offerings, repeated formulas, and prayed to personalized powers of nature: sun, moon, rain, wind, earth, air or fire, the most important being thunder (Indra).

As *prayer* had enabled salvation during Vedic times, *sacrifice* through Brahman priests gained prominence alongside literature called Brahmanas during the Brahmanic period. Lemuel refers to one elaborate sacrifice called Asva-Medha that involved slaying hundreds of animals in a prescribed order. The important literature known as Upanishads also appeared early. With Vedic deities and rituals of sacrifice less important, living by the four-fold *caste system* and knowledge of inner force or Ultimate Reality became more crucial to salvation. Whoever understood the truth of Cosmic Power ("Sarvam Brahma" which means everything is Brahma) and obeyed the Code of Manu came to realize the goal of release from transmigration. Temples with priests and idols (images) gained prominence too, Lemuel says.

Another strong dimension of Hindu salvation came through devotion. Perhaps Lemuel meant to include his description of the main story of the Bhagavad Gita in his discussion of *popular* Hinduism where he locates the two main epics: "The Mahabarata" and "The Ramayana." The Gita, also called "Song of the Adorable" or Celestial, is central to the well-known Hindu epic Mahabarata. It conveys a dialogue between Lord Krishna who is charioteer for Arjuna on his way to battle. The assuring message "Do your caste (military) duty and trust your God (me, Krishna) for the rest of your salvation" satisfies Arjuna, the leader of the Pandavas, Lemuel says. Teachings of Hindu Puranas, philosophical schools, and religious sects that honor Shiva or Vishnu provide more popular channels toward salvation. It can also be realized through multiple expressions of *bhakti* (devotion): idol worship, pilgrimage to sacred places, or through distinct ceremonies.

Lemuel suggests that because of attacks during this time against the Vedas and Upanishads made by Jains and Buddhist, *philosophical schools* emerged. Ways to salvation might take shape through schools named Nyaya (meaning of knowledge), Vaisheshika (atomic dimension of things), Samkhya (world origin), Yoga (attain perfection through human control—most popular), Mimamsa (ritualistic observance of Vedas), or Vedanta (Upanishadic philosophy). Religious ceremonies, like bathing in sacred rivers or expressing mantras or prayers, accentuate Saivite (worship of Siva) Power toward goodness. Or, Lemuel explains, extending loving devotion to Vishnu, or to Rama an incarnation of Vishnu, might best free loyalists toward salvation.

Lemuel notes the modern period of Hinduism through people.

- Ram Mohan Roy (1772-1833) found spiritual insight through truths from all religions rather than being limited to Hindu temples or worship forms.[8]

- Noted reformer Keshab-Chandra Sen (1838-1883) started his own *Samaj* (society) by combining creeds of diverse religions. His Church of the New Dispensation harmonized reason and faith with yoga and *bhakti* in addition to asceticism and social duty, according to Lemuel.
- Ramakrishna Paramahamsa (1834-1886), leader of perhaps the most influential modern movement, stressed goodness and salvation through any religion using meditation (*Samadhi* or concentration on God) as a prime method.
- Disciple of Ramakrishna Swamy Vivekananda (1862-1902) claimed human divinity—where each soul is identified with Brahma. Not a sinner, no person needs salvation or conversion; "New Age" thinking draws from this thought. Vivekananda introduced Hindu thought to people attending the 1893 Parliament of World Religions held in Chicago.

Lemuel concludes with ways that the Christian view of salvation that depends alone on faith in Jesus the Christ, rather than personal effort, differs from Hinduism's multiple ways.

Liechty, Daniel. (MC) "Church without Dogma" and "In View of Other Religions," in *Theology in Postliberal Perspective*, by Daniel Liechty. (Phila: Trinity Pr International, 1990) 59-72, 73-91.

Masih, Jai Prakash (GC) "Short Term Mission to Mennonite Churches in North India," *Mission Focus: Annual Review* (vol. 20, 2012) 85-91.
Masih, former pastor with BGCMC churches in India who now serves as a church planter in Chicago, was joined by Palmer Becker (GC) for a short visit (from September 11-22, 2012) to three Mennonite locations in India to teach "Who is an Anabaptist Christian?" Pastors from the three regions met for workshops in: the Bihar Mennonite Mandali (MC) of the Ranchi area (26 churches), the Bharatiya General Conference Mennonite Churches (GC) of Chattisgarh (28 congregations), and the Mennonite Church in India (MC) of Dhamtari area (21 congregations). The director of the united Mennonite organization of India, MCSFI, Emmanuel Minj met and initially hosted the visitors. He presented during storytelling an account of prayer and healing that he experienced with a sick, paralyzed Hindu man. (87) Gratitude for Anabaptist information and observation of needs were identified at each location, not insight into relating with Hindu neighbors as Anabaptists.[9]

Metzler, Edgar. (MC) "Interfaith Encounters in the Hindu Kingdom: Mennonites in Nepal," in *Borders & Bridges Mennonite Witness* *in a Religiously Diverse World*. Peter Dula & Alain Epp Weaver, eds. (Telford & Scottdale, PA: Cascadia Publ House and Herald Pr, 2007) 66-91.[10]

United Mission to Nepal executive director from 1989-1998, Metzler says that Prithvi Narayan Shah was known as 'father' of Nepal. Until the eighteenth century Nepal combined dozens of small kingdoms. Isolation marked the small, land-locked country for centuries. (69-70) In 1951 a king, thought to be a reincarnation of the Hindu god Vishnu, regained full power and opened the country's borders to foreigners and their ideas. By then friendly relations bridged Hindu and Buddhist religions; many folk revered shrines of both. The 1962 Constitution declared Nepal the world's only official Hindu kingdom, to be led by a Hindu king. Religion pervades society but people were not permitted to prod another to change loyalty; to do so could lead to imprisonment. (71-72)

The international, interdenominational UMM opened its first hospital (Shanta Bhawan later became Patan Hospital) in Kathmandu in February of 1954. This event took place in partnership with HMGN (His Majesty's Government of Nepal) and the local people. A School of Nursing began five years later led by Lena Graber (MC). In addition to specialized health programs, UMN organized multiple services over the next decades from its Kathmandu Headquarters to central and western regions. Services of education, skills training, engineering industry, hydro power development, agriculture and rural development emerged. As many as forty church agencies from sixteen countries cooperate as UMN. Hiring thousands of Nepali staff and handing over ownership and management to them has been intentional.

Metzler names Rudy Friesen from Manitoba as the forerunner in 1956 for "nearly 150 Mennonites to serve the official Hindu kingdom." [66] While serving in Christ's name for a half century, Miriam Krantz has built strong friendships with Hindus, Buddhists, and Christians. Dominant Hinduism (80 percent) mutually borrows from or blends with Buddhist (11 percent) religion. Not inclined to defame or ridicule other religions, UMNers avoid proselytizing—to "attempt conversion by coercion or offer of material inducement." (76)

Christians realize that respect for others' faith matters, not argument over religious issues. To "let God" follows. Twelve values shape UMN staff workers, expatriate and national: equality, special concern for the poor/disadvantaged, love and service, forgiveness, integrity, professional competence, participation in decision making, skills and values training, cultural sensitivity, conserve and enhance environment, identification with Nepal, and humility, Metlzer notes. (Of two thousand Nepalese, perhaps five to ten were Christian early on. (82-3)

Interfaith respect and understanding emerge in multiple ways. A group of airline, government, and local diplomatic corp officials asked Metzler to lead a memorial service for people from diverse countries and religions following a Thai Airways crash in Nepal in July of 1992. The service included prayers and readings from the sacred texts of Buddhists, Hindus, Muslims, Jews, Zoroastrians, and Christians. Comments afterward expressed appreciation for bridging across faiths in a spirit of service during such a tragic situation. (78)

Metzler, Edgar. (MC) "United Mission to Nepal," in *Serving with the Poor in Asia: Cases in Holistic Ministry*. Tetsunao Yamamori, Bryant L. Myers, and David Conner, eds. (Monrovia, CA: MARC, a division of World Vision International, 1995) 7-22.

Metzler identifies reasons why, despite restrictions against conversion, a church emerged wherever a UMN project developed.

- Because Nepali culture is basically religious, open discussion of religious aspects occurs.
- UMNers learn to know Nepali culture and language; those interested can read the bible formerly translated into Nepali.
- UMNers develop close personal relationships by living in community homes, not on separate compounds, and by inviting Nepali friends or co-workers into their homes.
- UMNers respect Nepali preferences for worship settings: their music, their sitting on the floor.
- They demonstrate Christian values of responding to needs with natural humility. (12-13)

Metzler credits UMNers from its beginnings in 1954 with openness to diversity of nation, language, denomination and theological background. Coming as professional workers intent to *live* one's faith, they know that integrity leads to expansion of God's broad kingdom. They accept restrictions against overt Christian witness. Such limits convinced nationals of expatriate interest in building the nation, receiving staff of different faiths, and training Nepalis to replace them. Restrictions prompted a more indigenous church to emerge, Metzler believes. [13, 15, 20]

As UMNers differed in relating with their Hindu context, so Hindu nationals saw the expatriates through diverse lens, from more fundamentalist, threatened voices to more open ones. When a thoughtful Nepali government agent asked Metzler "Where do Christians get this strong sense of duty to serve others?" Metzler responded, "It is not a sense of duty but a strong sense of gratitude to God." He both credits Christian faith and respects a Hindu sense of duty.

Murray, John C. (MC) "'Breaking Down the Dividing Wall of Hostility': Toward life-giving encounters with persons of other faith traditions," for Associated Mennonite Biblical Seminaries, Great Plains, (Fall 2009, Prof. Duane Friesen) 25 pp.[11]

Pastor and part-time teacher Murray expresses concern that Christians deepen their understanding of and respect for other religions. His direct encounter with Hinduism has occurred through the Menno clinic India, located in Andhra Pradesh State founded by Subbarao and Olga Yarlagadda, former Hindus. Murray has accompanied several groups of nursing students from Hesston College (KS) to the clinic for short-term, cross-cultural learning. Staff members there include Hindus: a priest administrator, and a nurse practitioner who faithfully worships through multiple senses in a Shiva temple. Murray hopes that students value the Hindu view that God is within each individual; develop and reflect on friendship across religions; discover how truth exchanged enhances personal faith; and understand the purpose of Hindu images.

Murray begins his article with current statistics of religious pluralism in the United States: as of five years ago 1,300,000 Hindus live here; their temples continue to multiply. Murray offers summary information about four major religions—Hinduism, Buddhism, Judaism, and Islam. Regarding Hinduism he mentions several major scriptures, goal achievement through four possible paths, and insight into the "manyness" of God. That "manyness" refers to the unknowable reality of God being revealed in many ways or that God is perceived through multiple ways. Informed Hindus use images to remind them of the reality beyond such an image as some Christians use an icon to "see" beyond the physical into the spiritual realm. Murray reinforces that the greeting *"Namaste"* credits *God* within the person being met, that sacred sounds like *"OM"* or *"Whoo"* expressed in meditation reflect the sacred language of Sanskrit. (6-8)

As religious people understand each other at deeper levels, walls of division can be broken and insight into personal faith can grow. Murray illustrates models for interfaith encounter noted by western interfaith scholars Diana Eck and Paul Knitter. He prefers a reverse order from theirs for presenting the theology of religion models, beginning with *love* as reflected in Knitter's fourth model of *acceptance*. Love enables root qualities of friendship and compassion to verify and enrich truth inherent within each person being met. (22-23)

Annotations from Murray's six-page outline titled "Encountering Other Religions" reflect how walls of hostility form. His formerly Hindu friend Subbarao reports a first encounter with a Christian who declared, "Your God is a stone and an idol. If you don't repent and accept Jesus you will burn in hell for all eternity." That comment caused a twenty-year delay in Subbarao's choosing to be a Christian. Murray learns also from Subbarao's mother who remains a Hindu. When asked why she tolerated a Christian who, when visiting in her home, commented on her religion with "disrespect and contempt," she said, "A guest in my home bears the image of God; I will treat him as God would with honor and respect no matter how he treats me." As people loyal to a given religion differ in what they believe about their faith and differ in how they respond to people of other faiths, not all Christians will be disrespectful of others. Nor will all Hindus be as gracious in response as Subbarao's mother. Tensions between religions and cultures have long existed—due to caricatures, false reports, or presuming to know absolute truths absolutely. Murray suggests that readers see Saul of Tarsus' comment about a "dividing wall of hostility" in Eph. 2:14.

Nafziger, Bethsaba and Dale. (MC) "Placing Nepal on the World Map for Quality Coffee" Brochure, and 'Pizza-making fosters faith in Nepal," by Mimi Hollinger-Janzen, *The Mennonite* (October 2, 2007), 24.

This husband-wife team manages the growing business called "Top of the World" in Kathmandu, Nepal. Local, Nepali women employed with the Nafzigers, like Reena Thapa, learn responsibility, practice integrity, and gain self-esteem as they assemble frozen pizzas and fry French fries or *aalu* chop (tater tots) to sell. Born and raised a devout Hindu in a village, Thapa has benefited from employment in the city with Nafzigers'; they helped schedule a minor operation to correct her hearing problem. She now actively engages with her husband in a small congregation. Having started the business out of her home in 2003, Bethsaba now gladly observes business growth at "Top of the World" alongside faith growth among her workers.

Dale describes his coffee business begun in December of 2011. Issues include access and opportunity to meet challenges whether of quality control, fair wages, credibility, or dealing with irregular supplies of essential electricity or water. As workers honor God through shared experience, they touch lives of customers and each other. Readers may find more at www.topoftheworldcoffee.com.

Dale first went to Nepal in 1978 as one of many Mennonite PAX fellows. UMN documents at Yale quote more than one director who commends the work accomplished by skilled PAX men—who create grounds and buildings, enable transportation and communication, or assist with medical, educational, and village development. The last to work with hydro-electric power at Butwal, Nafziger later learned that Mennonite PAX fellows were being memorialized there in a guesthouse. The current Hindu hostess has kept on the wall of the large dining room a "rendition" of the Last Supper that the guys had created out of iron rods—rods bent, painted, and crafted to replicate the stick figures from *Good News for Modern Man* scripture translation.

Neufeldt, Ronald W. (MB) "A Modest Retrospective," in *Re-Imagining South Asian Religions*: Essays in Honour of Professors Harold G. Coward and Ronald W. Neufeldt; Studies in the History of Religions. Harold G. Coward, Ronald W. Neufeldt, Pashaura Singh, and Michael Hawley, eds. (e-Book Brill Online) 15-23.

Neufeldt has studied, taught, and written extensively about Hinduism. Most of his academic years were spent in the Department of Religious Studies at the University of Calgary in Canada. He values re-imagining traditions that originated in South Asia. He commends key teachers along his academic journey: Robert Baird, University of Iowa PhD. major professor (beginning in 1969), Harold Coward his mentor for methodology and colleague at Calgary, and his students including those he has supervised at the graduate level.

What started as Neufeldt's focus on the Hindu renaissance through leaders like Ramakrishna, Vivekananda, Ranade, and Radhakrishnan led to a dissertation that delved into the Hindu Rig Veda text's influence on the German Max Muller. Muller is known as the 'father' of comparative religion. Neufeldt later added study of modern India through focus on the Sikh religion, Muslim Muhammad Iqbal, and the Theosophical Society. Attention to the topic of conversion, such as Hindu to Christian, prompted Neufeldt's interest in religion and law, therefore the system of courts; from there he studied current, radical Hindutva, an outgrowth from the school of Hindu Mahasabha.

Neufeldt reviews also his journey with the professional AAR organization, the American Academy of Religion. Formal study of Hinduism after 1978 led to a broader Section called Religion in South Asia (RISA). The latter deals with "shared history and social context of all religions" of South Asia. A further division led to the group's attention to Hinduism beyond Asia. Alongside broader religious studies such as ritual, Tantric studies, and Yoga, attention is given to Sikh, Jain, and Buddhist groups. Neufeldt values both the "study of traditions for their own sake plus connections and interactions among traditions." (21) He values having been involved with an entire field of study.

Neufeldt, Ronald (MB) "Christianity and 'Other Religions': Contributions from the Work of F. Max Muller," *Hindu-Christian Studies Bulletin*, (5, 1992) 9-12.

More than a decade after Neufeldt's dissertation was published (annotations of which appear in the *Academic* chapter here), this short article about Max Muller's gift to world religions appeared in print. Neufeldt, well aware of Christianity's limited attention to religions other than for the purpose of converting their members, introduces the founder of comparative religion, the German scholar Muller. As early as 1870 Muller understood that people of all historical religions (through faith) long for the infinite and, (rooted in sense perceptions), comprehend moral activity. Each religion, if carefully studied, he said, could be seen to move through three phases in its quest for holiness, for being in God's presence. Phases engaged were from the physical (natural phenomena) through the anthropological (self and neighbor) to the theosophical (infinite in nature and human beings). From Muller, Neufeldt explains that each religion has something to teach; that God works everywhere (beyond Judaism and Christianity); that although old, ancient scriptures like the hymns of the Hindu Rig-Veda hold truth. Such insight led Muller to observe the "true missionary spirit": appealing to truth in each religion, discarding what is not desired, and calling out the best from each tradition. Conversion might then form a new religion based on new understandings.[12]

Neufeldt, Ronald (MB) "Hindutva and the Rhetoric of Violence Interpreting the Past, Designing the Future," in *The Twenty-First Century Confronts Its Gods: Globalization, Technology and War*. David J. Hawkin, ed. (Albany: SUNY Pr, 2004) 157-72.
The ideology of *Hindutva* within the nation of India purports that 'true' Indians are Hindu, that to be Hindu is to be truly nationalist. Its desire is to recover a martial character supposedly lost from the past and to counter citizens like Muslim or Christian who do not claim India as their Fatherland and Holy Land.

Neufeldt explains how key reports or actions marked history after India gained independence in 1947. An Interim Report of 1947 included the "right to practice, profess, and propagate religion" and to prohibit conversion enhanced by coercion or undue influence. Leaders like Lokanath Misra of Orissa State understood justice to demand that ancient faith and culture be restored to their rightful place of supremacy, to protect against foreign religions that propagate. (164) Neufeldt shows that Misra feared that Muslim growth meant Hindu decline. The Niyogi Report of 1956 spoke against mass or deceitful patterns of influence, medical or educational services that lead to conversion, the use of foreign money to evangelize, and criticism of Hindu beliefs and practice, Neufeldt explains. (166) Hindu culture had always absorbed invaders; to nationalize involved loyalty to state over god. Freedom of Religion Acts appeared—in Orissa in 1967, Madhya Pradesh in 1968, and Arunchal Pradesh in 1978. While non-indigenous faiths endangered national interests, conversion back to Hinduism (a policy of *suddhi*) was valued.

Neufeldt observes how the *Hindutva* ideology can set up barriers and support violence between religious or cultural groups. If one defines the nation as Hindu and regards certain faith traditions as alien, then converts to such faith traditions can be seen as guilty of treason, to be dealt with in the way that treason frequently is—with violence, he concludes. (170)

Harold Coward, **Ronald Neufeldt**, & Eva K. Neumaier, eds. *Readings in Eastern Religions*. (Waterloo, Ont: Wilfrid Laurier Univ Pr 2007). Chapters by Neufeldt: 4 "Sikism" 247-63; 9 "Shinto 339-78; 10 "New Religions" 379-88.

Neufeldt, Ronald. (MB) "Reflections on Swami Vivekananda's Speeches at the World Parliament of Religions, 1893," *Journal of Hindu-Christian Studies* (6, no. 4) 3 pp. Available at http://dx.doi.org/10.78.25/2:164-6279.1073. 1993. Made available by Digital Commons of Butler University.

Swami Vivekananda is well-known from having spoken on six occasions during the 1893 World Parliament of Religions in Chicago. Neufeld reflects on that major event a century later. Themes presented by Vivekananda include: "Why We Disagree," "Hinduism," "Religion Not the Crying Need of India," and "Buddhism, the Fulfillment of Hinduism." Many who attended the Parliament were hearing a spokesman for Hinduism and India's Ramakrishna Mission for the first time. Regarding *Hinduism*, they learned the "centerpiece" for religious pluralism— "many paths, one goal." For Vivekananda that statement meant that "all religions are true." Swami explained the Vedas of Hinduism as less a book and more a revelation of "spiritual laws." (1) Neufeldt identifies Vivekananda's summary of Hinduism as: realizing, being, and becoming divine (to see or reach God). Not intent to believe a doctrine or dogma, the Hindu person strives to reach from one truth to another in order to realize the Infinite. While many world faiths stand within the umbrella of Hinduism, with Hinduism (not Christianity) being the highest, the common religion or sects point toward fulfillment in Advaita Vedanta, the essence of Hinduism.

Reflecting on "Why We Disagree" Neufeldt thinks that agreement is not necessary for religious harmony. Whereas Vivekananda hopes for unity through diversity, Neufeldt values being open to the significance of another while living together in disagreement. (3)

Neufeldt, Ronald W. (MB) Review of *Rammohun Roy in Hindu and Christian Tradition: The Teape Lectures 1990* by Dermot

Killingley (Newcastle upon Tyne: Grevatt & Grevatt, 1993) xii+181 pp. Produced by The Berkeley Electronic Pr, 1996, 2 pp.

Nyce, Dorothy Yoder. (MC) "Caring for Young Victims of Interfaith Rancor," *Mission Focus: Annual Review* (vol. 8, 2000) 107-18.
With the focus being broader, one reference to Hinduism in this article reports a study by the Indian psychoanalyst Sudhir Kakar about conflict between Hindus and Muslims in India. Kakar, a Hindu, constructed toy dolls to represent two families (marked by religious identifiers). Each child in the study is to arrange the dolls and tell an imaginary story. Types of findings that Yoder Nyce notes from Kakar's study include: Fighting between Hindu and Muslim dolls appeared in two-thirds of the boys' accounts. Forty percent of Muslim girls and twenty percent of Hindu girls created scenes of conflict; twenty percent of Muslim boys and seventy percent of Hindu boys enacted religious conflict. Muslim children were less informed than Hindu children of 'causes' for Hindu-Muslim conflict. Personal experience as a victim in a riot prompted religious hatred. (109-10)

Nyce, Dorothy Yoder. (MC) Review of Paul D. Wiebe's (MB) *Heirs and Joint Heirs Mission to Church among the Mennonite Brethren of Andhra Pradesh* and Peter Penner's (MB) *Russians, North Americans, and Telugus the Mennonite Brethren Mission in India 1885-1975*. *Mission Focus Annual Review* (vol. 19, 2011): 284-88. The review appeared also in *Mennonite Historian*, (38, no. 2 June 2012) 9-10. http://www.Mennonitehistorian.ca/. Annotations about both books appear in this bibliography.

Pankratz, James N. (MC) "Rammohun Roy," in *Religion in Modern India*. Robert Baird, ed. (New Delhi: Ramesh Jain, Manohar Publications 1981) 163-77.
Pankratz begins this chapter by stating: "More has been written about Rammohun Roy than about any other Indian who lived during the first half of the nineteenth century." Roy was: the first to establish his own press to publish his writings; the most prominent opponent of *sati* (a living wife's being cremated alongside her dead husband); an ardent protestor of British injustices; a strong advocate for Indian education alongside that from Europe; a strong supporter of traditional religious texts being translated and distributed; the center of religious controversies; and clear opponent of missioner' (Christian) criticism of Indian religious thought. (163)

Pankratz explains how some Hindu critics blamed Roy for being either a Christian or an atheist, for trying to destroy Hindu, if not all, religious traditions. While he opposed Hindu belief in more than one god and worship of images, he also questioned Christian belief in the Trinity. He especially countered Christian critique of Hinduism. Pankratz names the group for kindred thinkers that Roy founded, the Brahmo Samaj, in 1928 toward the end of his life. Key themes for Rammohun were, according to Pankratz: that all religions contain falsehood; that he and other *grhastha* (householders) were qualified to debate theological issues; that religious practices and beliefs had worth to the extent that they improved life for people. (165, 168, 172)

Pankratz further illustrates Rammohun Roy's thought. To stress reason and argument but overlook faith and "Divine Help" reflects the false in religions, he said. Falsehood also occurs when one group finds fault with another while denying its own inconsistent patterns. Roy justifies omitting accounts of Jesus' miracles when describing his life if miracle-working presumes that Jesus alone is superior. Pankratz explains how Rammohun stressed universal theology and brought balance to debates. He commended both the devotional and rational and was careful to convey honestly as well as question critically both Hindu and Christian traditions. That he critiqued religious authorities but failed to adhere to rules of diet expected of a spiritual leader caused some opponents to fault him for arrogance. Rammohun clearly presumed to know what was and what was not true religion; he based authority on knowledge and morality. (168-69)

Brahmo Samaj worship is congregational Pankratz says. It includes the meanings of readings from the Upanisads, *Brahma Sutra*, or Vedas, from prayer and song. Whereas Hindus note inherent value difference due to distinctions of peoples' role, color, or life-style, Rammohun stresses that people of any caste, religion, or nation may attend and expect to understand gathered Samaj events. He also counters outcomes from polytheistic worship dependent on images, insight available only to a few, and uncouth aspects linked with Krishna or Kali stories. He desires worship to be followed by greater well-being, unity, and freedom from priestly power.

Pankratz provides in conclusion a summary of Rammohun's religious thought. 1. His rational approach improved religious traditions of both faiths and avoided normative judgments; he refined Hinduism and questioned aspects of Christianity. 2. Individuals gained personal religious authority through reading what was printed, through exchange of insight rather than dependence on a few authority figures. 3. His emphasis on responsible social order (*dharma*) challenged stress on salvation. 4. Rather than focus ethics on self-denial, Rammohun led people to take care of each other. (174)

Pankratz, James N. "Response to Paul G. Hiebert," *Direction* (20, nol. 2, 1991) 15-18.

Pankratz, James N. (MB) Review of *Courage for Dialogue: Ecumenical Issues in Inter-religious Relationship* by Stanley J. Samartha. *Mission Focus: Annual Review,* (10, no. 4, December 1982) 2 pp.
Although this review does not name Hinduism directly, it examines essays from Samartha's years as director of the World Council of Churches' unit on Dialogue with People of Living Faiths and ideologies. Pankratz at the time served with MCC in Bangladesh a more Muslim country. He especially valued Samartha's chapter that presents a theological sketch of the Spirit of God at work among all people.

Penner, Peter. (MB) *Russians, North Americans, and Telugus The Mennonite Brethren Mission in India 1885-1975.* (Hillsboro KS: Kindred Pr, 1997).
Penner relies on primary sources—personal and official correspondence, reports and minutes, and conference papers from archives—in addition to a visit to India 1972-73 for writing this book. A few of Penner's comments suggest Hindu links: missioner A. E. Janzen's distinct relationship with a prince Raja when at the Wanaparty location from 1912-21; observation that missioners and MB Board members thought Britain was good for India while less sure about Gandhi's judgment of economic, political, cultural, and spiritual ruin that Britain had brought to India during 150 years. Further, Penner observes neglect in prior training of MB and Protestant missioners generally to cross-cultural, contextual exposure. Too little was known of the radical difference between standards and outlook of westerners with people of the East (as noted by Henry Krahn, 1957). Penner notes persistence of caste distinctions between MB Madigas, suppressed leather workers, and Malas. He observes MB caution or fear to minister among higher-caste Hindu Brahmans who in turn might choose to "remain secret believers rather than be identified with an organized church dominated by *harijans* (low-caste)." (114, 142, 151-53, 271-72)

Penner, Peter (MB) Review of *Christians in Andhra Pradesh: The Mennonites of Mahbubnagar* by Paul D. Wiebe. (Madras: Christian Literature Society, 1988) *Direction* (20, no. 1, Spring 1991) 115-18.
Penner reviews Wiebe's sociological dissertation that focused Christians in the context of Hinduism in Andhra Pradesh State in India alongside a report of a global gathering of Mennonite Brethren mission leaders held in Brazil. Penner refers to Wiebe's explanation of how three generations of North American MB missioners represented and impinged their civilization on the people who had practiced Hinduism near the AP city of Hyderabad. Wiebe observes that the 'untouchable' Madigas and

Malas caste groups continued their former separation from each other after becoming Christian. Penner says that Wiebe predicts that the church "will remain largely ethnic within the larger Hindu civilization."

Platt, LaVonne Godwin (GC) *Bela Banerjee Bringing Health to India's Villages*. (Newton, KS: Wordsworth, 1988) and *In Memory of Bela Banerjee A Coda to Her Biography*. (Newton, KS: Wordsworth, 1996).

Godwin Platt served with projects in Indian villages in the mid-1950s with a Hindu friend Bela Bannerjee. Bannerjee grew up from birth in a Brahman caste home known for its tradition of simplicity. Godwin Platt reports that in addition to reading Hindu scriptures, Bannerjee's mother had memorized most of the *Bhagavad Gita*. (12) Bannerjee was strongly committed to the Hindu reform movement known as Brahmo Samaj; it countered caste, sacrifice, and reincarnation.[13] Bela describes *work* within Brahmo Samaj as worship and *worship* as expressive of deep feeling not dependent on superstition or idols. She valued the quote "All religions come from deep inside." (113) "Do good to others" marked the Brahmo Samaj statement of faith comparable, Bela told Godwin Platt, with Quakers. (23) Godwin Platt describes Bela as a "dear friend" to many, as fluent in Indian languages, and as skilled with "treating patients, delivering babies, teaching health workers, and visiting with villagers." She engaged with groups attentive to multiple needs of the poorest as did the Kasturba Gandhi National Memorial Trust. (157)

Godwin Platt also writes of Bannerjee's final visit to the United States and Canadian friends in 1992. (*In Memory . . .*19-33) When faithful Hindu Bela died, having been cared for in Platt's living room, they acquired authorization from her family in India for cremation. They planned a memorial service in harmony with Hindu tradition, incorporating a garland of marigolds, an oil lamp with incense, a coconut, tape recordings of Indian songs, plus poems and music by noted poet Rabindranath Tagore. Dwight Platt later delivered Bannerjee's cremains to India to be scattered in the Ganges River.

Platt, LaVonne Godwin (GC) "Sokanda, the Son of Shiva," n.d., 8 pp unpublished short story.[14]

LaVonne and Dwight Platt were married in India's state of Orissa when he was on a two-year, rural agriculture assignment with Quakers. LaVonne's Hindu-focused, creative story about a fifteen year old Hindu fellow named Sokanda, here summarized, offers an example of Mennonite fiction writing.

Near where Sokanda lives, on a hill's summit with more than two hundred steps to reach it, stood a temple to Lord Shiva, Lord of the Dance. A Blue Roller bird—with flapping wings and harsh screams—

served as sign of the yearly festival event called Shiva Ratri Puja. Devout Hindus ascended the steep steps to offer the priest coconuts and garlands. While a farmer who performs the ritual might pray for fertile soil, a wife might plead for a healthy son. Sokanda longed for release from the cycle of rebirths. In constant pain, his handicap caused shortness of breath with any exertion. While Sokanda sensed this as possibly his last chance to pray at the temple, his parents refused his request to climb the steps.

When they and other relatives ascended the hill's summit, Sokanda and his sister Meena waited below near a rickshaw and driver named Bhimo. After scheming with his sister to buy two garlands—one for her to present to the priest in his behalf and one for him to hold as he prayed on seeing her enter the temple—she started up. He then bargained with Bhimo to help him (Sokanda) ascend. Reaching the fortieth step, Bhimo pleaded with Sokanda to rest and then be carried. A few steps later he fell. Bhimo called for a doctor; people headed up or down encircled them. As a doctor carried the still Sokanda down, he asked someone to tell the parents to come directly to the hospital.

Reaching the top, Meena had offered the priest the garland in Sokanda's behalf; with fingers to his lips and forehead, the priest chanted mantras. Looking down, Meena saw a commotion near their rickshaw. As the doctor's vehicle moved past, Bhimo placed Sokanda's garland on him. At the same time the Blue Roller plummeted nearby and then soared upward, lost from view.

Raj, Santos K. (MB) "Salvation as Release from *Karma*," *Direction*, (23, no. 1, Spring 1994) 27-28. Also see http://www.direction journal.org/23/1/salvation-as-release-from-karma.html;
Raj agrees with R. S. Lemuel's (MB) comment that "Hinduism and the caste system are inseparable." At the same time, however, that the Hindu individual is responsible for personal salvation, concepts of repentance and forgiveness are not apparent. Raj mentions other key Hindu concepts.
-    All religions and faiths journey toward the same God.
-    All ideas reflect partial Truth—incomplete toward more complete
-    Duty (*dharma*, the closest Hindi word for *religion*) within the caste system suggests "without feeling attached (sentiments) or concerned to know the result," giving shape to persistent *karma.*
-    *Karma* refers to the cycle of birth, death, and rebirth that depends on a person's merit accumulated during each life. It leads to final release of a person's soul into the One Soul, the creator Brahma—to lose identity and achieve salvation.

Since all of life's events are predetermined those that a Christian might think of as tragic are accepted by the Hindu as inevitable. Whereas *bhakti* (devotion) prompts a devotee to love a god form, some other god forms are more feared than loved, Raj adds.

Rampogu, Aseervadam. (MB) "Westernization of History in the Context of the Contribution of the Mennonite Church in India," *The Conrad Grebel Review*, (Winter/Spring 1997) 78-81.

Rampogu mentions that Mennonite mission agencies have been quite useful with socio-economic development activities, educational institutions, and social services. Their engagement with Indian religious faiths has brought change mostly to lower-caste people. Rampogu quotes K. M. Panikkar's view that Christianity more broadly has also indirectly brought "communal solidarity to Hinduism." Whereas through time Hindus were loosely linked through caste communities, Christian education prompted a deeper meaning of community. It also prodded Hindu thought regarding more freedom for women and, through Gandhi's example, resistance to issues like child marriage or the designation "untouchable." Rampogu encourages the church to better inform its people about non-Christian faith concepts, especially in order to speak intelligently with those who may be knowing a resurgence of faith. (80-81)

Rempel, Peter H. "The Shape of Global Anabaptist Missions for the 21st Century: The Whole Gospel to the Whole Broken World by the Broken Whole Church," *Mission Focus: Annual Review*, (vol. 8 2000) 23-36.

Remple begins this article with reference to the Mennonite World Conference meeting that took place under a large "shamiana" on the grounds of the Anglican St. Thomas School in Calcutta, India in 1997. A brief description of that occasion includes reference to Mahatma Gandhi, "the non-violent Hindu liberator of India from the time of his struggle for civil rights for the races of South Africa." (23) After presenting a history of mission activity, and in the context of looking ahead toward more global organization, one reference to other religions appears. The first of a list of seven items that from a global perspective "should be added or given more emphasis by the existing North American mission agencies in cooperation with those of other countries is: "dialogue with believers of other religions on basic human needs." Within one paragraph are noted *purposes* for establishing global cooperation in Anabaptist mission: to witness to the gospel of Jesus Christ . . . to make disciples. . . .to have a global council for "information sharing" . . . to enable missional ministries to cross cultural and national borders. (33) Remple's principles for shaping goals and structures in global missions include no reference to world religions.

Sawatsky, Walter (GC) Review of *A Time to Bind and a Time to Loose. A History of the General Conference Mennonite Church Mission Involvement in India from 1900-1995*. By Ruth Unrau, (Newton, KS & Winnipeg, Manitoba: GC Commission on Mission, 1996) and *Window to the World. Extraordinary Stories from a Century of Overseas Mission 1900-2000*. By Tina Block Ediger. (Newton, KS & Winnipeg, Manitoba: Faith and Life Pr 1999). *Mission Focus: Annual Review*, (vol. 7, 1999) 41-43.

Shenk, Calvin E. *Who Do You Say That I Am? Christians Encounter Other Religions*. (Scottdale, PA: Herald Pr. 1997).
Professor Shenk's lived experience among plural religions has primarily occurred in more rural eastern USA or the Middle East. He thinks that "pluralism, relativism, and openness"—what he labels "the new trinity"—cause westerners confusion about "belief, the meaning of truth, and acceptable morality." (29) During a short visit to India Shenk saw westerners gather near Hindu gurus or ashrams—to express devotion to Sai Baba (a manifestation of god) or Raj Neesh (guru who Shenk says "promotes diverse sexual practices"). (22) Shenk also ponders Hindu differences of meaning for *devotee* and *disciple*. (25)

   Annotations of Shenk's references to Hinduism, found in chapters 5, 9, and 13, follow expression of his bias toward an exclusivist, Christocentric view. (This segment fits more with *Theology of Religions*.)
- Jesus is Lord over all other lords and powers, many of which functioned as gods in other religions. (112)
- God is most fully revealed in Christ. Starting there, we see God's manifestation in other religions. (179) . . . Jesus as the norm for truth makes relative all other truth claims. . . Jesus is the fullest manifestation of truth . . . revelation in Christ is the norm by which truth found in other religions is evaluated. (180-81)
- The finality of Christ is a judgment upon other religions. (252) . . [yet] Witness to Christ that belittles or denigrates people of other faiths is counter witness. (256)

   Shenk recalls a conversation with a Hindu on an airplane.
   The seatmate asked, "Is God everywhere?"
   Shenk thought a while and replied, "Yes."
   The seatmate responded, "Then God is in the image."
   Shenk's later, written response: "However, the problem with the image is that God cannot be confined to time and space. Idols reflect ignorance of the all-pervading presence

of God. Human manipulation of images does not gain God's favor. God wants to move humans beyond the ignorance of images to a fuller revelation." (105)

Further insight from Shenk:

- Everywhere God is known in part, Shenk confirms. . . There are truths in other religions from which we can learn. (180) . . . Different religions turn on different axes. The questions which Hindus ask may not be the ones with which the gospel is primarily concerned. . . [For example] Hindus are disinterested in eschatology. (181)
- Movements like *bhakti* in Hinduism emphasize more personal aspects of God, Shenk states. (182)
- Keshab Chendra Sen, leader of reform Hinduism, said that he loved Jesus more than any other and that he wanted his life patterned after Jesus. But he was turned off by western forms of Christian life. . . . So also Gandhi admired Jesus but rejected Christianity because of the style of inconsistent Christians. (245)
- Sometimes western Christians idealize other religions. . . On visits to Hindu centers in India and in conversations with Christians from Hindu background, Shenk observes that Hinduism is not the "pure spirituality" that some in the west have come to believe. . . . We need to hear from people who have turned to Jesus Christ from other religions, to see how they experience Christ's uniqueness, Shenk says. (247)
- In one project Shenk interviewed first-generation Indian Christians from Hindu background to discover why they had become Christian. A Hindu lawyer was impressed with how Christians seemed close to God when they prayed. . . A student was attracted by Christian modeling of nonviolence, good family life, and disciplined ethical life. (248)
- Shenk heard a visiting preacher from North America speak in chapel at Union Biblical Seminary in India. When the speaker declared, "I can tell you, Gandhi won't be in heaven," Indian students were upset. For them, to pronounce another's destiny went far beyond a person's authority, Shenk learned. (250)
- Shenk also reports having heard a Hindu's judgment of Christians, "They went out to give and not to receive, to talk and not to listen." (258)

Shenk, David W. "We Are Brahman – Hinduism" in *Global Gods Exploring the Role of Religions in Modern Societies*. (Scottdale, PA: Herald Pr, 1995) 96-124.

Shenk begins this chapter with an excerpt from a conversation with a *swami* (religious leader) in a Hindu temple in Nairobi, Kenya. Basic to ancient Hinduism, according to Shenk, are distinct beliefs: that "all phenomena are Brahman"; that "everything in the universe is divine"; that "nature and divinity are a unity"; and that the caste system, law of karma, and universal, divine soul remain central for the educated Hindu. (96-98)

Threads of Hindu importance appear in this chapter. Resources notated here previously have explained the four main caste groups, the *jati* system of sub-castes, and the law Code of Manu from the third century B.C.E., all of which Shenk also discusses. Shenk's view of *karma*—a law of nature in which the soul (*atman*) is reborn depending on previous obedience to caste laws—precedes details from the Bhagavad-Gita, a portion of the Mahabarata epic. Shenk notes that the Gita story of Arjuna with his charioteer Krishna (*avatar* and incarnation of the god Vishnu) presents Arjuna's literal debate within over whether to go to battle against relatives. Shenk names devotion (*bhakti*), obedience (*karma*), and yoga as central paths for Hindus to use to seek and achieve salvation (110).[15] Shenk lifts excerpts from the important Hindu Upanishads text to note how its view of the place of the person within the universe differs from African religions, Judaism, Christianity, and Islam. (113) Shenk describes the person who comes to know the truth of *tat tvam asi* ("that art thou") as having realized *mukti* (enlightenment); the person's *atman* (soul) has become one with the universal Brahman. (114)

Shenk refers briefly to several Hindu notables and their developments. Reformer Radhakrishnan tried to make Vedanta philosophy and its claim to tolerance clearer for his current thinkers. For Radhakrishnan, religions were both on a continuum and one in essence. He understood that people could achieve within history though it is *maya* (illusion), Shenk reports. Gandhi, the voice and actor for peace and justice, borrowed insight from multiple religious sources. Shenk sees Gandhi's eclectic view—that "all truth, phenomena, religions, or ideas were expressions of God"—as part of a "dogmatic universalism" inherent within Hinduism. Gandhi's practice of *satyagraha* (soul force) plus integrity and compassion enabled his becoming "a moral conscience in India," Shenk notes. (121)

Solomon, E. D. (MB) "Vital Leadership for Andhra Pradesh," *Direction,* (30, no 2, 2001) 153-61.

Solomon's sole reference to Hinduism here reports an Indian MB pastor's daughter's having fallen in love with a Hindu, "a seeker in Christ." Aware of other instances of "love marriages" in her family the daughter told her parents of her interest in the fellow. Although they rebuked her and asked that she change her mind, she did not. When the fellow's parents contacted the pastor and his wife in hopes of coming to an agreement for their youth, the pastor flatly responded: "Either all of your family must become Christians or else you may have no relations with us." Before long the young couple ran away from home to a city to register for marriage. Learning of that action the pastor felt unable to cope; he left his parish, never to interact further with those who had chosen Christianity through his mission efforts. Solomon asks what better response might the pastor have taken to solve the situation? What aspect of leading might have enabled good will? Was requiring conversion of an entire family appropriate, he wonders.

Spare, Margaret Entz. (GC) "Doing the Gospel in Nepal" (Yale 188-5) Presented to the Mennonite Council of International Ministries, January 1998, in *Gospel in Nepal* No. 3, Mennonite Board of Mission "Insight Series," James R. Krabill, ed. (Elkhart, IN: MBM 1999) 15 pp.

Entz Spare does not state for how long she and her husband Dan served with UMN. Speaking for the UMN engineers, educators, nurses, nutritionists, accountants, agriculturalists, doctors and foresters who have found great joy in enabling the development of one of the world's poorest nations, she outlines her content. After explaining background to Nepal and UMN, she identifies "Strategic elements of holistic work," "Pitfalls/weaknesses of doing the gospel," and "The path ahead."

The Himalayan peaks along Nepal's northern border are known as "the abode of the gods." Most Nepalis, according to Entz Spare, claim loyalty to Hindu or Buddhist religions or to the blend that emerges from their co-existence. Officially the world's only Hindu kingdom, Nepal's cultural identity includes a social caste system and a sense that "all religions are true because they all originate in the divine Brahma." UMN expatriates understand the stipulation not to proselytize (offer material inducement to gain converts) or to engage in political activities. (2-3) The fact that churches emerged where UMN projects were located is a credit to God's Spirit at work despite 'closed doors,' Entz Spare says.

The effects of how people live cannot be stifled or denied. A physician may choose to pray for Divine assistance when performing surgery. A development professional who chooses to deal honestly when making purchases, will work with integrity also to increase literacy or decrease child mortality. Those skilled with electricity add more than convenience; they 'speak' on their own, Entz Spare adds. The Hindu worldview credits the spiritual being within rather than separate from daily experience and claims natural being as connected to the supernatural. So, religious concepts can be discussed freely between Christians and Hindus. "We [also] became acutely aware of the divisiveness of the gospel message within Hindu society," Entz Spare admitted. (6)

Many UMNers skilled to practice a 'secular' profession came to see legal restrictions as also useful. Entz Spare defines holistic ministry as relating everyday affairs with spiritual truths. She is convinced that God prepares people, whether the UMNer or Nepali, with occasion to engage a faith issue while doing daily work. The change involved with development integrates social, economic and religious aspects. (11-12) If faced with opposition unfairly, as through hassles with visa delays or opened mail, the UMNer can better understand Nepali Christian suffering. They also see the 'rightness' for Nepalis to be their own leaders along with their indigenous patterns in emerging churches. Entz Spare names the dual task of listening and learning as central for a Christian professional's search for truth within Hindu culture and context. In that, she clearly elevates "doing the Gospel."

Unger, Walter. (MB) "The Destiny of Those Who Have Never Heard: A Bibliographical Essay," *Direction*, (24, no. 1, Spring 1994) 54-63. Also http://www.directionjournal.org/23/1/destiny-of-; 11 pp.

Unrau, Ruth (GC) *A Time to Bind and a Time to Loose A history of the General Conference Mennonite Church mission involvement in India from 1900-1995* (Newton, KS: Commission on Overseas Mission, 1996).

Unrau wrote two books following several years' experience in India. Most of her content focuses themes other than Hinduism; occasional references to Hindu thought or practice appear via voices of a missioner or through her personal reflection.

When a nurse Augusta Schmidt (GC) pled with a Hindu husband priest to provide his wife with plenty of water, tea and milk after giving birth, unfortunately to an already dead child, he felt helpless to counter an old custom of not being given water for two days or food for five days after giving birth. A solution for the Brahman resulted when the liquids were ordered as "medicine." (5)

Ruth Ratzlaff (GC) told of superstitions surrounding the dread disease of cholera. A scourge like cholera needed a cause. To blame it on witches, on women who were thought to possess evil spirits, recurred. One man beat two neighbor women, causing one to die, after his wife, son, and mother succumbed to cholera within several days. To appease an angered cholera goddess, people needed to offer sacrifices at her temple. (37)

(GC) Orlando Waltner's shooting of a large tiger interrupted a missioner retreat held at a government rest house in a jungle. The dead beast, nearly worshipped by village folk, was kept safely between missioners named <u>Duerksen</u> and <u>Moyer</u> for the night. The next day local Hindu women came with coconut and fire on a platter "to do homage" to the animal while a man wrapped a few hair and some blood from the tiger into a paper to take back to his home. (44)

Unrau refers to the Hindu holiday season of Diwali in which celebrants receive goddess Lakshmi's blessings. Thousands of small earthenware bowls filled with mustard oil and a cotton wick line roofs, windows, shelves, and steps. Prayers, gifts, sweets, and fireworks are shared and business inventory is completed, to end the fiscal year. (46)

Missioner <u>Helen Kornelsen</u> (GC) knew that she needed to understand Hindu customs and superstitions in order to relate with Christian women whose ties to former fears lingered. A woman might not attend literacy classes if she had to pass a certain tree known to have evil spirits. Such spirits might also affect a group gathered under a peepal tree for Bible study or sewing classes, Unrau explains. (83)

While mission agencies valued single women for full-time assignments, western customs could also expect missioner wives to give prime attention to raising a family before being valued as professionals. But <u>Ella Bauman</u> (GC) "a valued obstetrician, pediatrician, and general practitioner" (137) gained further renown by serving several weeks in a refugee camp during the time of the awful bloodshed of Partition after India's Independence Day, August 15, 1947. Unrau reports that compounder Binod Kumar joined her to dispense medicines that she prescribed in one of multiple camps holding 250,000 wistful, fearful refugees. Many Hindus, Muslims, and Sikhs had to move from one side of the divide created between India and Pakistan to the other. Using four tents for wards and one proper building, one day found Bauman seeing nearly five hundred patients. With nothing about which to smile, "those who had all of their loved ones killed are most pitiful," Bauman writes. "One . . . reported losing fourteen members of her immediate family. Her face looked ready for certain revenge." (89-91)

During a time of famine a long-standing difference between Christians and Hindus resurfaced. A small Hindu idol was located under a tree in front of the GC Mennonite Church in Sirko. Some Christians preferred not to share relief grain with Hindus until that image was removed. Missioner <u>Edward Burkhalter</u> (GC) reports that an Indian pastor persuaded those Christians to befriend and share supplies with the Hindus since desperate need was their shared experience. (94)

The Jagdeeshpur hospital chaplain <u>Ibrahim Nand</u> (GC) was interrupted when he stood to share a meditation, having gone with a team to visit a village. A man shouted, "Because you associate with missionaries who come from cow-slaughtering countries, we will not listen to a word you say. Go away from our village." Nand paused to explain that he had read the classical Hindu Mahabharata and knew quite a bit of Hindu philosophy and religion. He asked, "Have you not read that one day King Ratideva had 21,000 cows butchered to feed a multitude of guests that he was about to entertain?" When the village pandit (teacher) agreed that such an account was true, the accuser left and those listening showed new respect. (106)

Unrau explains how missioners who first went to India had little training in anthropology, comparative religions, or Hindu culture. They knew something of geography and political history but learned through observing about caste, family relationships, superstition, and worship of images. They gained insight into Hindu and Christian differences of world view, for this world and what might follow. They experienced how loyalty to the Hindu group mattered over place of employment. Meeting a brother's need for cash, if holding an institution's cash box key, might matter more than honesty. To leave one's caste to become Christian showed disloyalty and polluted one, missioners were told. Ideas about purity differed, Unrau said. (107-8) Unable to separate religion from culture, Paul Dyck (GC) thought that missioners "always felt tainted by Hinduism." Yet he admits "how fabulous" the result was when a blind, Christian guest named Simon Patras, preached sermons through song "doing it in the Ramayana style." Both Hindus and Christians listened with keen interest. Unrau reports Dyck's confession: "Never in my life have I seen preaching as effective as that."(109)[16]

As nationals shifted between religious loyalties, so missioners shifted their approach, Unrau states. At times missioners made more contacts with high caste Hindus who might expect deference; during other times or locations they engaged primarily Harijans or Untouchables. At times orphans were the focus; other locations engaged secondary students or industrial workers. Some blocks of time led to 'touring' when missioners entered and camped in or near villages to present the gospel to first-time hearers. Other years found more attention being given to nurturing young Christians or providing literature in "reading rooms." . . . Then too, Hindus made their feelings known about changes in loyalty. They could persecute relatives or organize efforts to challenge folk to return to their Hindu roots. Unrau on several occasions mentions the *Arya Samaj*, a vital Hindu reform group. S. T. Moyer (GC) wrote, "Hinduism is so adamant that Christianity is ineffective. Only revolutionary changes will break up Hinduism— Christianity has not done it." (119)

Unrau, Ruth *Hill Station Teacher A Life with India in It* (North Newton, KS: Kidron Creek Publ., 1997).
Unrau here describes Mussoorie, called by some "Queen of the Hills," and Woodstock International School located in the Himalayan foothills. References to Hinduism appear informally.

- "There is no end to the study of Hinduism and no statement about it which cannot be contradicted" states P. Spear (203)
- Hinduism is basically monotheistic with multiple god forms representing facets of the Supreme Beings' personality. Three main god forms known as: Brahma (lord of all creation), Vishnu (lord of preservation), and Shiva (lord of destruction) may be worshipped along with a near-endless array of goddesses and god forms. . . . Villagers may know local gods to brighten their drab life. . . . Hinduism understands God to be accessible at the center with a million ways to achieve God, Unrau adds. (203)
- "Westerners (Jews, Christians) say 'In the beginning was the Word'" whereas Hindus say 'In the beginning was silence'" said Shridharani . . . Shridharani understands a Hindu's conversion to Christianity or the reverse as merely a change of labels rather than a spiritual experience. (204)
- For many Hindus life is full of suffering; the ambition is to escape from this world. Doing personal duty (*dharma*) leads to good *karma* (destiny) which enables being reborn into a better life, eventually to be absorbed into Divine Essence. (204)
- Many pilgrims and resident holy men can be seen around Dehra Dun (located at the beginning of the ascent to Mussoorie); the holy cities of Rishikesh and Hardwar as well as the Ganges River source are not too far distant. (205)

Wiebe, Paul D. (MB) "The Christian International School" An Important Face in the Work of the Church, 11 pp. mimeographed.
During Wiebe's thirteen years as principal of Kodaikanal International School in southern India he wrote yearly reports to board and other constituency groups.[17] Around 1990-91 twenty percent of KIS students had parents with citizenship of countries different from each other. Sixty percent of students were then Indian nationals, with perhaps seventy-five percent of South-Asian backgrounds. At that time 41 percent of KIS students were of Christian families and 41 percent were of Hindu families, while 12 percent were Muslim and the rest identified as Zoroastrian, Sikh, Jain, and Buddhist. Within such diversity "Christian outlines and emphases" are maintained, Wiebe writes. Basic values are promoted among students and staff—pursuit of truth, justice, peace— values practiced by all the world's great religions. Such schools remain "a place for introductions, reiterations, comparisons, reflections and soundings," Wiebe believes. (11)

Wiebe, Paul D. and **David A. Wiebe**. (MB heritage) *The Colors of the Mennonites in Andhra Pradesh*. *Devuni Prema Idhigo* (Behold the Love of God). Featuring photos by Rufus Gurugulla. (Winnipeg, Manitoba: Kindred Productions 2013).

Colorful indeed is this book about many MB churches (Half of the eight hundred groups of MB worshippers do not gather in church buildings.) in the area of Hyderabad in AP State of India. The Wiebe brothers, sons and grandsons of MB missioners, reveal genuine love for their inherited experience of cross-cultural insight. The noted MB photographer of some of the photos is "active in promoting inter-religious dialogue."

The Foreword writer, long-time, noted MB leader P. B. Arnold, refers to his ancestors of 150 years earlier who were sculptors of idols of the chief deities in Hindu temples where they lived. Legend explains that a sculptor would carve the eyes of an idol after completing its body. Then the deity's spirit, known to reside within the sculptor, enters the idol's body through its eyes. Others of Arnold's ancestors performed worship rituals to consecrate the image, he reports.

While most MB members in AP have Hindu heritage their vivid Christian worship becomes clear through colored photos and brief text.

Wiebe, Paul D. and **David A. Wiebe** (MB heritage), Compilers and Annotated by. *In Another Day of the Lord The Mission Days of the Mennonite Brethren Church of India in Pictures*. (Winnipeg, Manitoba: Kindred Productions 2010).

Here the adult Wiebe twins use primarily black and white photos to tell the MB mission story in India from 1899 through the early 1970s. Seventy-three North American missioners served during this period, seldom as many as twenty at one time. All but a few people living in the area of early MB service were Hindu.

A few references to Hinduism appear scattered through the text and photos. For example, photos identify: representations of deities under a banyan tree; a "chariot of the gods"; members of the welcoming Brahmin family outside their home with its Vaishnavite markings; a priest at a temple pilgrimage site and a village temple; a devotee being prepared to do penance or ask for blessing; progression at the annual Rath (temple cart) Festival; pilgrims and others bathing in the waters of the Krishna River at a pilgrimage site; and a procession during Siva Ratri observances. (25, 30, 32, 34-35).

Wiebes describe *caste* as

the order of civilization that grew out of the encounter between those who entered India over the centuries, as conquerors, and those who were there earlier. . . . Dalits, descendents of the original inhabitants of the land, were suppressed beneath the Brahminically defined *varna* ordering as it was constructed.

(*Varna* means color; castes and the several hundred *jati* groups—perhaps 10-15 within a village—make up the broader, complex social system.) "Being Indian" means understanding caste and its implications—*dharma* or duty—that determine present and future lives, Wiebes explain. (38-40) . . . Dalits were formerly known as "untouchables"—depressed classes to be avoided; conservative orthodox Hindus thought that to touch them was a sin. (50)

Wiebes report that during early MB missioner years Hindu-Muslim conflict was more dangerous in their area than conflict with Christians. But the decision to become a Christian could cause sporadic, public beating or humiliation such as refused access to public wells; homes could be burned too. Non-Christians did not want Christians to prosper, Wiebes explain. (94, 100)

Wiebe, Viola Bergthold (MB) & **Marilyn Wiebe Dodge**. *Sepia Prints Memoirs of a Missionary in India*. (Hillsboro, KS: Kindred Productions, 1990).

Missioner Viola Wiebe and one of her adult daughters provide informative, respectful descriptions from decades of experience meeting Hindu people and practice in India where the majority of the population is loyal to Hinduism.

- Wiebe & Dodge report about a *sadhu* (Hindu holy man) who traveled with them in a train *bogie* (car). Neither Papa (Viola's husband/Marilyn's father) who had read of *sadhu* feats of endurance—"sleeping on nails, walking on fire, standing in one position for a long period of time to acquire spiritual merit"—or the *sadhu* conversed; neither knew the other's language. (7)
- Whenever missioners entered a village headman's home to ask for permission to camp and conduct meetings ("touring") in his village, they could not leave his verandah before being served a cup of tea. The same response of hospitality occurred when entering most any Christian, Hindu or Muslim person's hut. (74)
- When she was age seven, Laxmi's Hindu parents arranged for her to marry a caste boy several years older than she. He died before the ceremony took place leaving her a widow. Attracted to the Christian church, she was baptized at the age of twelve, much to her family's disdain. When a Christian couple took Laxmi into their home, her name (the name of a Hindu goddess of wealth) was changed to Gnanamma (which means wisdom). She later became a very effective Bible woman (visitor to Hindu or Muslim homes to share stories and songs with women). (90)
- Subamma, with wet hair from bathing in a nearby river as part of her morning *puja* (worship), joined the group meeting with a Bible woman. Viola asked Subamma if she had plans for a trip

to visit relatives. She explained that she first needed to consult the *pujari* (priest) to find out from the astrologer the position of planets and stars in order to advise her about traveling. The astrologer would accept whatever gift she gave in return: like rice, ghee (clarified butter), chicken, or eggs. (96)

- When the Wiebe twins were baptized in a stream, onlookers approved saying, "Don't we all need to go into holy waters to be purified? Wasn't our Krishna River one of the largest and named after the black, Hindu deity and hero of the Indian epic Mahabharata?" . . . Wiebe & Dodge explain that bathers in the Krishna River might be lepers, high class Brahmins, *Marvadis* (merchants), or peasants. All Hindus who submerge themselves to wash away all sins then cup their hands to drink water, letting it also run through their fingers three times while saying prayers. . . The Wiebe baptism event conveyed to bystanders that to follow Christ's example is part of a renewed life. (91)
- When two women came screaming and dancing toward Wiebes, John (husband/father) moved toward them speaking in Jesus' name and commanding the spirits to depart. When the women became quiet, their "masters" (those who controlled them and earned money raised through the drama that they caused) became angry because of such intervention. (It halted their rupees made at the women's expense). (97)
- On the occasion of Deepavali, the Hindu Festival of Lights, Mahbubnagar's Collector wrote asking Wiebes for several gallon tins of butter oil to use for lighting lamps for the festival. Because that oil had been sent for poor people to use in cooking, they chose not to give it for the lamps. (125)
- In October 1955 Wiebes set out for *Kurmurti Jatri* (a fair) when once each year Hindus of the area bathe in the 'holy' pool on the hill . . . Wiebes talked with people as they gave out medicines before spending the night with Christians in their *pallem* area. Early the next morning they were awakened by a clanging of bells and shouting of "Sita-Rama!" (Hindu deity names) after which people rushed to the pool to wash away their sins. . . Later, when meeting some who had attended the event, John asked "What have you received?" The reply: "We went without peace; we return without peace." (132)
- Visiting in Kathmandu, Nepal through its picturesque streets and around the noted Stupa (Buddhist Swiumbunath), Wiebes watched the people touch and spin the prayer wheels as they passed. The Great eyes painted on all four sides of the Stupa watched the throngs below, the authors write. (135)

- When holding meetings in a village, Wiebes and two preachers were called to the home of a Hindu *pujari* (priestess). When they were seated on mats on the dirt floor, she pointed to niches carved into the walls holding *bommalu* (idols). Having heard the missioner's messages, she no longer wanted the idols and asked Wiebes to throw them into the well. John said, "Amma, since you worshipped them, you need to throw them away." No doubt fearing that she might be struck dead or that fire would come from heaven, she cautiously gathered them into a basket and took them to the well where she threw the basket and contents into it. Together they returned to her room to speak and pray together. (138)
- Common superstitious beliefs among Hindu hospital patients included: that no water be given to feverish or diarrhea patients; that evil spirits attack a person wearing white when in a hospital ward (white is the color that widows wear); that the sacred *tulasi* plant purifies blood, the authors write. (151)
- Villagers of the region were involved in a system defined as sacred in which a person performed duties as socially defined. . . . . The most frequently approached, favored deities were those associated with particular illnesses and those that protected or granted favors. Many religious practices of daily life helped to accumulate favor or avoid disfavor among deities. (171)

Yoder Lawrence M. "Contemporary Global Pluralism: The Approach of Hinduism," in *Practicing Truth Confident Witness in our Pluralistic World*, David W. Shenk and Linford Stutzman, eds. (Scottdale, PA: Herald Pr, 1999) 102-15.

Lawrence Yoder's exposure to Hindu thought centers in Indonesia, some of which resembles Hinduism in India, the prime country of its origin and presence, while some differs. Distinct location needs to be clarified as do scattered ideas noted in Yoder's Introduction. Yoder credits Persians for having originated the term *Hinduism*. He sees it as their label for religious practice and belief among all who lived along northwestern India's river called Sindhu (Indus). Rivers enabled sacred ablutions and bathing that enhanced ritual purity. Yoder names *dharma* (the law or way) as the Indian name for its religion which had two ancient sources: third millennium BCE and 1500 BCE. Recent scholars may debate the invasion of light-skinned Aryan peoples from the northwest during the latter period. Yoder names the "Republic of India" his source for defining anyone not a Muslim, Christian, Parsi, or Jew as Hindu. (102)

Yoder identifies basic categories of Hindu thought and practice. He finds the basis for the main caste system division into exclusive social groups to be the cosmic Purusha or *atman*. From his mouth the gods created the Brahmins, from his arms the Kshatriya, from his thighs the Vaisya, and from his feet the Sudras. (104) In addition to the caste system, other unifying Hindu themes that Yoder names are: Mother India as the source of life, the sacred river, reincarnation with the law of *karma*, and suffering. For Hindus, paths to salvation include works (duty and sacrifice), devotion (*bhakti*), and knowledge (*jnana*, a central school of thought being *monism*). Within *monism* one thing alone exists which is Brahman-Atman or the Ultimate. (104-07) Yoder explains *monism* and issues of mysticism from the perspective of Javanese religion. Having lived in Indonesia more than a dozen times, Yoder's view of Hinduism reflects Indonesian culture's particulars, as stated.

Zimmerman, Earl (MC) "Calcutta Connections: Mennonite Service in India," *Conrad Grebel Review*, (Winter 2001) 4-28.
With the focus of this article clear from the title, Zimmerman does not write much about Hindu thought or practice. However, he very informatively reports the story of activity in India of both MCC (Mennonite Central Committee) and the combined, Indian Mennonite organization MCSFI (Mennonite Christian Service Fellowship of India). The social crisis that plunged East Bengal (now Bangladesh) in 1946 into chaos left little question whether MCC's theology and practice of service was needed. The brutal time before and partition of India and East Pakistan prompted thousands of Hindus to be driven from their homes. Burnings and lootings of villages and religious riots left four thousand dead and more than ten thousand injured. Instead of celebrating in Delhi on August 15, 1947, Gandhi stayed in Calcutta to "fast, pray, and spin" Zimmerman reports. In addition to useful details reported with endnotes, Indian leadership with MCSFI is named: P. J. Malagar (MC) to begin followed later by R. S. Lemuel (MB), Shant Kunjam (MC), and Emmanuel Minj.

Zimmerman, Earl (MC) "Kolkata Reflections", http://kolkatareflections .blogspot.com/2007/11/blog-post.html; "Religion, Politics, Tombs and Temples," (November 9, 2007) 3; "Christmas in India," (January 6, 2008) 3; "Mennonites in India," (September 16, 2008) 3.
Zimmerman and wife Ruth lived in Kolkata, India, as MCC representatives for India, Afghanistan, and Nepal. His November post refers to the Aryan tribes that invaded India around 1500 BCE from Central Asia bringing "their Sanskrit language (predecessor of Hindi) and their religious beliefs (predecessor of Hinduism) with them." Discussion of the birth of Buddhism in north India and its embrace, including nonviolence, by emperor Ashoka in 262 BCE was followed by the

Muslim Mughal empire in 1525. During Mughal emperor Aurangzeb's (1658-1707) reign he imposed Islam on subjects and destroyed Hindu temples, the legacy for ongoing Hindu-Muslim tensions in the land. Religious tolerance through Babur and son Akbar (1556-1605) had led to open interreligious conversations and Hindus being included in government offices. Zimmerman credits such diverse histories as reason for some Indians, like the deeply devout Hindu Gandhi, to embrace secularism following Independence (1947). Zimmerman poses two guiding questions that face MCC staff:

> How do we deeply respect and learn from other religious traditions yet live and witness from the center of our own faith? Can we invite people to join us in the new life and community we find in Jesus, yet avoid the religious superiority that thinks that we alone have the truth?

The January post finds Zimmermans vacationing in the "stark beauty" of the snow capped Himalayan peaks near Mussoorie, U.P. State. Tensions had flared into communal violence between Christians, Muslims and Hindus. Zimmerman expresses his intent to learn more from Jesus' example of "living out of the center of God's love for the whole world." His September post refers to Hinduism having existed in various forms since the beginning of recorded history. Then he invites readers to imagine details from the time of the beginning of western Mennonites' entering India—blind spots and strengths—as part of a perplexing colonial era until leaving in the 1970s. With MCC he anticipates working with a "promising new generation of Indian church leadership."

---

[1] Alle Hoekema. "Christianity in Asia," in J.A. Lapp, Snyder, *et al.*, *Churches Engage Asian Traditions*.

[2] Indian Bible women who took the Christian message into homes deserve credit too. Missioner Thelma Miller Groff (MC) describes Bible women as "effective—good at meeting women, telling scripture stories, and authentic prayer"—in the video titled "Holy Respect—No Less" created by Dorothy Yoder Nyce (1996) 31 minutes. Also informative is Indian James Taneti's "Telugu Women in Mission" (DMin thesis, Western Theological Seminary, 2012). Taneti is known to present MB leaders in Andhra Pradesh.

[3] Late nineteenth century restrictions on Asian immigrants to the USA, enhanced by exaggerated views that Indians could not assimilate with "white men" (126) led to a 1917 Asiatic Barred Zone Act that deprived people of South and Southeast Asia origin from freedom to settle here.

[4] Gerber Koontz and Alexis-Baker might have examined why intellectual, Indian Christians who have lived life-long in religiously plural India found Hendrik

Kraemer's book prepared for the 1938 International Missionary Conference less than satisfactory.

[5] It therefore can be meant also for Hinduism.

[6] Formerly held at the Centre for the Study of World Christianity, University of Edinburgh, these UMN materials were donated to Yale in 2008 and 2010. The writer wishes to thank archivist Martha Lund Smalley and Special Collections Assistant Kevin Crawford for assistance in making available ten boxes of material requested for perusal on May 6, 2013.

[7] (February 28, 1984) 146-47.

[8] See Ronald Neufeldt and James Pankratz for more detailed discussion of this reformer.

[9] The writer has tried to locate Masih's paper ("Proclaiming the Gospel to Hindus") and others presented at the Council of International Ministries meeting held January 23-26, 1998 titled: "Pluralism and the Christian Gospel: Encounters with Hindus and Hinduism."

[10] A significant paragraph about this chapter appears in Gerald Shenk's review of the Dula & Weaver book in *Mennonite Quarterly Review*, April 2009, 355.

[11] The writer valued conversation with Murray in Newton, Kansas on July 9, 2014. He told of his encounter with Hinduism when guest of former Hindus doctor Subbarao and wife Olga Yarlagadda at the medical, dental, and eye clinic in Chilivuru, Andhra Pradesh State, India.

[12] A footnote names two achievements of Muller's: his Sanskrit edition of the Rig-Veda and his *Sacred Books of the East* series most of which he edited from 1875 to his death in 1900.

[13] Readers are cautioned not to confuse the Brahmo Samaj with Hindu reform members of the *Arya Samaj*; the latter strongly opposed Christian activity, including where GC Mennonites were located.

[14] Read by this writer at the Archives of the General Conference Mennonite Church, Bethel College, Newton, KS. July 1014. On that day she also had a conversation with the Platts in their home.

[15] Other writers may see and claim the Gita account's *mythical* depth, and other informants name *knowledge* (*jnana*) as the third path.

[16] See Chad Bauman's writing about blind Simon.

[17] That Ronald Fleming (GC) was principal for a few of the same years at Woodstock School, an international, Christian school located in the Himalayan foothills of the north, reflects well on Mennonite leadership in ecumenical education.

Academic

Asheervadam, I. P. (MB) "The Historical Setting for Mennonite and Brethren in Christ Churches in India," 15 pp, retrieved 6/8/2014. http://archive.bethelks.edu/ml/issue/vol-56-no-3/article/the-historical-setting.

Asheervadam is currently Principal and Professor of Church History at the Mennonite Brethren Centenary Bible College in Shamshabad, India. He believes that if major groups within India's diverse, multi-religious, multi-cultural population—like Backward Castes, Scheduled Castes, Scheduled Tribes, and all other minorities—were distinctly named and counted, the actual number of Hindus is considerably less than the eighty percent usually stated. Asheervadam's purpose for this essay is to study the background context for Christian mission efforts in general in India and more particularly in north Bihar State. Attention is here given to Hindu influence, not the Bihar content. (1)

Asheervadam names five periods of India's general history or rule: 1. Ancient (3250-2000 BCE—Before Common Era), 2. Hindu (2000 BCE – 100 CE Common Era) with Hindu rulers when both Hinduism and Buddhism developed, 3. Islamic (1000 - 1757 CE), 4. East India Company and British Colonialism (1757 - 1947), and 5. Independent India since 1947. By 2000 twenty-nine states divided India mostly along language lines.

The Hindu caste system and the designation of out-of-caste people as "untouchable" (due to menial work assigned to them by Manu's law) provide important statistics: Dalits (downtrodden), the name preferred by them instead of *untouchable*, make up seventy percent of Indian Christians. Ninety-nine percent of MBs come from Dalit groups which Asheervadam describes as a "condition of hope." Seventy to ninety percent of people in different faiths in India are from Dalit origin. (3, 6) Religiously, Dalits could not enter Hindu temples until several decades ago; nor did Brahmins serve them as priests. Many Dalits choose religious identity other than Hinduism for reasons of self-respect, human dignity, desire to be treated as equals, and to escape oppression of high caste groups. B. R. Ambedkar, known to enable many Dalits to shift to Buddhism, said: ". . . freedom cannot be secured without conversion." Thousands who followed Veerabrahmam, a former devotee of the Hindu Shiva, embraced Christianity in Andhra Pradesh State during the first half of the nineteenth century (where MBs later emerged). (3-5, 7-8)

Asheervadam, Injamuri P. (MB) Review of *Christian Identity and* Dalit *Religion in Hindu India, 1868-1947* by Chad Bauman, *Mission Focus: Annual Review*, (vol. 17, 2009) 190-94.

Asheervadam begins his review by lifting from Bauman's Introduction an account of a political cartoon that appeared in 2003 during elections in Chhattisgarh State.

> A nationalist organization called the Hindu Raksha Manch (the Hindu Protection Platform) depicts the Christian Bishop of the region next to a fierce-looking *goonda* who is menacingly holding a *lathi* (firm stick used by police) over a man presumably being forced to become a Christian. Behind these three is a prison full of others awaiting the same "fate." Referring to the Bishop, the caption for the cartoon reads: "Agent of the Pope—A Servant of Madam" (Sonia Gondhi) . . . Changing religion means changing nationality (*dharmantaran yani rastrantaran*). Change the government in Chhattisgarh and we can stop conversion.

Asheervadam makes clear that Bauman's book raises important issues about "conversion, nationalism, and Christian mission." He explains that the reformer Guru Ghasidas, about whom Bauman writes, accepted but altered certain ideas of Hinduism like purity and pollution while rejecting other Hindu symbols like ritual hierarchy. Annotations below will elaborate. Asheervadam concludes how symbols and cultures go through a process of hybridization when a person changes religious loyalty. "No religion is purely indigenous and no religion is purely foreign" he adds.

Bauman, Chad M. (MC) *Christian Identity and* Dalit *Religion in Hindu India, 1868-1947*. PhD dissertation from Princeton Theological Seminary, 2005 (Grand Rapids: Eerdmans Publ Co, 2008).

Bauman's extensive study and exposure combines with others' scholarly work, British colonial texts, missionary letters and papers, and interviews that he conducted with one hundred Chhattisgarhi people. This writer will be selective with annotations from such rich content.

One aspect that Bauman carefully examines is *conversion* and why it is so "politically charged" in India. Those who oppose a person's shift from one religious loyalty to another, as from Hindu to Islam or Christianity, say that such change counters national strength. Such converts turn from an expected loyalty to *Bharat Mata* ("Mother India"). In that shift India's unity and autonomy are threatened, Hindus charge. Some laws then denounce change that involves "force, fraud, inducement or allurement." (3-4) Bauman understands conversion to be transition from one worldview, way of life, or community to another one through a process of acculturation within social and cultural features. (75)

Bauman's Introduction distinguishes the Hindu sectarian community of *dalits* (broken or oppressed folk) and the Satnamis of Chhattisgarh, founded by an uneducated *guru* named Ghasidas of the Chamar caste. From early in the nineteenth century until his death in 1850, Ghasidas encouraged followers to change their patterns: to not worship idols, eat meat, or depend on *brahman* religious figures, and to be devoted instead to a single deity called "Satnam" (True Name). Nearly all area Chamars had joined the Hindu reform group of Satnamis by the end of that century. Ghasidas had returned in the 1820s from a solitary retreat (some sources say "to a forest") to the well-known Hindu Jagannath temple in Puri with a message. Bauman suggests that message to have been inspired by the Hindu *bhakti* (devotional) tradition through Indian *sants* (poet-saints). It enabled the Chamars to gain a new, more dignified self-image and a worldview with a sense of more equality of castes. So, when the first German Evangelical and American Disciples of Christ missioners arrived in 1868, religious restlessness dominated the area. (5, 15-16)

Bauman analyzes the development during eighty years of three groups: Hindu reformed Satnamis, Christians, and a mix of people neither strictly Satnami nor Christian. He understands *religion* to be a dynamic, diverse, contested system of symbols that condition people's personal experience of the world into a broader worldview. Worldview, Bauman says, emerges through symbiosis of lived and imagined experience. It is neither resistant to nor insulated from change affected by social power and authority. An example exists when more urban experience changed the former Chhattisgarhi people's division between Hindus living on the plains and "jungly" *adivasis* (original inhabitants) who were less caste-oriented and located in the hill area. (6-9)

Bauman notes ruptures due to religious unrest among nineteenth century lower castes in Chhattisgarh. He understands that all cultures ever-undergo change. To become Christian involved less a break from Chhattisgarhi culture and more a process of mixture, a mutual informing between "old" and "new" worldviews. Missioners proposed that rather than reject Guru Ghasidas' message, Christianity fulfilled it. Satnami-Christians then evaluated new insights through traditional criteria and former cultural patterns in light of new criteria. (13, 19) As a scholar Bauman looks at culture through history, comparison, syncretism, and method. With the latter, missioners might name a shift in Christian focus from *belief* as prime to daily *practice and ritual* as of first import—what a person *does*. Whereas Americans understand *secularism* to mean "keeping religion out of government" or the latter out of the former, Indians see it as "not privileging one religion over another." (25-27)[1]

Although much more insight could be lifted from Bauman's dissertation only a few distinct points linked to Hinduism are added.

- People in rural areas of India tend to connect with "small-time Hindu gods and local goddesses." (36)
- *Sanskritization* refers to the process in which a tribal or 'low' Hindu caste individual or group shifts toward being part of higher castes. (53)
- Members of the Hindu reform group named Satnami never shifted as a "mass movement" to become Christians; by 1931, 2.5 percent of them had made that shift of loyalty. (68)
- Hindus commonly think that devotion toward a chosen deity does not exclude worship of other deities. (159)

Bauman, Chad M (MC) with Arun Jones, Brian Pennington, Joseph Prabhakar Dayam, and Michelle Voss Roberts. *Christianity and Hinduism: An Annotated Bibliography.*2012 Available from http:///digitalcommonsbutler.edu/facsch;

Bauman, Chad M. (MC) "Hindu-Christian Conflict in India: Globalization, Conversion, and the Coterminal Castes and Tribes," *The Journal of Asian Studies (72, no. 3,* 2013) 633-53. Available from Doi: 10.1017/S0021911813000569.
http://digitalcommonsbutler.edu/facsch_papers/270.
In this article Bauman reviews anti-Christian rhetoric in India, discusses patterns of communal violence, and argues that "only theories linking local and even individual social behaviors to larger, global processes like globalization can adequately honor the truly 'webby' nature of the social world." (Abstract, 633)

In answer to the question of *why* Hindu-Christian conflict increased in and after 1998, Bauman notes the fact of the more politically stringent BJP's (Bharatiya Janata Party) gaining central power including the Prime Minister's role in 1998; the backlash felt by RSS (Hindu nationalism-oriented organization) after the destruction of the Babri Masjid (Muslim mosque) in Ayodhya which led to deadly Hindu-Muslim riots in 1992; the fact of Italian, Christian Sonia Gandhi's becoming Congress Party president; and the offensive western, Christian evangelical efforts. But for him the major reason centers in the way Indian Christianity came to symbolize the powerful impact of *globalization*. Bauman defines that term as increased "connectedness of national and regional economies, peoples, and cultures" through increased transportation and exchange of ideas. (634-35)

Highlights of Bauman's historical survey of Hindu-Christian relations in India include:

- Coming of the "Syrian" Christians to South India during the sixth century (Hindus accepted them as ritually pure);
- First mass shift of lower-caste Hindus to Christianity through Francis Xavier and missioners;
- Evangelical British East India Company's effort to reform Syrian Christians from their Hindu-linked syncretism that had enabled their acceptance among upper-caste folk;
- Increase of European missioners (19th century) which led to violence from those threatened by national Christians;
- Elite Hindu efforts to conserve and revive their suspicion toward Christian power-mongering and disloyalty (late 19th century);
- Creation of policies that provided rights and benefits for only *non*-Christians among the lower classes;
- Formation of the Hindu *Arya Samaj* association (1875) that challenged conversion to Islam and Christianity and that, due to fear for Hindu decline, developed campaigns for "purification" (*shuddhi*) of such converts if they returned to Hindu loyalty;
- Assistance and sensitivity toward famine victims (late 1890s) that led to Christian growth which in turn prompted growth of Hindu societies like the All-India Hindu "Mahasabba" (1907);
- Strong Indian identity prompted by V. D. Savarkar's 1923 tract "*Hindutva: Who is a Hindu?*" which led to founding of the RSS organization (1925) intent to propagate *Hindutva* thought. BJP and VHP (World Hindu Council, 1964) groups also worked to reverse Christian missioner 'success.'
- Partition, the massive divide of peoples at the time of Independence (1947), killed mostly Hindus, Muslims, and Sikhs, but tradition-focused Hindu groups continued to counter Christian efforts among lower-caste Hindus. (636-41)

Bauman's further discussion of theories of communal violence and globalization—focused on psychological, political, and economic issues—illustrate both Hindu-Muslim and Hindu-Christian patterns. He explains how communal violence, especially against Christians, "results from the interplay of local exigencies and global flows of wealth, power, and money." (644) Christian conversion threatens the nation's presumed (by many Hindus) Hindu nationalist agenda which conflicts with globalization.

Bauman, Chad M. "Is Conversion Violence?" Presentation at New Perspectives on Faith, Goshen, Indiana, Handout: "'Religion' and

'Conversion' from a 'Hindu' Perspective," 1 p. (Sept. 30, 2012). See www.newperspectivesgoshen.org.

Before noting several of Bauman's compiled Hindu understandings of the interlinking cause and effect of the terms *religion* and *conversion*, several other points from his speech deserve annotation.

- Many Hindus became suspicious of mass conversions; they fear that unarmed folk can be induced, that India might disintegrate.
- Some Hindu politicians promote fear of non-Hindu religious actions for political affect.
- Many *Dalits* (lower-caste) see conversion as a means to improve their status; upper-caste Hindus show little intent to assist *dalits*
- St. Thomas Christians engaged more with upper-caste Hindus in south Indian involvement.
- Most Hindus think of conversion as "uncouth," as destructive of culture, as likely to seriously diminish the number of Hindus. Bauman illustrates such concern with a painting by Shoury titled "Harvesting Our Souls."
- Many Indians understand 'freedom of religion' as being free from intrusion or aggression from others.

The next two paragraphs summarize Bauman's sixteen sequential points of agreement that he heard from Hindus during discussion of his title question "Is Conversion Violence?" Presenting the question with responses to a mainly non-violent, Mennonite audience enabled their understanding of the Hindu thought process.

"True conversion" has distinct meaning for Hindus, according to Bauman. Many Hindus experience conversion as effort to change another's loyalty or label. Such effort shows lack of respect for one's own community and lack of knowledge about true religion. Bauman also heard from Hindus that such religious labels can be meaningless. The hope within all religious traditions centers on moral transformation— change from being less to more good, from a base or weak nature to one that is increasingly sublime. Therefore, those who encourage others to change religions are rude or intrusive, perhaps even violent. They are being political or underhanded; they fail to understand "true religion" which characterizes Hinduism.

Among Bauman's sixteen points of how Hindus perceive *religion* and *conversion* appear the following: Some Hindus say that *secularism* privileges the western Christian in calling religion not to interfere with politics. Since Hindus explain religion to be about *practice*—to move up in morality—"true conversion" reflects being transformed from a more base posture to one more sublime *within* one's birth or chosen loyalty. Hindus see their need to 'wake up' to the disadvantage of being as tolerant as they are lest those who evangelize in order to convert people from one loyalty to another see that approach as a "right." Since no particular religion provides a superior concept of Truth or means to salvation, many Hindus claim that religious affiliation depends on birth.

Bauman, Chad M. (MC) "Redeeming Indian 'Christian' Womanhood? Missionaries, *Dalits*, and Agency in Colonial India," *Journal of Feminist Studies in Religion*, (24, no 2, 2008) 5-27.

This study by Bauman of women's experience among reformed Hindu Satnami, Satnami-Christian, and Christian *dalit* groups in the Chhattisgarh region of India contrasts with most historical writing of Christian missions in India. [2] Bauman gives reason to question if shifting from Hindu to Christian loyalty improved life "without qualification" for women. Readers will benefit from keeping in mind several of Bauman's facts: 1. That several religious shifts emerged—from Hindu to Hindu reform known as Satnami, to Satnami-Christian, or Christian loyalty. 2. That German Evangelical and American Disciples of Christ missioners brought Victorian-era norms with them. Some norms resembled upper-caste Hindu constraint of women to home duties (in part to protect them) and their subordination to husbands. 3. That steps useful to describe women's history might reflect three R-words: *Retrieval* (to uncover and preserve lost voices of women), *Reconstruction* (to retell accounts more inclusively), and *Re-theorization* (to provide a more practical theory, aware that combating one form of oppression may validate another). (5-8)

After reviewing the story of Guru Ghasidas' influence on Satnamis, as explained in Bauman's first resource above, he notes injustices toward Indian women that scandalized missioners—child marriage, temple prostitution, widow abuse, and seclusion (in the *zenana*). While conversion to Christianity lessened such behaviors, other western-brought goals like the "cult of true womanhood" negated mobility, spontaneity, and self-indulgence, similar to some Hindu limits. The financial and low social status experienced by *dalits* required many Chhattisgarhi women to work outside the home, especially in fields. That missioners seemed pleased when Indian wives could focus instead on being dedicated homemakers under the protection and control of their husband hardly reflects only progress, Bauman cautions. (11-12)

Bauman discusses themes of weddings, widows, and divorce, comparing details from within a typical Hindu context. While divorce was discouraged for Satnami-Christians and Christians but common among Satnamis, the option for a widow who wished to retain property, even children, among them all was either to remain unmarried or marry a brother of her husband (called *levirate*). Again, restriction for Christian married women surfaced—less freedom to disagree with their husband. Whereas "Satnami women said whatever they wanted to their husbands, Christian women said nothing to theirs" Bauman learned from interviews. He recognized western Christian ideals for "wives to be submissive, restrained, and self-controlled." (13-17)

Bauman discusses important areas of education and being professional including reference to Christian women trained as teachers, nurses and Bible women. As Christians became more confident and Satnami-Christians more inclined to express a desire for autonomy, conflicts occurred with missioners who retained paternalist attitudes toward Indians. (17-21) Bauman also discusses *agency* for women—to combat oppression—as western feminist scholars do, again noting caution. When agency focuses too narrowly on resistance to oppression or subversive norms, the full complexity of women's experience may be overlooked, he suggests. To presume that women ever-gain freedom from restraint through becoming a Christian "falls flat" in light of some evidence that Bauman discovered. (23)

Bauman, Chad. (MC) "Sathya Sai Baba At Home Abroad in Midwestern
America," in *Public Hinduisms*. John Zavos, Pralay Kanungo,
Deepa S. Reddy, Maya Warrier, and Raymond Brady Williams,
eds. SAGE, www.sagepublications.com; 141-59.

Professor Bauman wrote this informative chapter after a year of fieldwork at the Indianapolis, Indiana Sai Baba Center. Of interest is the fact that when his content was going to press, the central figure, *guru* Sai Baba, "gave up his bodily form" in India (24 April 2011). The Friend with whom SBC Indian Americans had walked 'spiritually' no longer existed to share advice. But his influence continues for thousands in India and around the world.

Born in 1926 and victim of powerful seizures at age 13, he then proclaimed himself "Sai Baba" a reincarnation of the Muslim Saint Shirdi Sai Baba who had died in 1918. Miracles that marked his early attraction for followers diminished in importance in later decades. Before long, Sai Baba further declared himself an *avatar* of God Siva with his consort Shakti. Bauman explains how Sai and his devotees claim that his name and form, as with all Hindu Gods and Goddesses, manifest the one divine principle. A famous segment of his message lingered throughout his life:

> There is only one religion, the religion of love . . . only one
> caste. . . Select scriptural stories, values, and saints from all
> faiths. . . Persist therein and "you will find that you are
> coming nearer and nearer to Me (Sai); for all names are Mine
> and all forms are Mine. (151)

As is characteristic of Sai Centers in most U.S. states, activities at the one in Indianapolis concentrate on devotion, education, and service.

Devotion (*bhakti*) to Sai Baba becomes the focus of Sunday morning and Thursday evening gatherings where many *bhajans* are sung. Bauman describes the evening gathering room where a large statue of the Hindu god form Ganesh stands on a pedestal alongside a chair over which a saffron robe formerly worn by Sai Baba is draped. Also noticeable are framed pictures of the late and former Sai figures, a bell, candle holders, a small oil lamp and a brass container for *vibhuti*, plus a "Byzantine-style icon of Jesus' face." Following the chanting of "*OM,*" devotees sing many *bhajans*—*songs* linked to diverse regions of India, to Hindu, Muslim, Jain, Sikh and Christian sources. "Amazing Grace" is sung nearly every week, Bauman adds. Devotees perform *arati* at the altar, hear readings from Sai's writing and a meditation, and express the other noted Hindu chant, the *gayatri mantra*. (144)

The key educational dimension, known as *bal vikas* (childhood development), focuses on basic values of non-violence (*ahimsa*), compassion, truth (*sathya*), right conduct (*dharma*), moral courage, moderation, modesty, love for God and God's creatures (*prema*), peace (*shanti*), and service. A monthly soup kitchen for homeless people and engagement with elderly folk illustrate how children along with adults implement service. Parents are convinced that children learn basic values through simple but sincere devotion to their flexible *guru* Sai Baba. That education enables them both to connect to India and Hindu traditions and to fit in to the American setting, Bauman says. Many Indian Hindus in America value emphasis on universal human values. They credit all secular traditions or religions (including Hinduism) rather than trust a limited, Hindu focus on scriptures dependent on Sanskrit, or complex rituals that rely on a priest present at temples. (145-48)

Bauman's article ends by noting how some Sai devotees distinguish between religion and the spiritual—". . . that religion is about rituals and institutions whereas spirituality" (such as Sai devotion that may also include the former) "focuses more on transcendent principles and values." (153) In parts of North America loyalty to a religious *guru* might also replace loyalty to region, language, or caste for some Indian Americans. (156)

Bauman, Chad M. and James Ponniah. "Christianity and Freedom in India: Colonialism, Communalism, Caste, and Violence." Religious Freedom Project, (December 2013) 35 pp.

The setting for an academic conference titled "Religious Freedom Project," where Chad Bauman and his Indian acquaintance James Ponniah presented this paper on Hindu-Christian conflict in India, was the Pontifical Urbaniana University, Rome, Italy. During that event participants were surprised to be invited to a private audience in the papal residence with Pope Francis. He "appears intent on improving interfaith relations," Bauman thinks. The group's papal audience lasted only a few minutes; his request "Pray for me," was spoken in English.[3]

Content for Bauman and Ponniah's paper, researched over five years, covers four areas: 1. Demographic data on the Indian Christian community and a history of tensions between India's Christians and Hindus; 2. Source and severity of social, legal, political, and violent pressures experienced by present Indian Christians; 3. Effects of those pressures on the life and practice of Indian Christians and on Indian social and political life in general; and 4. Christian contributions to Indian civil society. (3) Information was gathered from two hundred people in, or in villages near, sixteen Indian cities.[4] The extensive information provided by Bauman and Ponniah includes such diverse points of interest as:

- Conclusions of the noted, 1956 Niyogi Committee Report: that Christianity was growing rapidly at the expense of Hinduism; that foreign Christians desired both religious and political loyalty of Hindus; and that Christians used superior medical and educational institutions to attract Indians who then might convert to Christianity. (9)
- Other Freedom of Religion laws emerged and changed over time with varied stipulations about conversion; these prompted mixed meanings of terms, false charges, and threats.
- Officially, Christians did not form castes; experience proved otherwise for some.
- A reservation system, with those qualified known as Scheduled Caste, benefited certain people for financial, educational, or job opportunity. SC members who converted to Christianity could lose such options; that fact led many of them not to change or identify religious loyalty. (12)
- "Everyday" violent attacks pursued specific communities or targets like pastors or evangelists, while "anti-Christian riots" were widespread, Bauman and Ponniah explain.
- Rumors can prompt violence—in 1982, during a popular Hindu temple festival in a southern village, word spread that some Christian men had molested Hindu women during their ritual baths. When police fired to quiet the crowd, six Christians were killed which, in turn, led to violence nearby when hundreds were injured. (14)
- Anti-Christian violence can erupt at Christmas time as in Kandhamal, Odisha in 2007; it ignited there again eight months later. Controversy centered on a Swami (Hindu holy man). Although a Maoist revolutionary group called Naxalites claimed responsibility for his death, Christians were blamed. Fifty people lost their lives in addition to dozens being beaten or raped;

refugee camps emerged when thousands of homes were destroyed. A Christian mob also destroyed 120 Hindu homes, Bauman and Ponniah report. (14-15)

* Increasingly, Christians see the need to shift from their isolated living toward more ecumenical support with Protestants and Roman Catholics. They also are more ready to cooperate with non-Christian traditions like Buddhism. (25, 27-29)

Bauman and Ponniah conclude by expressing several positive views. Conflict between Christians and Hindus need not prevail even when tensions between religious minorities and a majority exist. If Christians more often validate commendable aspects like Hindu piety and devotion, or if high-caste Hindus admit their felt threat to supremacy from lower-caste Christians gaining new skills and strength of self, both can benefit. The authors also suggest that conflict need not keep people loyal to either religion from separately or together improving life for all in India. (30-31)

Bauman, Chad. (MC) Review of *Bourgeois Hinduism* or *The Faith of the Modern Vedantist: Rare Discourses from Early Colonial Bengal*, by *Brian Hatcher*. (New York: Oxford University Pr), *Journal of Religion*. (vol. 89, 2009) 452-54.
Bauman reviews this book from 1841. It contains twenty-one discourses by members associated with a Truth-Promoting Society, one of whom was father of the noted poet Rabindranath Tagore. Early missioners were influenced by such Bengali societies regarding cultural goals and middle-class values, values that had in turn been inspired by Hindu scriptures, the Upanishads. Reference is also made to Rammohan Roy, founder of the Brahmo Samaj Society begun in 1928.[5]

Bauman, Chad. (MC) Review of *Divine Mother, Blessed Mother: Hindu Goddesses and the Virgin Mary*. By Francis X. Clooney, (Oxford University Pr, 2005), *Journal of the American Academy of Religion* (74, no. 3, September 2006) 779-81.
Here Bauman reviews a resource useful for academic purposes written by Clooney, a noted scholar of Hindu thought. Hindu Goddesses known from the 8th, 12th, and 18th centuries are examined. To take a goddess seriously involves viewing her as 'real,' not merely symbolic, Clooney suggests. Bauman notes that Clooney recommends that readers have knowledge from both Hindu and Christian mythology; that scholarship includes Marian hymns.

Bauman, Chad. (MC) Review essay: "Indian Christian Historiography from below, from above, and in between." Review of *India and* *the Indianness of Christianity: Essays on Understanding the Historical, Theological and Bibliographical,* Richard Fox Young, ed. and *A Social History of Christianity: North-west India Since 1800* by John C. B. Webster. *Church History,* (80 no. 3, 2011) 622-29.

Bauman raises the question *"Is the history of Indian Christians more missionary or Indian?"* as central for the first resource. Several ideas surface. Lutheran Indian historian Daniel Jeyaraj reports in his chapter how interdependent missioners and Indian Christians were in Tranquebar, South India. Bauman observes that Mennonite Wilbert Shenk's chapter gives little attention to Indians with whom missioners related. Bauman notes that upper-caste Hindu *pandits*, when teaching missioners Indian languages, definitely influenced their understanding of Hinduism.

Bauman describes Webster's book as mostly observation with little theory. Issues raised by Webster include: Christianity's local and regional influence, compared to national; Muslim and Sikh influence compared to Hindu; Lower-caste involvement from 1873-1918; How Christian conversion prompted Hindu reform movements; How a focus on historic missions can neglect attention to other groups' growth, such as Pentecostals; How few Indians are named in the history as recorded.

Charles, John D. (MC) "Hinduism (Brahmanism)," in *Present Day Religions.* Mission Committee of the Mennonite Board of Missions and Charities, (Scottdale, PA: Mennonite Publishing House, 1921).

J. D. Charles wrote this book when a professor at Hesston Academy in Kansas. In addition to the chapter on Hinduism he wrote chapters about Buddhism, Confucianism, Taoism, Shintoism, and Sikhism. Topics in this chapter include: origin, caste, scriptures, the Supreme One (Brahma), and salvation. Concerning comparative religion Charles calls students to proceed from the "high ground of true religion to facts and aberrations of non-Christian religions." He understands the purpose for idols—made from stone and metal, wood and clay—to be either to appease a god's wrath or gain its favor. He judges the central caste system to be "the worst of all wrongs." (28)

Whereas Vedic hymns, prized ancient literature for many Indians, had at one time praised the One True God, (monotheism), according to Charles, that ancient faith knew shifts: to seeing God in everything (pantheism) prior to belief in polytheism. The latter offered options for knowing the One—through the triune Brahma, Vishnu, or Siva along with a pantheon of thousands of divinities.[6] Charles notes details about Hindu god-concept, scripture and theology: The "Supreme One (Brahma) though too far off to be worshipped was part of everything and everything was part of Brahma." Salvation realized the union of a person's soul with Brahma. Through prayer, good action, and obedience to laws a person eventually gains merit through a process of transmigrations or rebirths, Charles explains. (30-31)

The noble religious book called Gita is "more Christian" in sentiment than other Indian literature Charles thinks. In addition to commending the prominent place given to prayer by Hindus, Charles faults several features of Hinduism: that touching a low-caste person cannot be pardoned; that the duration or number of re-births might be reduced through strict adherence to law or acts of merit; that widows consecrated to Krishna may become prostitutes when resident in temples (27-29) In the study of religions, Charles cautions against either becoming liberal to the point of granting salvation through them all, or so narrow as to refuse to learn or receive good ideas from others. Since all religions provide interest and instruction, he expects a student who compares religions to keep focused what is "true." Charles ends each chapter with review items such as: Name commendable features of Hinduism and defects in Indian views of God.

Flueckiger, Joyce Burkhalter. (GC) *Everyday Hinduism* (Lived Religions). Wiley Blackwell Series on "Everyday Religion." An Introductory Textbook, 2015.

With a PhD from the University of Wisconsin, Burkhalter Flueckiger has been Professor of Religion at Emory University in Atlanta, GA. This textbook, forthcoming at the time of Yoder Nyce's compiling this annotated bibliography, will be an important resource for classroom (and likely more general) settings.

Flueckiger, Joyce Burkhalter. (GC) *Gender and Genre in the Folklore of Middle India.* (Delhi: Oxford University Pr, 1996).

Professor Burkhalter Fluechiger's writing has appeared broadly— academic articles in journals and chapters of books. Her first book describes six representative Indian folklore genres (types/works of literature) and ritual performances. Her attention to women within indigenous culture through song, the Hindu Ramayana epic tradition, rituals, and events of celebration emerges through observation, tape recordings, and personal conversation. She notes the relationship between genre and community—to which community a tradition "belongs, which social group is engaged where and how, and ways in which female performers challenge male *brahmanic* views of gender.

Distinct for Burkhalter Flueckiger as an academic fieldworker over fifteen years' time is her 'belonging' to the community and culture being studied. She had grown up through childhood in the Chhattisgarh region of central India, other than when away to attend boarding school. Chhattisgarh remains authentically part of her being. [xv] Her (GC) missioner parents who lived in the area for over forty years had instilled a love for India impossible to absorb or duplicate through books alone. In addition to the language, she knows "ways of talking" including *dehati* (village) Hindi. Interested to join in home rituals, she is welcomed into either high or low caste families. Being in her "mother's place" enables her to be known as *sister*. [xvii] A questioner who asked to which caste she belongs was hoping to find out *how* she lives, not what beliefs mattered for her. Knowing that she genuinely wishes later to teach Americans about Hindu and village life, an uncommon trust flowered with the Indian folk. A further bridge emerged for her; she lived with the only Christian family in a village while learning in depth from Hindu practice.

Basic facts valuable for folklorist Burkhalter Flueckiger include:

- Learning how celebrations for major deities affect agricultural patterns of double rice crops among people, fifteen percent of whom are tribal folk. (5)
- Knowing how distinct caste dialects and oral traditions fit into the broad Hindu hierarchy of social structure. (14)
- Determining who is available to perform which genre (*tradition* might be a preferred word, 21), whether sung or danced or whether indigenous, within a community. (15)

Burkhalter Flueckiger's first taping of a week-long festival honored the elephant-headed deity named Ganesh, known broadly as the "remover of obstacles." Consistent with that descriptor, people worship Ganesh before beginning a project, whether a performance, journey, or construction. A clay image (*murti*) of Ganesh might sit on the village owner's verandah or some more public space, paid for collectively by villagers. Hindus who honor the *murti* do so by "taking *darshan*," by appearing within its auspicious sight. Festivities end by taking the *murti* to a water source like the village pond (tank) to be immersed.

Burkhalter Flueckiger discusses distinct festivals from the Phuljhar area of Chhattisgarh in separate chapters. The second chapter describes a female festival tradition called *bhojali*. For that event unmarried girls form ritual friendships while growing and exchanging wheat seedlings (*bhojali*) as part of a nine-day festival to honor the goddess named Bhojali Dai. Young girls line their baskets planted with bright green seedlings within a dark temple or household shrine area. Each evening the friendship pairs lead and sing songs. They tend (soak or pour water over the sprouts) and serve (worship) their representative of the goddess. (27) On the final festival day the young girls in procession carry their baskets on their heads to the village pond where, on immersing the basket, the deity is understood to leave. Leaving, she extends a blessing to each participant. (29)

A related festival called *javara* engages some married women who are possessed by the goddess. To be "possessed" reflects the goddess' favor for the woman's having expressed prior, deep devotion. Favor may also be shown the woman through her becoming fertile. *Bhojali* may also anticipate ripening into fertility for a young girl. (38) Songs and friendship suggest what lies ahead—hoped for marriage and motherhood. (48)

Other chapter highlights inform. While chapter three describes a festival called *Dalkhai*, now less actively combined with the country-wide Holi festival, the fourth chapter explains the *sua nac* (parrot dance). For that event tribal girls who labor on the land perform dances for landowners in their courtyards. Burkhalter Flueckiger learned the Gond tribal folk's understanding of how the goddess Lakshmi, known for wealth, transforms the harvested paddy into ritual wealth.

Chapter five focuses on the *kathani kutha* genre, widely known over the Chhattisgarhi language area. In that event which deals with regional epics, individual performers tell stories, prompting the audience to be the performers. While Burkhalter Flueckiger explains the meaning of *epic* within and beyond the immediate area in chapter six, her seventh chapter elaborates how a particular genre called *pandvani* reflects distinctly the local region in contrast to the Hindi, all-Indian genre of the noted Hindu Ramayana epic.

In the book's second section Burkhalter Flueckiger translates full texts of two performances, *Song of Subanbali* and *kathani kutha's* from chapters three and five respectively. She wishes to reflect both the oral composition and performance quality of texts. As folklorist she also clarifies how performance identifies levels of community: the broader folklore region that shares a stock of songs and dances, the more immediate community that determines distinct rules for performances, and the performers themselves. Festivals distinctly reflect a portion of Hindu experience.

Flueckiger, Joyce Burkhalter. (GC) *In Amma's Healing Room Gender and Vernacular Islam in South India*. (Bloomington, Indiana: Indiana University Pr 2006).

While Burkhalter Flueckiger focuses this book on Amma a Muslim female healer, a few annotations explain the healer's involvement with Hindus. A "hierarchy of spiritual powers" enables Hindu deities to exist in a Muslim world, Burkhalter Flueckiger explains. For example, a disciple of the healer Amma named Hussein might practice a skill that draws on powers that enable Hanuman, a monkey character from the Hindu epic Ramayana, to serve as a messenger in a non-Hindu context.

(99) Healer Amma is convinced that in her healing space what matters is that "all breathe in and out" rather than distinct labels like Hindu or Muslim. The spiritual crisis that a patient presents matters more than religious division. Amma shares rituals across boundaries of tradition, and Allah, or God known to both traditions, meets the need. (168-71) Patients do not think in terms of power through a specific religion; nor might they know what is written on the amulets that Amma gives them. Powerful spiritual forces exist within a broad "spiritual plane that crosses boundaries of difference," Bukhalter Flueckiger learns from Amma. Amma combines Hindu and Muslim terms like *shakti* (spiritual power) and *avatar* (descent) along with *babas* (saint or ascetic) and prophet. (173-74) While healer Amma may call upon Hindu Kali or Hanuman's service or power, she does not worship those forms. (194) Sacred water matters beyond boundaries too: Muslim pilgrims drink from and take bottles filled from the *zamzam* spring site in Mecca; Hindu pilgrims utilize water from the Ganges River for later rituals and blessings. (189) Interreligious linkage also appears in this book when a patient asks Amma if Joyce herself is another disciple. Amma replies: "She doesn't need to be a disciple; she loves God and I love God, so we have a connection." (17)

Flueckiger, Joyce Burkhalter (GC) "Wandering from Hills to Valleys with the Goddess: Protection and Freedom in the *Matamma* Tradition of Andhra," *Womens's Lives, Women's Ritual in Hindu Tradition*, Tracy Pintchman (Oxford University Pr, 2007) 35-54.

Flueckiger, Joyce Burkhalter (GC) *When the World Becomes Female Guises of a South Indian Goddess.* (Bloomington, IN: Indiana University Pr 2013).

With a strong heritage from missioner parents (Edward and Ramoth Burkhalter, GC) who followed an earlier great aunt Martha Burkhalter (GC), Burkhalter Flueckiger grew up in India. The focus of her academic teaching and writing has been with World Religions. Her third book surrounds celebration of a South Indian, Hindu goddess. Directly after reading *When the World Becomes Female* this writer sent a letter of thanks to her friend Joyce:

> . . . What a gift of sensitive information you've given us readers! I feel like I've met and started to know quite a number of people directly linked to the Gangamma festival. Your having met them in person at different times over multiple years gives authenticity and recurring insight into places and patterns. Thanks for the flavor, for the respect, for the awareness of struggle to "bear" the power of this goddess.

Thanks for your effective way to process fieldwork—blending your narrative with materials recorded from others . . .

Burkhalter Flueckiger saw goddess Gangamma worshippers (who total nearly a half million) at three annual, week-long *jatara* (village festival) events beginning in 1992. A year's fieldwork in Tirupati, South India followed. Intent to see the festival, rituals, and participants within the broader religious world, she values learning to know individuals, especially women, linked to the traditions. Thousands of religious Hindu pilgrims daily visit Tirupati, in part to also honor Sri Venkateeshvara, an *avatara* of the god named Vishnu, notable in that region of Seven Hills.

The Gangamma festival reinforces the empowering dynamic of *shakti* (female power). It is shared by the goddess with women and 'taken on' or acknowledged during the week of celebration by men. Those men are transformed into the *vesham* (guise) of women via clothing, jewelry, and braided hair. The meager amount of female power that men inherently have causes them to fear (even discredit) women. Such power comes forth for men involved then as they go door to door to be fed by women, as they appear before the stone form of Gangamma in her two major temples within the city. Women's *shakti* is known to intensify during festival days as they cook and serve *pongal* (rice with lentils) and apply facial *pasupur* (turmeric). Gangamma is known for *ugra* (anger, desire, or passion); it makes her "too much to bear" for all but a few, select people. The festival goal includes calling her to provide personal protection and the gift of fertility, for people and land.

Burkhalter Flueckiger knows that both rituals and narrative introduce Gangamma and the "world become female" (as the book title suggests). She explains accounts of several noted performers (chapter 4) and includes insight from direct encounters with Annapurna's performance of three different stories about gender relationships. (123) Many Hindus live in "multiple ritual, narrative, imaginative worlds" Burkhalter Flueckiger says. Those worlds are often divided between more academic and non-textual, village Hindu traditions. (150) Useful insight follows about *amma*, a familiar, honorific suffix, and *matammas,* women who exchange their *tali. (*A groom ties a *tali* around his bride's neck during their wedding to symbolize her being bound to him.) Information about *devadasis*—women who, rather than know human marriage or widowhood, "marry" a male deity to serve him at a temple—and much more appears.

Along with Endnotes, Glossary, Reference material, and Index, this resource expands any reader's understanding of Hinduism, useful for Mennonites who value interfaith exchange.

Graber, J. D. (Joseph Daniel) (MC) "Hinduism" - Research Notes, HM 1-503, Box 3 Folder 2, Mennonite Church USA Archives, Goshen, IN. Outline format, n.d., 17 pp. Graber credits materials by: Malcolm Pitt, John Noss, and Ruda Krishna.

Reasons missioner and mission administrator Graber gives for studying this eastern religion include because Hinduism: represents eastern religions; reflects India's numerous sub-cultures; contains documents from pre-Moses' time; and conveys creative genius. He does not identify the fact that he had been a missioner in India, was therefore exposed directly to Hindu thought and practice. From Northrop's *Meeting of East and West*, Graber notes that while western people seek God's will, eastern folk "seek the essence of God above all else." Never too open to outside influences, India's primeval religion derived from a fairly advanced Indus culture. The timeless, eternal Vedas extended much further back than when they were first written down in 1600 BCE. (1) Graber explains that the one main God then called Shiva was known in India before the Arian invasion[7] of 2000 BCE. That civilization enabled what is now known as Hinduism to develop. Those Arians were musical; they loved their Sanskrit language and knew war as an art, Graber adds.

During the Vedic period, which extends to 600 BCE, priests used the four books or collections of hymns (*samhita*) in distinct ways. The most important (ten books) of Rigveda wisdom convey praise to multiple ancient deities. While the Summa Veda is to be sung, the Yahurveda is the manual that priests used for activity with sacrifice. People and institutions then reflect a more settled time. With the last Veda, the Atharvaveda, (accepted after 800 BCE) priests were to know or recall and then dispense the useful traditions.

The Rigveda story of creation sacrificed the primeval giant into four distinct classes (*Varna*) from body parts upper to lower—mouth, arms, thigh, and feet. Graber outlines classes starting with the highest Brahman who know the sacred hymns and magic spells in order to serve all others. From the Kshatruja (royal, warrior or Rajanya class) come kings followed by Vaishya levels of commoners like trained or untrained farmers or menial workers. Whereas those three Arian classes are known as "twice-born"—meaning born through biology and Vedic study—the lowest class, Sudras, are not. (2-5)

Graber continues to discuss the gods of Vedic thought, only a portion of which content is annotated here. Vedic thought "tried to go behind the Gods into the ultimate essence from which even the gods evolve," he says. Gods were to be worshipped because they represent and have control over forces of nature that ever need to be engaged or appeased. While Indra, revealed in rain or storms, is the first among gods for Arians, Varuna, who creates order for the world and is morally strong, is lord over Gods and men [*sic*]. Once the need for sacrifice lessened in Hindu practice, the Vedic gods declined; modern Hindus more often reject them, Graber reports. (3) Another contrast from that early era is the fact that reincarnation is not found during the time of the Vedas; Arians had little concern for after-life. Graber notes their belief that after death a person who had been faithful in ritual went to the third layer of heaven—*Svarga-loka*.

Christians often overlook a fact that Graber explains regarding Hindu practice: "The many Gods are just a way of conceiving the One God." People have never been able to identify that single, all-pervading force that uses names like Brahman (source of all dynamic energy of the universe), Prajapati, Purusha, Pram or Atman. Names can detract from the force's actual meaning. Vishnu, while not very important during Vedic times, has become quite important today. Both Vishnu and Shiva, known for multiple consorts, represent either the good or bad so are worshipped by many Hindus, Graber adds.

He then notes three aspects of post-*Vedic* religion. Those three *ways* toward what Christians call *salvation* will be discussed by other Mennonite writers: *bhaktimarga* (way of loving devotion), *karmamarga* (way of action), and *jnanamarga* (way of knowledge). (7-8) Two basic differences related to the *bhakti* way are emotionalism or feeling and the fact that even outcaste folk practice that way. The cult of Krishna, an incarnation of Vishnu, is also valued highly within the *bhakti* pattern.

Graber gives several pages of outline space to *puja*—the worship of images—and *dharma* (duty). Such content looks to the number of gods worshipped, where the ritual takes place—within a person, family or temple—and whether for the worshipper's merit or deity's wellbeing. Graber notes varied features of Hindu worship: daily morning care of *ishta-devata*—attending to a personal god form that best suits personal needs; *sucertas*—five representative forms to honor; or *advaita* (meaning non-dual)—the worship of One Great Being. "The Hindu monotheist offers *puja* to only one God," Graber says. A worshiper goes to the temple where God dwells in a single or multiple forms, to offer gifts, ask for strength or a particular benefit, have sin destroyed, or appease the god. (7-8)

The caste system first emerged between 600-200 BCE through literature about d*harma* (specific duties). The idealized Laws of Manu— "one place for each person"—presumed to bring morality to bear: people of other castes expected to be below the Brahman class of priests. Graber also lists life stages for the three upper, "twice-born" caste men: student, householder, forest dweller and *sannyasin*. The latter involves abandoning the world, to be an ascetic who depends on others. Not "twice-born" the Sudra caste serves the Brahmans; they neither gain property nor study Vedas. Outside of caste then follow the

Panchammas, those who lack dignity, known also as Untouchables, Scheduled Castes, or Dalits. They have no choice of work as with basket or leather workers. Hundreds of further subdivisions of caste are known as *jati*, Graber adds. (9-11)

A final focus of Graber's study of Hinduism is the Bhagavad Gita or "Song of the Lord." This account, located within the Mahabharata epic, borrows basic doctrine from the Hindu Upanishads. It forms a theistic document (qualified *monism* which equates good and evil with a sense of moral failure that remains), Graber says. Gita teachings address God, world, and salvation. God, known as Krishna an incarnation of Vishnu, is interested in and can be served through human, ritual devotion within the material world, a world that is important to the divine. Social concern matters also but duty (action) is understood alongside grace. Knowledge of the need for God's grace frees a person from the binding, recurring law of *karma*, Graber explains. (17)

Hiebert, Paul. (MB) "Conversion in Hinduism and Buddhism," in *Handbook of Religious Conversion*. H. Newton Malony & Samuel Southard, eds. (Birmingham, AL: Religions Educational Pr, 1992) 9-21.

Only content related to *Hinduism* is presented here, starting with a few general statements:

What counts within Hinduism is conduct, not belief, Hiebert explains. . . . Religion in Hinduism suggests personal spiritual pilgrimage; its goal (*moksha*) is for each person to realize his or her purpose. (10) . . . . Salvation or release (*moksha*) refers to learning to know through deep, inner light the true nature of reality. . . . All religions engage reality. . . Many roads lead to *moksha* or full enlightenment. To realize that we are part of oneness with God, that too is reality. (12)

Three key paths (*marga*) may lead to God in Hindu experience:

1. *Karma marga* – path of duty, as through offerings, pilgrimages to shrines, performing rituals;
2. *Bhakti marga* – path of total devotion to or worship (praise) of god (all god forms being manifestations of the One God); a personal caste god or a chosen deity saves (11). Presumably ninety percent of all Hindus are *bhaktis*, worshipers of a manifestation of Vishnu or Siva.
3. *Jnana marga* – disciplined path or way of wisdom or knowledge that leads toward the goal of enlightenment or inner oneness with the universe and God. (12)

Hiebert mentions further aspects of *conversion* within Hindu thought:

- While the term is primarily used by Jews, Christians and Muslims, for Hindus *conversion* is part of the Hindu worldview.

- *Conversion* begins a person's pilgrimage toward the light which means to seek God, truth, light, and good, Hiebert explains. (11)
- Levels of discussion of *conversion* within Hinduism include: 1. changing in belief (an evolutionary progression, toward enlightenment) and practice that leads to self-realization; 2. assimilating into a religious community; (9) 3. becoming a Hindu through birth or by entering the Hindu social order—taking one's place in the caste system; (14) 4. being transformed (as a tribal person) into a caste and ending former demeaning customs (like eating meat); 5. inviting a Brahmin priest to perform rituals for you; and 6. performing actions such as to: build temples, celebrate Hindu festivals, adopt Hindu rites of passage, or pursue a distinct vocation. (15)
- Hiebert notes further that each person has personal *dharma* (duty) or law of growth. To claim one's own religion as the 'only right way' or to try to convert another person to your way reflects spiritual arrogance and denies personal duty. (13)
- Gandhi used the term *conversion* for a changed relationship, not label or traditions, within the nonviolent search for truth. The person improves the world while becoming a *satyagrahi*. (14)

Hiebert, Paul. (MB) "Critical Contextualization," *Missiology*. (12, no.3, July 1984) 287-96.
In this article Hiebert addresses the question of how people deal with past customs when changing religious loyalty. Three options appear. First, a Hindu who shifts to Christianity might reject the former, traditional religion as *pagan*. A person's meaning for the term *pagan* changes too. Different customs might replace rejected ones. Or, a former custom might simply shift 'underground,' to be used on occasion. Second, a person in the change process might simply continue to accept former patterns without critique while complying with new expectations. Or, third, "critical contextualization" might occur—where careful examination of a former custom's function, alongside study and assessment of prior action or events, follows in light of new scripture or rituals. Deep insight into the history and culture of each religion matters

Hiebert, Paul. (MB) "*Karma* and Other Explanation Traditions in a South Indian Village," in *Karma An Anthropological Inquiry*, Charles F. Keyes & E. Valentine Daniel, eds. (Los Angeles: University of California Pr, 1983) 119-30.
MB anthropologist Hiebert observes that underlying Hindu rites and myths (the meta-narrative by which the cosmic story of reality is known) is a sense of good and evil. *Karma* shapes myths that appear in popular village Hinduism—stories portrayed in temple rituals, village festivals,

and street dramas, or sung by mothers to children. (119) The focus is not on how *karma* increases or is conveyed but how it works itself out in people's lives. (125) Common to village myths is the corporate nature of *karma*. Whereas philosophers explain *karma* for the individual—each person reaping rewards (evil or good) for previous actions—village myths convey how *karma* affects those who surround a person. (126) Village myths disclose that only God alters evil results of a person's bad karma. Knowing how to thwart possible consequences requires consistent discipline. To hear stories or express cyclical rituals helps the people as a whole to claim order and meaning for what otherwise might be chaotic in life. (129)

Hiebert, Paul. *(MB) Konduru. Structure and Integration in a South Indian Village*. PhD dissertation. (Minneapolis: University of Minnesota Pr, 1971).
Hiebert did dissertation field work during 1963-65. His anthropological study finds the centuries-old social structure of a south Indian village meeting modernity. Not only does this study encounter dozens of caste groups, Hiebert ponders the honor given to higher animals such as cows. He learns how customs regulate caste, how castes cause factions. Using anthropological, comparative categories he was aware that people might worship deities named Shiva or Vishnu of the Hindu Great Tradition alongside supernatural beings of the Low Religion.
   Hiebert's insight reflects disciplined study:
   • Caste - which provides village stability (30), becomes a key part of this study, there being eighty-four caste groups among three thousand people in Konduru. People of thirty of those Hindu castes worship both Shiva and Vishnu. Brahma castes provide religious services for worshippers in homes or temples. Astrologers calculate auspicious times for certain tasks—like lighting lamps or calling people to work . . . Low level, Sudra Muslim castes include Turks (largest group), Fakirs (traveling mendicants or entertainers), and Kartikes (village butchers).
   • *Upanayana* – This initiation ceremony for a Hindu boy (age 8-11) of 'twice born' castes (not *sudras*, the low castes) marks the onset of his wearing the "sacred thread" (cord) across his left shoulder under his clothes. The cord indicates his becoming a full caste member.
   • *Deva dasi* – These Hindu dancing girls marry the temple deity (never being a widow) and train for dance, song, and love.
   • Divinity - Many supernatural beings inhabit groves, fields, wells, or houses—known as gods, demigods, spirits, ghosts of the dead, winds, or powers, Hiebert explains. A home may enshrine multiple god forms. Great gods that live in the heavens may

appear to worshipers in temples where priests assist with worship practices. While "High" religions (Hinduism, Islam, and Christianity) have scripture, institutions and traditions—'great' rights and beliefs—'little' ones have local myths and practices. "Low" religions promote local goddesses or powers with no distinct scripture or rites. Local or regional Hindu goddesses, often feared by villagers, may reside in trees, rocks, or streams. Their desires may be satisfied through sacrifice of animals. . . . While most Hindu deities are available to all castes, several are tied to specific groups, such as Lakshmi with merchants.

- Hiebert explains how rituals have both religious and magical elements. Magic may guard against danger or cure disease. To intone mantras (sacred chants) such as "OM" (first and last letters of the alphabet) guarantees true wisdom. A diviner gives medicines or recites powerful names or mantras. Omens discern good or evil. Hindu rituals connect with many gods or manifestations of gods that punish evildoers and reward the faithful. Konduru has two temples plus several shrines. The most important, yearly temple *jatra (*festival) celebrates and reenacts the marriage of god forms named Rama and Sita. Holy places are closed to low caste Harijans who have their own gods and shrines.
- Hiebert's Appendix materials include extensive data: section II – "Supernatural Beings of the Konduru Hindu Community" and III – "Important Hindu Marriage Rites Observed by Various Castes in Konduru." 178-80.

Hiebert, Paul. (MB) "Missiological Issues in the Encounter with Emerging Hinduism," *Missiology (*28, no. 1, January 2000) 47-63. Western Mennonites relating with or wishing to better understand Hinduism today can benefit from Hiebert 's discussion of Neo-Hinduism. This major religious movement credits and claims: Vedas as Hindu scripture, different ways to salvation, worship of many gods (60, note # 7), importance of gurus, temples, festivals, and pilgrimage (*tirthayatra* – seeking to be purified). Hiebert suggests that engagement with the Hindu world needs to be rethought in order to distinguish those who focus on good will and tolerance from some who are increasingly aggressive.

Political/Religious Issues that Hiebert encourages westerners to know:
- Political organizations: VHP - the World Council of Hindus; RSS – the reorganization built on Hindu nationalism (52); *Sangh Parivar* – brotherhood of Hindu nationalists linked with RSS (60, note 11). The ideology of "*Hindutva* that attracts many Indians caught between a traditional past and modernity or

globalization." (55) BJP – Indian Peoples' Party that challenges the notion of a secular state, redefining the nature of nation.

- Ayodhya – The city where ancient temples, believed by some Hindus to mark Rama's birth place, were destroyed and replaced by Muslims with a mosque which in turn was destroyed by Hindu mobs in 1993. Major riots with deaths, rapes, and property loss followed in various cities. (59, note # 1)
- Ratha Yatra refers to a religious pilgrimage.

Hindu defined by Hiebert:

1. Geographic – Persian word for *Indian*; people located beyond the Indus River (48);
2. Religious order - rooted in 10th century BCE caste system of "eternal religion"; 4 major *varna* (color) categories with countless sub groups (*jatis*);
   Brahmanical terms: *ekajivam* – (all of life is one), *karma* (law of rewards and fateful action (49), *samsara* (cycle of rebirth), *moksha* (release from rebirth cycle), *adivasi* (aboriginal people), *devas* (deities), *guru* (teacher);
3. Oriental – Sanskrit, Vedas (ancient religious texts);
   Europeans started the term *Hinduism* as a coherent, unified religious tradition of the Orient;
4. Political – wealthy Hindu kings who struggled for control;
5. Religion – includes encounter of Indian religious philosophy with Enlightenment and Christian thought.

Several Notable People introduced by Hiebert:

- Swami Dayananda - He spiritualized Hinduism by stressing "back to the Vedas"; founded *Arya Samaj*. (51).
- Ramakrishna Mission Leader Ramakrishna and disciple Vivekananda. This Mission includes a strong *bhakti* (devotion) and tantric or esoteric focus.
- Savarkar – Noted promoter of the concept of *Hindutva* which promotes Hindudom or a theocratic state of political economy, totalitarian idealism, and aggressive cultural nationalism.
- Annie Besant – Through the Theosophical Society she tried to bring all religions together incorporating the Vedanta doctrine of *karma*, rebirth, and yoga.

Missiological Issues: (See Hiebert's informative notes on pages 60-61.)

- Experience of persecution for Indian churches;
- Development of meaningful response to *Hindutva*;
- Attention to the on-going, central task of evangelism;
- Response of Dalit and tribal societies to the gospel ;
- Engagement with pluralistic *diaspora* Indian communities. (59)

Hiebert Paul. (MB) "World Views" in *Cultural Anthropology*. Paul Hiebert. (Philadelphia: J. B. Lippencott Co, 1976) 356-69. Also, see Appendix 2 chart in *"Transforming WORLDVIEWS,"* 337-41.
Anthropologist Hiebert suggests that for Hindus the term *religion* explains the reality of all things. *Religion* entails assumptions and beliefs as well as myths, rituals, sites, and objects. Assumptions about the nature of reality and morality underlie peoples' actions; when used to explain responses to the universe, assumptions can be called "world view." Hiebert uses numerous terms to distinguish the world views of middle-class Americans, shaped more by Greek and Judeo-Christian thought, and those of south Asian Indians, influenced predominantly by Hindu views. Differences persist; no English word has exactly the same meaning for Hindu terms like *maya*, *karma*, and *dharma*. While one culture credits demons for producing diseases like smallpox or pneumonia, another culture finds them caused by viruses.

Other world view distinctions that Hiebert notes:

Whereas most Americans take the material world seriously, seeing the natural world as real and orderly, many Indians see the natural world as a transitory, ever-changing creation of the mind. (*maya*)

Whereas Americans see time as linear—not repeating itself, with people having only one life to live—the Hindu world view sees the universe as ever-repeating itself; an individual is often reborn. (358)

While Americans have a moral obligation to share knowledge and truth, each Hindu individual within each caste is duty-bound (*dharma*) to fit into or fulfill the task to which their caste is destined. (361)

While a Hindu's life goal remains to be released from hardships into self-realization, from the cycle of rebirths, the American world view measures success and security by results (pragmatism). (362)

Kaufman, Edmund G. (GC) *Basic Christian Convictions*. (North Newton, KS: Bethel College, 1972).
When Kaufman became president of Bethel College, Newton, Kansas, in 1932, he also began to teach a basic course useful for upper-level students, to enable them to "re-evaluate and reintegrate their thinking" about faith. This course continued for many years. Annotations draw from Kaufman's attention to *Hinduism* in a unit "Patterns of Religion."

- A religion of "divine immanence and an hereditary social structure or caste system";
- Without a definite founder;
- Brought to India by Aryan invaders between 1500-2000;
- Six distinct types developed:
    Early nature worship before 1,000 B.C.E. with 4 Vedas (Books of Knowledge) as scripture; prayer as means for salvation;

Priestly (1000-800 BCE) with Brahmanas as scripture; priestly sacrifice as means for salvation;

Philosophic (800-600 BCE) with Upanishads as scriptures; meditation on Atman (self) as part of Brahman (God) brings salvation from reincarnation;

Legalistic with Laws of Manu (250 BCE) as scripture; ritualistic ceremonies as means of salvation;

Devotional (about 1 CE) with Bhagavad Gita as chief scripture; Krishna's emphasis: to do duty as caste member;

Popular (1-250 CE) with Puranas as scripture; varied beliefs, idolatry, worship of Brahma/Creator, Vishnu/Preserver, and Siva/Destroyer, Krishna, Kali, and many more gods present in temples, or through pilgrimage, ceremonies or festivals.

- Historic castes: Brahmans, Kshatriyas, Vaisyas, and Sudras along with outcastes and untouchables;
- Features: caste system, reverence for Vedas, belief in *karma* (reincarnation) with salvation from reincarnation when self merges with Brahma through prayer, sacrifice, meditation, ritualism, and devotion. "Brahma is all and all is Brahma."

Kaufman also provides details for the religion of Jainism which began as a reform movement of Hinduism founded by Mahavira (599-527 BCE). (5-6) Also originating from India, Buddhism and Sikhism have links with Hinduism but they choose to be known as distinct. Later in the book Kaufman discusses Hindu deities when addressing "The Trinity and World Religions." (186)

Kaufman, Gordon D. (GC) *God, Mystery, Diversity Christian Theology in a Pluralistic World*. (Minneapolis: Augsburg Fortress, 1996).
Key ideas from son of Ed, Gordon Kaufman here includes direct links to Hinduism as well as more general ties with other religions. Kaufman understands religious pluralism in India, its profound reality within Asia. He lived, learned, and taught theology in both India and Japan for periods of time. His deeper crediting of Buddhism enhances his personal integrity with being Christian and Mennonite.

- Knowing that *theology* means "thinking about God" Kaufman nudges Christians to keep it focused on *God* rather than Christ. Then when thinking about Christ theologically (known to Christians as symbol through story, preaching, devotion or reflection 111), Christ will not displace God (idolatry). Each great religion has its particular way to express "transcendence"; all share the responsibility to contribute to and learn from others' views. (19, 151)

Correspondence (June 16, 2014) from Duane Friesen (GC) to the writer comments also on Kaufman's reference to Hinduism on page 19 of *God—Mystery—Diversity*, a collection of essays that grew out of Kaufman's sabbatical spent at United Theological Seminary in Bangalore, India. Kaufman names a stance expressed by notable Hindus Radhakrishnan and Vivekananda that rejects exclusivist and imperialist claims. It suggests that "all religions point in the direction of the infinite, ultimate or 'God.'" But because religions in their *difference* need to be understood in specific historical and contextual ways Kaufman differs with the Hindu view that many valid paths lead to the same goal, Friesen explains.

- Kaufman notes how India's caste system based in birth has the potential to dehumanize those of low or out-of-caste. They cannot counter that "order of life" without risking disdain. (32)
- Kaufman also questions "claims to truth made simply on grounds of religious authority." He welcomes learning from Buddhists about suffering, from Hindus about spiritual discipline, from Judaism and Islam about the risk of idolatrous talk about Jesus as savior. (40)
- In a pluralistic world Christians will avoid arrogance and the tendency to reify Jesus the Christ as by suggesting that salvation is lodged only in the church. Kaufman believes that most Christians overlook the critique of their "falling into idolatrous attitudes toward Christ (and the church)." (115, 119)
- Religious Truth itself is pluralistic. People, whether Hindu or Christian, engage in dialogue about distinct claims and practices brought by religions from varied historical contexts. What religions regard as true reflects how those loyal to them understand human life, Kaufman says. He confesses that "truth is never final or complete or unchanging." As diverse people dialogue about it, with no single tradition's view to be seen as normative for all others, it (truth) continues to emerge and be transformed. (189-192, 200, 135)

Kaufman, Gordon D. (GC) *In Face of Mystery A Constructive Theology*. (Cambridge, MA: Harvard University Pr, 1993).
Within broad discussion of theology Kaufman includes several references to Hinduism. Regarding the symbol "God," what he calls a "point of reference," he cautions against authoritarian claims that might be idolatrous. Religious traditions like Hindu or Buddhist have their distinct value orientations, ways of life, and traditions of God-talk too. (28) Through time, human thought has depended on a concept of *world*, whether based on a Copernican view or Sankara's world of Advaita

Vedanta, Kaufman says. With the latter "only Brahman is truly real" since human ignorance prompts ordinary events or objects to be simply *maya* (illusion). (113, 302) Rather than reify (make wholly other) or know "God" as excessively anthropocentric (since people are created in God's image), Kaufman encourages welcoming insight from all peoples including Hindus, into what is ultimate mystery. (459)

Several Mennonites discuss Kaufman's writing and thought:

- Weaver, Alain Epp. "Imaginative Construction: The Theology of Gordon Kaufman," *Mennonite Life*, (September 1991) 22-26.
- Weaver, Alain Epp, ed. *Mennonite Theology in Face of Modernity Essays in Honor of Gordon D. Kaufman*. (North Newton, KS: Bethel College, 1996). In addition to Kaufman's personal chapter writers include Duane Friesen (GC), J. Denny Weaver (GC), and Tom Finger (MC).

Lapp, George Jay. (MC) "Strengths and Weaknesses of Hinduism," Draft of unpublished, paper written for degree completion at Goshen College, n. d., Mennonite Church USA Archives, Goshen, IN.

Lapp was encouraged by mission administrators and missioner colleagues to pursue this study during a furlough year. Chapter titles for the study are:

I.   Historical Development of Hindu Society
II.   Literature upon which Hinduism is Based
III.   Deities of Hinduism
IV.   Hindu Philosophy and its Relation to Hindu Religion
V.   Elements of Hinduism
VI.   Caste
VII.   Man and Status of Woman
VIII.   Fruits of Hinduism
IX.   Hindu Concepts of Deity and Man's [*sic*] Relation to Him [*sic*
X.   (not included, which prompts curiosity)
XI.   Tales and Sayings for the Common People
XII.   Christ for India

Rather than repeat discussion of Hindu themes from Lapp or other Mennonite writers, notations highlight only scattered comments from Lapp's serious study.

The power of conservatism pervades Hindu society, Lapp believes.

Puranas – legends from the eighth century and after. . . Each deals with praise for one god form.

Gayatri – Vedic prayer: "O earth, firmament, and heaven, we meditate on the great Light the Sun. May it enlighten our hearts."

Pilgrimage is often done to fulfill some vow. Lapp laments the "highhanded wickedness" of some Hindu priests around shrines "to deceive pilgrims." However, Lapp is also grateful to have "met those of the priestly class who are earnest in their endeavors to know the truth." . . . He believes that a day will come for awakening of truth among them.

"Caste has within its power both religion and philosophy and so fixes the standard of society that each individual and every detail of life is controlled by it."

Fruits (examples of weakness) of Hinduism, according to Lapp, include: false charity; fatalism; bigotry (to hold blindly to a creed); peoples' being guided by custom, not reason; false fears through life and false hopes in death; great gulf between the educated and illiterate Hindu.

For many Hindus "the quarrel is with Christianity, not with Christ." . . . Educated India "will never definitely embrace Christianity until Christian doctrines have been recast in a less alien mould." . . . the missioner "finds that only a sound Gospel can prove itself true."

No other religion needs to be so carefully studied by missioners as does Hinduism, Lapp declares.

Lehman, Martin Clifford (MC) "Manuscript of Studies of Harishchandra." PhD dissertation, Yale University 1932, HM I-139, Box 2, Mennonite Church USA Archives, Goshen, 160 pp.

Lehman states purposes for this disciplined study of a noted Hindu poet:
- discover the religious concepts of a Hindu writer from the last quarter of the nineteenth century;
- trace dependence on a religious system that preceded Harishchandra;
- describe and analyze concepts with reference to earlier and his current settings; and
- evaluate the poet's subsequent effect on religious and secular life

Harishchandra was born the son of poet Gopalchand in the sacred Hindu city of Benares in September of 1850; he died at age 35 after a twelve year literary career. Harishchandra was raised in wealth; both parents died before he was ten years old. Able to read both Hindi and Sanskrit at an early age he became India's first vernacular literary critic. Lehman describes him as "famous" by 1880. He donned at age nine the sacred cord of the Vishnu religious sect—founded by Valla before 1531— Lehman reports. He opposed religious differences within Hinduism; "There was no time to quarrel." (7) By age eleven he protested some base rites that he saw performed at the noted Hindu shrine at Puri. While on pilgrimage to Benares he engaged with cultural leaders like the *Arya Samaj* founder Dayananda.

Lehman's second chapter introduces Harishchandra's writings. Many of the 175 works were dramas in prose or poetry. Lehman notes diverse themes:

- conflicts between different Hindu sects;
- history including gurus of the Vaisnava sect;
- versions of the famous wars known in the Mahabharata epic;
- conditions in India when Valmiki wrote the Ramayana epic;
- devotion to Krishna and verses to recite for morning devotion to Radha and Krishna;
- historical religious relationships between Mohammedans and Hindus; collection of Mohammedan hymns; and a comparative study of Mohammed, Krishna, and Jesus;
- evils that western culture will bring to India; evil inherent in religious practices like *sati*; and
- justification for cow reverence.

The third chapter of Lehman's thesis explains "Settings of Writings" and the fourth focuses on "Religious Concepts of God, in Terms of Deities Referred to by Harishchandra." Harishchandra wrote extensively in *Braj Bhasha*, a dialect used especially for poetry; writings devoted to Krishna appeared in a branch of Vaishnavism. With religion ever a part of Hindu life, the Hindu mind struggles to perceive western separation of life into religious and secular (27) Harishchandra did not approve of how the British government handled the severe famine in India's eastern coastal area. To better digest his subject, Lehman visited Benares (a pilgrimage center where much religious discussion occurs), Puri, Poona, Lahore, Calcutta, and Madras.

Lehman helpfully discusses twenty terms for *God* that appear and recur in Harishchandra's poetry.[8] Fourteen uses of *Hari* occur, a name applied to Vishnu the Preserver or multiple other gods. The amount of *Hari* usage alongside devotion for *Krishna* reflects the poet's preference. *Krishna*—hero of the Mahabaratha epic, similar to *Bhagavan*, plus his *Gopis* (semi-divine milkmaids)—was known for moral power and was the most popular incarnation of Vishnu, Lehman adds. *Rama*, another Vishnu incarnation and hero of the Ramayana epic, was assisted by *Hanuman* the monkey-faced god. *Iswara*—without an image, the Lord or god of the universe—occurs seven times. *Brahma* the Creator, source of revelation, is named the "personified emanation of the Supreme Being," Lehman explains. Also present are goddess names: *Devi* (more frequently used for the wife of Krishna, Siva, or Vishnu); *Parvati* (*shakti* or creative energy of different gods, notably of the Vedic destroyer god *Siva* whose son is known as the elephant-headed *Ganesha*); *Radha* (chief mistress of Krishna with multiple names); *Lakshmi* (goddess of wealth and beauty known as wife of Vishnu); *Kali* (who manifests most fiercely Siva *shakti*, also called *Durga, Uma,* or *Parvati*); and *Savitri* (wife or energy of Brahma identified with the goddess of learning *Sarasvati*). (33-49)

Harishchandra's heartfelt allegiance stands out: *Krishna* (16 references), *Hari* (14), *Radha* (8), *Vishnu* (7), and *Bhagavan* ("blessed" 5). He experienced *Krishna* as "the one from whom all comes; the one who decides a person's fate; the one on whom everything depends" (such as forgiveness of sin). (57) Siva was less important for Harishchandra, perhaps due to phallic worship involved, Lehman adds. Lehman understands deities to be objects of the poet's devotion; they served his literary purposes. For the poet, as for many Hindus, to mention a god name represents also the whole Hindu pantheon. From this study of devotion and validation of deity, Lehman acknowledges Harishchandra's orthodox Hinduism, personal theism, and dependence on the Divine. "God is praised as the savior of the world and sufficient in power and virtue for any emergency to which people come." (72-73)

Further sections of Lehman's thesis followed.

Section V. "The Idea of God as Shown by Concepts of Heaven, Hell, Death, Revelation, Tradition, and Salvation"

Section VI. "The Concept of Man [*sic*]: Soul, Body, Sacrifice, Prayer, Monism, and Dualism"

Section VII. "Conceptions of the Cosmos: *Samsara, Karma,* Caste, Transmigration."

Section VIII. "Ethics Shown in Writings of Harishchandra"

Section IX. "A Summary of the Religious Conceptions Revealed in Harishchandra's Works"

Section X. "The Derivation of the Religious Conceptions in the Writings of Harishchandra"[9]

Loewen, Jacob A. (MB) "A Fresh Look at the God Concept," Lectures for a Mennonite Missionary Study Fellowship, March 12-14, 1987, 150 pp Xeroxed including 30 pp titled "Comparative Listing of the Translations of God's Names."

Loewen's lectures are titled:

1. "A Fresh Look at the God Concept for Missionaries—Introduction,"
2. "God and the Gods: The Panorama of Deity in the Scriptures,"
3. "The Implications of Culture for Deity Concepts,"
4. "The God/Gods of Western Christianity,"
5. Two-part lecture: "Translating God's Name: Introduction" and "How European Languages have Translated Them."

While much general wisdom marks this resource, the focus here draws from Loewen's specific references to Hinduism. When touring with his wife in India Loewen valued seeing "magnificent Hindu temples, reading Hindu literature, and talking with warm, open Hindu priests and devoted worshippers." A teenage guide at a temple in Bhubaneswar explained the distinct parts of the building, paid homage to images, and rubbed paint with his finger from one to make a mark on his forehead. When the guide asked if he could mark Loewen's forehead too, Loewen responded: "By all means. And what will it do for me?" To that question, the guide said, "Oh, sir, I am happy and want you to be happy too. And if I bless you, you bless me." (Lecture 1/page 19)

In response to another of Loewen's questions "Why so many deities?" the guide explained that as with Christianity, Hinduism honors manifestations of the one god.

> Whereas you Christians say that you believe in and worship only one god, in practice your one god has manifestations in three different persons. Then when you meet multiple manifestation of god in other religions, you . . . condemn them as so many idols . . .Now Hinduism, like Christianity, believes in only one god. Like Christians, Hindus believe that god is known in more than one form. In fact, we Hindus believe that god is revealed in enough forms to meet every person's need. (1/20)

Loewen assures his listeners that he's "still chewing on that sermon." Then he tells them about touring a cave temple on Elephanta Island near Mumbai, India. There the guide concluded: "There is a part of god in every human being and the function of religion is to help that divine element in a person to develop to the fullest." (1/20)

Encounters with world cultures and religions can help Christians to read the Bible more honestly, Loewen believes. Honesty includes claiming texts: scriptural reference to power residing in sacred objects; Moses' recognition of the potential power of Yahweh's presence if touched by worshippers, given as reason for building a fence around the foot of Mt. Sinai (2/22); and Israel's viewing Yahweh as a warrior god over their territory. Yahweh was known to shift from being Abraham's personal god to being god of the tribe before being god of the Hebrew nation as a whole. For the Hebrew people to claim one god did not imply that other names and forms of god did not exist. Loewen reminds missioners that they do well to understand that a single, male-identified God with many scriptural, male references to the Divine seems quite foreign to many people of the world. (2 & 3/23-44)

Most world religions recognize the need for both female and male aspects for deity. (3/45) Loewen heard with interest a Hindu priest's explanation of deity pairs and their sexuality. The Hindu deity Shiva, known as the dancing Shiva, is thought to be passive except when his female counterpart Parvati prompts his creative art of dancing. (3/46) Loewen understands Israelite history better through this basic pattern. As they shifted from a pastoral existence to dependence on agriculture, changes emerged in Israelite culture—their social organization and religious god-concept. Doubting whether the pastoral Yahweh god form could provide needed fertility when more settled in Canaan, Israelites, for centuries, turned to worship Baal, the Queen of Heaven, and fertility deities. (3/50-53)

Loewen's anthropological insight prompts questions that linger: "When one tribal god is seen as the only true god, all other people who worship other gods must be seen as infidels . . . When peoples' concept of god separates them from neighbors, prompting a self-satisfied feeling of superiority, healthy relations with others falter. . . . When a preliminary concern is elevated to being ultimate—as Lordship of Christ for Lordship of God—idolatry can emerge, Loewen understands. (3/56)

Neufeldt, Ronald W. (MB) "A Lesson in Allegory: Theosophical Interpretations of the Bhagavadgita," in *Modern Indian Interpreters of the Bhagavadgita*. Robert N. Minor, ed. (Albany: SUNY Pr, 1986), 11-33, notes 230-32.

This chapter by Neufeldt complements a collection of Mennonite writing about Hinduism as it notes leaders who provide insight into the important Hindu text called Bhagavadgita or simply Gita. Many Hindus yearly celebrate performances that highlight this popular text which is part of a larger epic titled *Mahabarata*. The title of a second notable Hindu epic is *Ramayana*. Through both Indian and western interpreters of the Gita, Neufeldt acquaints readers with the Gita story and why Hindus find meaning in it. Readers also are exposed to the Theosophical Society, an organization known for decades in India and the west, and to *allegory* as a method for viewing the story.

Indian Subba Row's account of the Gita provides practical, spiritual guidance for a person's development toward realizing immortality, Neufeldt says. (13) Guru Krishna, representative of Logos or the light, teaches Arjuna the human student. Arjuna has reached a life stage that requires deciding whether to continue to follow lower passions or to identify with his higher being. Arjuna identifies his dilemma—whether to face his kin in battle or, allegorically, the 'battle' between higher and lower elements.

Neufeldt includes Mohini Chatterji's description of Arjuna's ego within the Gita story. Within a framework of belief it moves through a series of kingdoms—from vegetable and animal through human and into the divine. (15) Internal opponents drive Arjuna to doubt; as grief and fears attack him, he loses faith. When he takes action to overcome the enemies prior to pursuing the path of knowledge, Krishna explains that action is inferior to knowledge. Neufeldt says that Theosophists differ. They assert that "knowledge of the true nature of reality" dawns during rather than apart from ongoing action. (18)

Neufeldt also notes an anonymous Indian figure, simply called 'A. Brahmin,' who includes points from history in interpreting the Gita. For example, he suggests that the 'war' (that goes on in human hearts and minds between higher and lower selves) took place about five thousand years earlier. Krishna, understood as either a "ray of dark glory" within the human heart or as a divine being sent down (*avatara*) to watch over and protect a person's evolution, advises the student. The student will carry out required duty in the spirit of service to all; he is to serve or love others in the context of being true to his *dharma* (duty) or caste. (19) Neufeldt explains 'A. Brahmin' to mean that Arjuna, in the midst of a symbolic conflict, represents a human unit that has reached a stage in the evolutionary process for saying farewell to an earlier stage so that a higher, less personal stage might evolve. (18)

Known by a pseudonym, Dreamer explains how the Gita guides a student on the path of non-attachment, love and sacrifice. From one stage, even if advanced, to the next higher one the aspirant Arjuna struggles. To give up powers of attachment or virtues, weighty as they may be, takes effort, Neufeldt hears the Dreamer to suggest. Caste confusion can occur with evolution; forces for good can subdue forces of self-assertion.

Neufeldt notes a more recent interpretation, based on earlier lectures, that appeared in 1966. Focused on key Gita chapters (4, 13, and 15) Pandit Bhavani Shankar suggests stages or realizations through which Arjuna and all human units travel: the physical ego or center as an expression of divine life; the supernatural body as a reflection of the one life; the spiritual ego or causal body as a mere reflection of divine life (not limited); and the real battlefield—individual death before rebirth. The Gita, Shankar says, is a book that discusses sacred "doctrines of the origin, trials, and destiny of humanity." (22)

Neufeldt names several westerners who explain the Gita— William Judge, Annie Basant, and Charles Johnston. The American Judge suggests "reading between the lines" in order to perceive the high, psychological meaning that underlies the Gita for Hindus. He names the two allegorical 'sides' for battle—*material* (that which drags down) and *spiritual* (that which aspires). The Kuru people represent the former and the Pandus (to which Arjuna belongs) the latter. So the 'battle' reflects preparing the spiritual rule of life to take over the material. Krishna's universal message nudges Arjuna to forego as a warrior former, lower drives like money or the ego in moving toward selflessness and hope.

Annie Besant, though a westerner, thoroughly identified with Indian causes. For her, the universal Gita text is to be *lived*. Due to a crisis prompting the need for a savior, an *avatara* Krishna, a part of the human spirit, comes to lead. Besant also sees India as the *avatara* coming with wisdom to benefit world affairs among other nations. The conflict, seen as allegory, whether between mind and passions for Arjuna or for him with his relatives, represents the struggle for skill in action—to move on toward higher levels of development. That action needs to be done as sacrifice, without attachment, in order to realize "the union of the many in the One." (27) Evil and good, which people create through ignorance and passion, can be transcended through living within unity, Neufeldt hears from Besant. To realize unity then leads to further activity.

Neufeldt offers several concluding qualities of the Hindu scripture known as Gita: its symbolic and philosophical nature, with multiple levels of meaning in the search for truth; its disclosure of life's evolutionary process; and its essential message of selflessness that calls all of us, like Arjuna, to counter our lower selves while looking to savior figures like Krishna for instruction. (28-32)

Neufeldt, Ronald (MB) "Conversion and the Courts," *Journal of Hindu-Christian Studies*, (13 no. 1, 2000) 12-18.
In this article author and professor Neufeldt discusses the turmoil that has persisted in India over conversion from one religion to another. Article 25 of the 1947 Indian Constitution addresses conversion with the position of religious minorities implied. It has been debated and reinterpreted through the decades. Neufeldt suggests that *propagation* is "the single most important issue for the future of Hindu-Christian relationships." (1) He explains different states' Freedom of Religion acts—from Orissa, Madhya Pradesh and Arunachal Pradesh.

Issues discussed include: undermining another's faith; methods used like force, fraud, material inducement, or exploitation of one's poverty or ignorance; Hindu misperceptions; fundamental rights; propagation as part of religious duty; and reasons for conversion. Not endorsing questionable means to prompt change, both Catholics and Protestants identify two possible reasons why people might choose to shift loyalty: 1. to satisfy basic physical wants, because of Christian beliefs themselves, due to exemplary Christian living, and 2. to escape from one's depressed class. But Christians have been faulted for causing uneducated folk to think that God is displeased if they do not convert. Also troubling is the charge that change disrupts public order.

Even justices can deliberate to the point of countering those who first framed the Constitution, Neufeldt suggests. If people in a community publicly fault others for converting, supporters of the strong-willed VHP (Vishva Hindu Parishad) group will publicly protest and attempt to prohibit such conversion. Neufeldt understands the original Constitution framers to have called for justice for minorities, hoping precisely to prevent dependence on a majority voice like VHP.

Article 25 had guaranteed "freedom of conscience to every citizen."(15)[10]

Neufeldt, Ronald W. (MB) *F. Max Muller and the Rig-Veda* A *study of its role in his work and thought*. PhD dissertation from University of Iowa (Calcutta, India: Minerva Assoc Publ, 1980).

Attention now turns selectively to Neufeldt's dissertation.[11] Neufeldt's study explains how the ancient, Hindu Rig-Veda scripture influenced the life and thought of the noted German Max Muller, presumably the first scholar to engage the discipline of comparing religions. Key ideas from Muller's insight noted by Neufeldt will form brief paragraphs here.

1. Muller credits India's ancient literature as the oldest historical religious documents that reveal how religious thought and language began, grew and spread. He calls it "the oldest work of speech and thought in the 'Aryan' world." Because similar literature did not exist in antiquity, interpretation and comparison are difficult. (11, 46, 93, 167)
2. In 1853 Muller noted three major points about the Rig-Veda: no parallel exists for revealing the intellectual life of a person; the Rig-Veda depicts a person's intellectual development; such growth reveals that strata of thought exist. (20-21)
3. Religions had concepts of the infinite and of law and order. (101) Sacrifice and ritual were secondary to the human attempt to perceive and name the infinite. (116) The Rig-Veda reveals that Indian ancestors believed that divine powers existed in rivers and mountains, in elements such as thunder and rain. Rig-Veda deities follow a pattern of evolution: "from metaphorical names to mythological beings to divinities." (50)

   (Views that differ also appear in Neufeldt's discussion of Muller.) Monotheism may have preceded the Rig-Veda's multiple gods. (27) Or, the idea of One God may follow from the earlier concept of many gods; stages of henotheism or polytheism prepare for a monotheistic state. (164)
4. No other documents allow a student to go as far back in history or show such clear lines of development as does the Rig-Veda. (115, 168) Materials useful to study religion are: language, myth, sacred books, customs and traditions. (112) Thought and language are inseparable; "no words are possible without sensations"; to speak implies that thinking or concept occur. (124-5) Such insight Neufeldt draws from Muller.
5. Principal elements of 'real religion' in the Rig-Veda include: belief in gods with power, kindness and immortality who appear as ideal immortal beings; belief in gods as creators of heaven and earth who authorize laws of right and wrong; belief in

human immortality. (31) Muller used the Rig-Veda as a model for how religions develop, Neufeldt explains. (114)

6. All religions share some features. They: without reason have intuition regarding god, believe in divine rule of the world, distinguish between good and evil, and hope for a better life. (96) With either religion or language, everything new is old, everything old is new. No religion is fully new; it may only combine certain elements in different ways. (176)

Neufeldt, Ronald W. (MB) "In Search of Utopia: *Karma* and Rebirth in the Theosophical Movement," in Karma *and Rebirth Post Classical Developments*. Ronald W. Neufeldt, ed. (Albany: SUNY Pr, 1986) 233-56.

Views of *karma* and rebirth vary. This chapter by Neufeldt describes the Theosophical Movement's distinct approach to *karma*. That society was founded in New York City; its active group located in Madras (now Chennai) in India's southern state of Tamil Nadu shows Helena Blavatsky's strong influence. It stresses freedom of thought. It understands *karma* as a "moral law of retribution," Neufeldt quotes. Cause and effect, which individuals bring upon themselves rather than being punishment by a god, is important for harmony and progress. Blavatsky suggests that "all pain and suffering is simply the result of lack of harmony which in turn is caused by some form of selfishness which will eventually be removed through the functioning of the law of *karma*." (240) As *karma* evens things out, progress to a higher state of existence follows. Once a person, rebirth does not regress to lower levels, theosophists think. Theosophical understanding finds that society ever-moves toward improvement. (247-52)

Neufeldt, Ron (MB) "Justice in Hinduism" in *The Spiritual Roots of Restorative Justice*. Michael L. Hadley, ed. (New York: State University of NY Pr, 2001) 143-60.

Here Neufeldt discusses issues of justice originating from classical Hinduism—*dharma-sutras* (earliest 600-400 B.C.E.) and *dharma-shastras* (200-100 B.C.E.) While the current legal system shows British influence, classical insight continues, Neufeldt observes. The most influential religious-legal document or text case of *dharma-shastras* is Laws of Manu. Suggesting order for well being, rules or laws, *dharma* basically means *duty*. Because the divinely sanctioned Hindu social system was defined by the caste system, duty depended on status or life stage. *Dharma* was upheld as members of each caste performed distinct duties. "To fulfill one's *dharmic* obligations was to place oneself on the path to liberation or salvation," Neufeldt explains. (146) Hindu laws, designed for study in order to regulate actions, were to govern every aspect of human activity.

Along with classical influence through *dharma* came *karma*. With position in society determined by personal actions or *law of karma* in previous lives, "each act had potential for either merit or demerit in this life or in future lives." (147) Aspects such as parents, caste status, experiences, intellect, and length of life all evolved or were inherited through *samsara*, or transmigration. Punishments (the "means to keep human beings on the path of *dharma*," 148) or rewards followed certain acts. Manu names eighteen causes for legal action, some being more serious than others, along with four kinds of punishment—admonition, reproof, fine, and corporal punishment. Offences and penalties depend on various details including whether an offender mistreated a person of higher caste or was once or twice-born, Neufeldt notes. Twice-born refers to members of the three upper caste groups, those Hindus who are permitted to explore Vedic knowledge.

Neufeldt notes types of crimes or misconduct, punishments, and results from penance in detail. Points of interest include distinct cases in which a Hindu priest is a victim, minor penances as for killing a cow, conditions for a fault described as unintentional, or the degree of pollution that accompanies a sin—whether separation from the present community results or whether *karma* affects a future life. Key justice concerns with Manu laws include retribution, deterrence (with "intent to preserve the divinely ordained order of society," 154), and restoration (ultimate or temporal). Ancient lawgivers expected penance to purify an offender—it could 'burn up' bad *karma* or enable a person to admit and atone for having violated *dharma.* Or, the victim might be less inclined to seek revenge. Restoration could restore the 'bruised' social order or restore the sinner to a former place within that order.

Neufeldt offers a final example of the power of penance both lived and noted in the film titled *Gandhi.* During interreligious killings in Calcutta, when Gandhi is near death from fasting for personal or collective failings, a crazed Hindu with blood of Muslims on his hands approaches Gandhi confessing his defeat. Gandhi offers a profound way out—the Hindu should locate and raise a Muslim boy as a Muslim. In that, he called the Hindu to own and practice the fact that all religions and scriptures contain truth. Since all people are God's children, the truth through which the Hindu could live penance, or be restored, would be to carry out selfless, nonviolent service for a child of those he had so wrongly violated. (157)

Nyce, Dorothy Yoder. (MC) "Henry Martyn's Short Stint in India and Persia: Prior and Later Influences," *Mission Focus: Annual Review,* (vol. 20, 2012) 170-88.

Having known the name Henry Martyn through interfaith efforts in India, Yoder Nyce wondered what prompted the man's being noteworthy. Research at the Henry Martyn Centre, Cambridge, England, revealed that he went to India as a chaplain in 1706 with the British East India Company. What he accomplished within six years, leaving due to severe health problems, amazed all. His story credits Martyn's "extraordinary learning," and perfectionist, scholarly skills with translation of biblical texts into Urdu (Hindustani), Persian, and Arabic. While he modeled effective interaction with Muslims, his openness to people loyal to diverse religions led him to daily journal about encounters with Hindus too. He recorded details like: an event of "immolation when a widow threw herself onto her dead husband's pyre; people bowed profusely before a black, lifeless image of Krishna; noise-making linked with festivities when goddess Kali effigies were thrown into the muddy Hooglie River at Calcutta, and his own polluting touch that prompted his cook to throw out perfectly good, cooked rice. Not intent to proselytize children through occasions of worship or schools that he started, "he wished children to learn to fear God and become good men." [sic] (177-79) Yoder Nyce values the legacy that Martyn left.

Nyce, Dorothy Yoder. (MC) "Hinduism: A Study of Its Development and Belief," for a Religions of the World course at Goshen College with Marlin Jeschke, (October 10, 1966) 19 pp.

Yoder Nyce took this course directly after having lived and taught at Woodstock School in India for three years. She felt a need to clarify some of what seemed complex about Hinduism—that which she had pondered, read about, or observed while in India. The validity of her outline then surprises her fifty years later. Yoder Nyce basically deals with Sruti and Smriti literature divisions that attend to Samhitas, Brahmanas, Aranyakas and Upanishads with the former and the two Hindu epics, shastras, and puranas with the latter. While stations and stages of life are discussed regarding the Brahmanas, windows into *karma*, life paths, and Brahman-Atman shape much of the Upanishads section. With the Bhagavad Gita central to the Mahabharata, only mention of the Ramayana epic follows. A far-too-brief introduction to the Law of Manu within the Shastras precedes noting the Trimurti deities succinctly outlined in a chart. (16) Anyone knowledgeable about Hinduism knows the brevity with which such subjects were presented. A quote from Hindu Swami Prabhavananda concludes the effort:

> . . . India . . . strives for unity, not by calling for a common doctrine, but only by pointing to a common goal, and by exhorting man [sic] to its attainment. The path, she assures us,

matters little; it is the goal that is supreme. And what is the goal? It is only—once again—to realize God. (18)

Nyce, Dorothy Yoder (MC) *Multifaith Musing: Essays and Exchanges.*
(Goshen, IN: Self-published, 2010).
In addition to three essays that appear in this book[12] Yoder Nyce gives prime attention to Hindu-Christian engagement through imagined conversations.

The first essay, titled "To know one [religion] is to know none," quotes Max Muller. To enable "knowing" Hindu rituals, Yoder Nyce reports having visited Hindu temples in India noting: bell ringing on entering or blowing of a conch shell, milk poured over an image, a priest or *sadhu* (holy man) honored, the right hand whisked through a camphor flame, or blessed *prasad* (consecrated food returned to worshippers) received. She reports further "knowing": that Hindus express awe through terms like *Aum/Om* or *Vac* (meaning spoken word), that they experience divine energy when watching sacred dance steps (as with the Bharata Natya classical dance form), and that a power presides in the innermost heart of a temple (*sanctum sanctorum* or *garbha griha*). (22-23) Yoder Nyce's extensive Resource listings with lectures suggest sources for more "knowing."

Yoder Nyce notes learning from mentors. Indian scholar K. P. Aleaz suggests that "Christians need Hindus to help us understand Jesus; Hindu views of renunciation may help explain Jesus' call to give up the self." And Harvard interfaith professor Diana Eck teaches about *consciousness*. For the Hindu, *consciousness* reveals a person's ability to hold two viewpoints at once; seeing many god forms, there is One. An oft-quoted, ancient Rig Veda text states "Truth is One; the wise call it by many names." Yoder Nyce values language that credits God's manyness while being One. Also from Eck, who lived and studied for seven years among Hindus in India, is awareness that adherents construct God-language but "never exhaust or grasp the Divine" she says. (23, 25)

Nine major exchanges created by Yoder Nyce focus on diverse themes that reflect interreligious experience: wisdom, water, and crossing cultures as through drama, dance and temples. A Christian dialogue partner names hymn titles that refer to the universal image of sacred water in ways that prompt a Hindu speaker to identify: a river as feminine nurturer or healer, the sacred rite of bathing in a river to purify oneself of sin, or "crossing over a river at the time of death." This book also includes a one-act play by Yoder Nyce in which Hindu, Muslim, and Christian university students exchange views about experience of ongoing conflict between their religions. While Christian scripture texts are discussed by two imagined Christian seminary students, several key Hindu scriptures are explained in another exchange between two Hindu presenters to a Christian audience gathered at an Indian ashram. After an exchange that enables a Christian to distinguish diverse Hindu goddesses, a Hindu and Christian converse about Asherah of the Hebrew Bible; highlights of the female divine presence among ancient Israelites emerge.

A few annotations from Yoder Nyce's Appendix material appear in the *Theology of Religions* chapter in this resource.

Nyce, Dorothy Yoder. (MC) "The World Missionary Conference, Edinburgh 1910—A Context for Review," *Mission Focus: Annual Review*, (18, 2010) 100-23.

In addition to information about this major 1910 event for ecumenical missioners, a distinct feature of Yoder Nyce's study is her access to original questionnaire responses of some Commission IV members who focused "The Missionary Message in Relation to Non-Christian Religions."[13] One-third of the 187 respondents studied Hinduism. Co-chair of the group, noted Indian theology professor A. G. Hogg, reports types of response:

- Not a philosophy like Hinduism (except for ritual acts), Christianity is based on certain facts.
- Hindus understand Jesus as an incarnation (*avatara*) of God.
- The Hindu sense of *sin* is slow to awaken.
- Hindu life and thought are pervaded by the idea of merit.
- Hindu speculative philosophy begins with suffering; pain's mystery is the most acute problem.
- The system of caste is divinely appointed, not to be disturbed.

Examples of attitudes needed toward a religion like Hinduism that Yoder Nyce values from respondents' wisdom include:

- Respect and reverence, never attack, another's ancestral religion; show respect and deep empathy for, not argumentation with, people.
- Teach to construct, not destruct or wrongly present, others.
- Recognize Hindus as children of, loved, and blessed by God in light of their trust.
- Be well trained in fundamentals of others' faiths; know points of contact and fundamental differences—in order to make confession, not misjudge or be arrogant.
- Hindus accept Christ's love, renunciation of life, not Christianity.
- For a missioner to suggest that Hindu thought is irrational while Christian doctrine is rational causes Hindu hearers amusement or disdain. (104-06)

Nyce, Dorothy Yoder. (MC) "Wisdom or Folly: Thoughts of Religious
   Superiority" Review Essay of *The Myth of Religious Superiority A
   Multifaith Exploration*, Paul F. Knitter, ed. (Maryknoll, NY: Orbis,
   2005) *Mission Focus: Annual Review*, (vol. 14, 2006) 211-30.
Yoder Nyce, in highlighting the folly of judging one religion alone as
superior, looks to two Asians—K. P. Aleaz from India and Wesley
Ariarajah, originally from Sri Lanka. Aleaz names early, open-minded,
non-Indians in India who accepted more dimensions of Hindu thought
or practice than do most traditional westerners—first century Thomas
Christians, Roberto deNobili, and Bartholomaus Ziegenbalg. Ariarajah,
from having lived among neighbors of diverse religions, knows that a
"theology of religions is part of being a religious person or community."
(214) Yoder Nyce commends their affirmation for claiming possible
plural paths to salvation when engaged with Hindus or other
religionists. To credit plurality need not diminish being faithful to a
particular identity. Effective Hindus and Christians in dialogue know
more than their own prime expression of Truth. Further, people loyal to
all religions have more to learn during their quest for the sacred, Yoder
Nyce adds. To cooperate, whether in dialogue or actions to meet global
needs, with that which (those who) differs entails witness. To confess is
expected, not to exclude. When meeting the Divine (however named or
formed) the religious goal is to grow in personal faithfulness and
communal responsibility, Yoder Nyce gathers from informed writers.

Pankratz, J. N. (MB) "The Response of the *Brahmo Samaj*," in *Modern
   Indian Responses to Religious Pluralism*. Harold G. Coward, ed.
   (Albany: SUNY Pr, 1987) 19-38.
In addition to a dozen chapters that present responses to religious
pluralism from other organizations or individuals, James Pankratz
discusses how the Brahmo Samaj founded by the dynamic Rammohun
Roy responded.[14] Rammohun had earlier explained why he, a "Hindoo,"
established and attended a Unitarian congregation in Calcutta in 1821.
He valued that Unitarians reject polytheism and idolatry. He endorsed
their professing and promoting divine unity—an idea based in both the
ancient Hindu Vedas and Christian scripture. Pankratz notes themes of
Brahmo Samaj worship: unity of the One God or Universal Being, direct
experience of God, value of *reason* and *revelation* for understanding
God, worshiper tolerance because aware that all views of God are
partial, weakness of worship through images, and service to others. (22)
   To understand Rammohun's approach to religious pluralism
Pankratz highlights five major motifs: "universal brotherhood of all who
worship the Author and Preserver of the Universe"; critique of
"polytheism, incarnation, idolatry" and certain patterns of worship;
worship that expresses God's unity via "scripture, prayer, sermons, and

hymns"; tolerance toward those whose forms of worship differ; and affirmation of each nation or culture's worship forms and insight into the One True God revealed everywhere. (23-24)

Pankratz notes Rammohun's public efforts. He debated with both Hindu and Christian opponents. He recruited educated Hindus in various cities and he questioned some Christian missioner methods. Difference of view also caused splits among Brahmo Samaj adherents. Keshub Chunder Sen, for one, promoted devotional (*bhakti*) singing, Vaishnava imagery, and the spiritual goddess. He formed four classes of devotees—the *yogi*, b*hakta*, *jnani*, and *sevak*—based on how each expressed religious life. Later, some countered his authoritarian approach, Pankratz says. (28, 30-32) Despite occasions of turmoil, consistent views toward religious pluralism remain. Those views center belief in One God who loves all nations and wills their mutual respect. Without Hindu expansion or national synthesizing as broadly as hoped for, the Bramo Samaj combines critique of religious thought with tolerance toward religious plurality, Pankratz notes. (33-34)

Wiebe, Paul D. (MB/MC) *Heirs and Joint Heirs Mission to Church Among the Mennonite Brethren of Andhra Pradesh.* (Winnipeg, Manitoba: Kindred Productions, 2010).

A great nephew, grandson and son of MB missioners to Andhra Pradesh State, Wiebe was born in India.[15] Wiebe continues to return to engage in different projects with the MB church of India. A professional sociologist, Wiebe creates and responds to questions like: Who among Telugu folk (Telugu being the main language of AP state) responded to missioners? Under what conditions does social change occur? How does a mission program evolve into a church program? While this book focuses more on the *MB church in Andhra Pradesh*, annotations here highlight from the system of Hinduism, aware also that many people in AP cities and large towns are loyal to Islam.

Differences within Hinduism are as great as those between Hinduism and other noted religious systems, Wiebe says. (2) Ideas within this paragraph appear scattered through Wiebe's first thirty pages. His first chapter provides a fine review of Christianity in India. Regarding Hindus, that the whole of life is religious is clear. A person is Hindu who belongs to and follows caste laws; the caste system provides social order for India's diversity, Wiebe explains. Four main caste levels plus *Dalits* and 200-300 *jati* groupings mark peoples' styles and occupations. Hindu reform movements such as *Brahmo Samaj* (founded in 1828 by Ram Mohan Roy) and *Arya Samaj* (founded in 1868 by Dayanand Saraswati) emerged to challenge Brahmins or to counter vile attacks on Hinduism by Christians or Muslims. Christians who converted from Hinduism also rejected aspects of the Hindu system, less directly its caste and sub-caste features. While Gandhi encouraged Hindus to read Christian scripture, he also told them that Hinduism offered similar and additional features of value. Wiebe notes that many Hindus feel free to scapegoat minority groups; they perceive Sikh, Jain, and Buddhist religions more favorably because indigenous to India while Christianity and Islam, having come from outside, can more easily be ignored or excluded.

With India's social life based on the caste system, MBs of AP primarily were of the low Madiga and Mala *jatis,* Wiebe explains. Ninety percent of AP Christians are of *Dalit*, tribal, or animist background. (30) Intent to spread the gospel—to change and recruit members through diverse ways from the system of Hindu power—few "kingpin" missioners "felt that they had more to learn than offer." Few went to India expecting to "appreciate indigenous beliefs or ritual systems," Wiebe suggests. (129-31, 201) In 1970 over fifty percent of MB members had Hindu parents when they were baptized. Hindu influence persists: bonding relationships, spirits and beings with powers, and stories from sacred texts. Such influence shapes members' sense of good and evil, their patterns for festivals. Drawn to greater individual worth and dignity as Christians, recruits choose to leave the bottom of the *jati* hierarchy, Wiebe adds. (171, 149, 188)

While some missioners "gained deep insights into the great traditional teachings of Hinduism," others denounced them with fury. Most missioners stressed a world view or bias against "heathendom" and for salvation only through Jesus Christ's name. Wiebe believes that quite a few more Indian people value Jesus' life and teaching than are counted on church rolls. While some educated, Hindu Indians dislike missioner efforts to evangelize, they value good educational and medical efforts begun by missioners. As Indians took over leadership roles with MB schools, western influence lessened. Differences then emerged between Christians who remain in villages (the majority of whom remain in ways disadvantaged) and those who left. (231, 282, 235, 239, 247,252)

Wiebe observes that family, caste and other features of identity continue to attract Indians to distinct cultural and social patterns from their Hindu past. Ancient Indians had not distinguished supernatural and natural worlds; no word for *religion* existed among ancient Indo-Aryans. Then, as the caste system lost some of its strength, extremist defenders of Hindu nationalism correlated moral order with India's being a "holy nation." V. D. Savarkar 'father' of Hindu nationalism defines a *Hindu* as one who "regards this land, from the Indus to the seas, as his fatherland as well as his holy land," Wiebe notes. Severe anti-Christian violence by Hindu extremists—perhaps due to Christian weakness or their presumed lack of loyalty to India since linked with colonialists—shape several other states more than AP.

Wiebe explains some discontent. Noted Indian historian Romila Thapar, well-aware of the extremist, Hindu RSS' wish to re-write India's history, describes their intent to "saffronize" India's system of education. (To "saffronize" makes a verb of *saffron*, the sacred color of Hinduism.) Extremists intend to "downplay and denigrate the contributions of minorities in India," she says. (318, 315) In AP politicians may prompt Hindu nationalists to spread their religious message during morning chants over loudspeakers, healing campaigns, or fairs. They distinctly resent conversion; they welcome returnees back into Hinduism but ban folk from leaving it, Wiebe notes.

Slightly over two percent of India's population and only four percent of people living in the area of the MB's eight hundred congregations (only half with church buildings) are Christians. Wiebe fully believes that while missioners spread their message, the most important actors in mobilizing the church have been local people who embody the message. (306, 316-317,336, 342, 347, 357)

Wiebe, Paul D. (MB) "Religious Change in South India: Perspectives from a Small Town," *Religion and Society*, (22, no. 4 December 1975) 27-46.

Wiebe notes two perspectives on religion in India—Hinduism's great and little traditions plus structural forms of social life that link with systems of religious belief. As might be expected, higher castes reflect the "great" tradition and lower castes the "little" one. To be a Hindu means to belong to a particular caste. As the title suggests Wiebe examines what religious structural changes are taking place in rural, south India as reflected in a town named Peddur (pseudonym). Within such a town occur tradition and multiple changes within caste, within people's religious orientation. Among varied details of Peddur, there are twenty-two caste groups and two sections. Within one section live the four main caste groups (the three 'twice-born'—Brahmin, Razu and Komti—and the lower Sudra); within the other *pallim* live out-of-caste or 'untouchable' groups like Madigas (leather workers) and Malas (coolies or workers with coarse cloth). (27-28)[16]

Wiebe understands sacred dimensions of town life. Diverse features link Peddur folk: the bazaar, staff (police or doctors), transport (buses), news (via radio or newspaper) as well as trade, marriage and kinship, plus religious events of pilgrimage, fairs, or festivals. Hindu rituals for life-cycle events differ by caste; *puja* (worship) precedes activity like construction or drama; and forehead markings indicate loyalty to a distinct deity. Sociologist Wiebe includes many details about Peddur's people: useful charms and superstitious features of encounters with a snake, cat, widow, or even stacked, new pots. Days or hours on which to travel or stay at home, are so determined. (29-30)

Places have religious meaning too, according to Wiebe. Small Hindu shrines along the roadside, goddess locations linked with a distinct disease, household alcoves for convenience of worship, or a *neem* tree important to women who desire pregnancy—all of these options shape life's sacred being for Hindus in Peddur. Two large Hindu temples, with hereditary or salaried priests for lords Siva and Vishnu, plus eight other, scattered temples mark Peddur. Wiebe helps a reader to understand distinct features about priests, land links, or special occasions for Brahmin families within these "holy Hindu havens." (31)

Many changes have and will continue to occur in Wiebe's south Indian town of Peddur. Along with more frequent intermarriage between people of different castes is the fact that patterns of authority remain caste-related. Whereas school children of Madiga and Mala caste groups used to sit separately from each other and a high caste teacher never touched a student of low caste, such habits are changing. Members of low caste groups may enter temples from which they were earlier restricted. On fewer occasions need a high caste person purify by sprinkling with water an object that a low caste person had previously touched. Wiebe reports numerous other distinct changes within government, education, politics, and travel. Yet places that sell alcohol may still provide separate glasses for owners, caste people, and untouchables. And competition persists between Hindu or Christian Malas and Madigas. Power differences can emerge between or within caste groups. Hierarchy persists within social organization that affects the interplay of culture and religion, according to Wiebe. (35-39)

While most Hindus who live in a place like Peddur understand terms like *karma* (religious action or duty) and *samsara* (cycle of death and rebirth), they would less likely talk about shapeless, nameless ultimate reality, Wiebe says. They may speak of levels of beings known for varied powers, levels under the creator God Bhagavuntudu. At a lower level are approachable male gods known to dominate at specific sites, like Venkateshwarluswami at south India's town of Tirupathi. A Hindu from Peddur might go there on pilgrimage to gain ritual merit, or a barren woman with her husband may venture there to give offerings and make a vow to the god for help with pregnancy. Wiebe explains that goddesses linked with illnesses are thought to be on another level. A specific goddess may be thought to cause smallpox if dissatisfied with peoples' actions. Whereas worshippers approach a male god, a goddess more often visits people in response to them. (40-41)

Another level of religious beings centers in spirits. Certain incidents may cause a person to become a spirit, as when he or she dies sooner than expected. Birth may so destine or be the fate of another.

Wiebe explains that spirits around Peddur may be understood to take on a former animal form, may live at a particular place (as in an abandoned house), or appear at certain times. Sprits cause most people fear; a select few may know the right incantations to force a spirit out of one who is possessed. Or a person thought to have an 'evil eye' can cause crops or food to spoil, or a child to cry. (41-42)

Caste levels also influence the measure of strength shown by beings. High caste Brahmins are known as teachers, priests, or those with power to judge on ritual matters. Their role will vary when affecting a Mala who is 'untouchable' compared with relating to a Komti merchant, one of the higher, 'twice-born' castes. But Wiebe observes that the power of Brahmins in Peddur has shifted. Known to be ritually elite within the social hierarchy and to have authority for auspicious dates or times, the overall position of priests has decreased. A further reason for perceived divergence depends on whether the one who assesses knows only a local setting or has experience in the broader region where Hindu resurgence may be growing. However, Wiebe concludes that "all of the various forms of spiritual beings have relevance at all of the caste levels." (42-45)

Yoder, John Howard. (MC) "The Disavowal of Constantine: An Alternative Perspective on Interfaith Dialogue," in *The Royal Priesthood Essays Ecclesiological and Ecumenical*, John Howard Yoder, Michael G. Cartwright, ed., (Grand Rapids: Eerdmans Publ Co., 1994) 242-61.[17]

With this chapter the writer takes the liberty to presume that what Yoder writes "speaks" directly to encounter with Hindus even though he names no specific religion. Several writers reflecting on Yoder identify this chapter as a key source for his view of interfaith concerns. Yoder wrote elsewhere about Christian engagement with Judaism and Islam, drawing from his experience in Jerusalem and Algeria. For example, he repeatedly identifies Judaism as "*not* non-Christian," based on personal experience in the country of Israel and his sincere claim to Jewish history as a Christian. Therefore, to think of this address to Christians as possibly relating also to a Hindu is presumed.

Along with Yoder's disavowal of Constantine's endorsement of Christianity during the third century is his confession that Christianity has failed to fully follow Jesus the Christ, as through denial of continuity with Judaism and a pattern of church hierarchy. He validates restoring diversity of religious truth and expecting cultural change, wherever. Ideas important for interfaith engagement include:

- Repentance for attitudes or actions that harm understanding of God, personal or another's.

- Not all of any religion is good. (Truth or good can be learned from any religion is also implied.)
- To discover or enable religious exchange is the responsibility of anyone, not only religious elites.
- Yoder credits Islamic specialist Kenneth Cragg's insight: one truly understands another's faith when you "feel at home" in it to the extent of questioning one's chosen religious loyalty.
- Truth claims must be non-coercive. Alongside truth content, one in dialogue attends to the utter dignity of the partner, to a sense of solidarity with him or her. A triumphal, domineering claim for Jesus in itself denies Jesus, if the neighbor (partner) feels disrespected on hearing it.
- In dialogue Yoder's wish is not for less talk about Jesus but more. Jesus' message stresses love of enemy, dignity for the lowly, repentance (readiness to learn from another and adapt), service, and avoiding coercion. [18]
- Dialogue involves acknowledging the potential legitimacy of the other's religious system for salvation.
- Yoder distinguishes *ecumenical*—common commitment to Jesus the Christ and biblical scripture—from *interfaith*—common dimensions such as scriptures or good will, not Jesus.
- Yoder explains that Gandhi refused to claim Christian identity because during his lifetime the term *Christian* meant empire, racism, and uniqueness of Jesus only. Instead, Gandhi reconceived features of Indian language—although he knew about nonviolence from within Hinduism he added to that insight from Jesus' teaching and example.

---

[1] Comparable space for or mutual crediting of religions may also be known as *communalism* in India.

[2] This study was named winner of the 2008 Elisabeth Schussler Fiorenza "New Scholar Award."

[3] Source: Bauman's correspondence of January 10, 2014 with the writer.

[4] Extensive historic details and reasons for the rise of anti-Christian violence in the late 1990s were noted in Bauman's article above titled "Hindu-Christian Conflict in India."

[5] Information about Rammohan Roy appears in articles by James Pankratz.

[6] Other writers in this resource will explain the Hindu insight into God's manyness and oneness.

[7] Graber consistently uses the spelling for *Aryan* with an *i*, *Arian*.

[8] Interested readers will wish to read more than these annotations provide.

[9] The writer's notations for these sections are too lengthy to include. She regrets not examining Folder2 in Box 2 titled "Manuscript, Part II 1934."

[10] The controversy has surfaced repeatedly, as again in 2015 the radical RSS group endorses that all subcontinent people be Hindu. To be other than Hindu is not true to being Indian, they charge.

[11] The writer is indebted to Dr. Lewis Brubacher for gifting a copy of Neufeldt's published dissertation to her. He also provided copies of several of Neufeldt's articles.

[12] Yoder Nyce gave two speeches at meetings of New Perspectives on Faith, Goshen, IN, the first, "To know one [religion] is to know none" quotes the German scholar of comparative religions Max Muller and the second, "Paradox of World Religions: Conflict and Peace-building." In the third essay here titled "Encounters: 'spiritual beings having a human experience'" diverse episodes of personal contacts with religions in India are narrated.

[13] Historian Brian Stanley provided the writer with these materials for reading at the Centre for the Study of World Christianity, New College, Edinburgh University, Edinburgh, Scotland.

[14] Pankratz' unpublished PhD dissertation "The Religious Thought of Rammohun Roy" was granted from McMaster University in 1975.

[15] MB missioners Susie Wiebe and N. N. Hiebert went to India in 1899; Daniel and Katherina Bergthold, and daughter Viola arrived in 1904; Viola returned to India from the States with her husband John Wiebe in1927. Wiebes' son Paul and wife Donna Beth are now members of the Mennonite Church. Paul's PhD study focused on Christians in Andhra Pradesh. He was principal of Kodaikanal International School in south India, from which he had been graduated, for thirteen years. He knows India and the MB church there very well.

[16] A chart of Peddur appears on page 36 of the Wiebe brother's book *In Another Day of the Lord*.

[17] Yoder presented this lecture at the Ecumenical Institute for Advanced Theological Studies, Jerusalem in 1976.

[18] The writer wishes that Yoder would make clear that Jesus' message primarily focused, *not* on himself, *but* on the vision, openness, and radical nature of **God's** kingdom.

Anecdotes

Most of these segments appeared in brief articles or correspondence found in archival materials at Mennonite Church USA Archives, Goshen, Indiana or in "Manuscript Collections" from Mennonite Library and Archives, Bethel College, North Newton, Kansas. With thanks to staff and archivists Colleen McFarland (Goshen) and John Thiesen (Newton), the writer thanks Joe Springer at the Mennonite Historical Library, Goshen College, Goshen, Indiana, for alerting her to *India Mission News* a several-page newsletter compiled, edited, and sent from MC missioners in India from 1922-34.[1] Regretably, no research was done in Mennonite Brethren archives in California. Most writers are identified; anecdotes unattributed follow those named.

Augsburger, Myron S. (MC) "Coolie Discipleship," *Gospel Herald*, (February 23, 1988) 128-29.
During a trip to India Augsburger recalls meeting a beggar when leaving a temple. The beggar, standing at the bus window near Augsburger, repeated statements in English: "I am a family man; I am a holy man; I hate you, but five rupees would help. . . ." Augsburger ponders: 'Only five rupees? That's less than fifty cents; so easy to give but terrible to perpetuate a social system of injustice. How long does one work for justice where a rigid, Hindu caste system locks a quarter of the population into perpetual servitude?' he wonders.

Bauer, Evelyn (MC) tells of Chandra Lela who was married at age seven to the son of a Hindu priest; the son died before they began to live together. Still a child, she with several servant girls went with her father from Nepal to India on pilgrimage to Hindu shrines. Not only did the father die en route; two of their servants died of cholera. Although known to have a good Hindu education and knowledge of scriptures, Chandra Lela was despised as a child widow. Doing everything to please the gods and to receive pardon for sins—bathing in the sacred Ganges, gifting images and priests, and repeating names of gods an excessive number of times—she began to lose faith in Hinduism. Bauer reports that before long Chandra Lela met a missioner who introduced her to Jesus; she then gladly endured persecution by Hindus for becoming a Christian. After 27 years she returned to Nepal to share the peace that she had come to know.

Bauman, Ella G. and **Harvey** (GC) [Tape 266.97 # 17, interview of Ella by James Juhnke 1977, Bethel College Archives, Newton, Kansas and– MLA – 127, # 23.

Married in 1924, the Baumans left for India in 1925, the first General Conference Mennonite trained doctors from the USA. Except for furlough years they were located at the Champa "station" to serve the surrounding region until leaving India in 1961. During their first few years Hindu patients feared being touched by "foreign doctors." Having felt polluted they would follow an appointment with a bath. Types of Indian or Hindu customs that, according to Baumans, interfered with medical work included: use of cow dung as a preventative for cholera; a stipulation that a new mother not ingest water for five days after giving birth; and use of burnt flesh to combat certain internal health problems. Baumans adapted to some Indian remedies that later American doctors refused. Ella also complements early missioners with having respected Indian culture more than did some later ones—early ones first served immediate physical needs. Later missioners, perhaps due to specialized training, felt drawn to "the gospel" for their first response.

Baumans faced and survived turmoil. Dr. Harvey observed the *Arya Samajists* (Hindu reform movement that encouraged Hindus to return to the ancient *Vedas*) to "do all that they can to run us out of Surguja." The *Samajist'* technique was to convince those Hindus who rent space to our workers to insist that those workers leave. Mary Lou Cummings writes (*Full Circle Stories of Mennonite Women*, 28-39) about Dr. Ella's harrowing adventure of walking several miles at night from a train station during a rain storm to a Reformed Mission at Sakti where boarding school children were very sick with flu and pneumonia. Bauman's clear "inner relationship" with God never failed. Her medical care given to Hindu and Sikh refugees at the time of Partition is told elsewhere in this book.

Beachy, Miriam (MC) reports that conflicts may surface along with deity worship during festival times. Hindu village leaders may pressure all villagers to help pay for celebrations. When a Christian named Simon told the leader that he could not give for such a Hindu event, the village leader threatened to drive him from his plot of land. Simon decided to compromise—he would give money with the stipulation that it be used for *food* for the celebration, not for worship of the Hindu deity. When the next festival occurred, he told the leader to go ahead and drive him away; he would not make a donation. Thereafter, Simon felt that God had intervened when no one asked him for a donation. Beachy explains the need for pastoral care when such interfaith occasions arise.

Brunk, A. C. (MC) People of the Dondi congregation finished replacing the earthen floor of their church building with cement. For that project a generous Hindu gave one thousand bricks free of charge. The ordinary labor was done by men, women, and children of the church. Enough benches were also made for those attending plus visitors; all costs were covered by the church's budget, Brunk reports.

Burkhalter, Edward and Ramoth (GC) *With No Regrets A Memoir of Ramoth Isabelle Lowe Burkhalter.* As told to Mary O'Brien Tyrrell, (St. Paul, MN: Memoirs Inc. 2007).

When missioner Ramoth realized in 1978 that recruiters were persuading young Hindu girls or women from Jagdeeshpur to pursue prospects for jobs or marriage overseas, she recognized the guise for trafficking women. Seeing their need for training beyond primary school, their need for skills to provide income, Burkhalter began ASHA Handicrafts. *ASHA* is the Hindi word for *hope.* Before long she had a group of young women sewing, tatting, and making children's clothing, along with designing cutwork for export. In addition to being paid well, the seamstresses were empowered; their new self-esteem was a "wonderful side effect," Burkhalter says. (91-92)

The six Burkhalter children commend Ramoth at the end of her memoir by saying:

> . . . You taught us to love the world and the people we met in our daily life . . . . You taught us to love those who are different. . . . You taught us to love and appreciate the experiences and outlooks that living in India provided. . . . A deep spiritual life within the family has been formative and lasting. (107-10)

Burkhalter Martha (GC) Perhaps, more anecdotes have been written *about* than *by* this exuberant, unmarried missioner who, among other distinct actions, adopted an Indian baby girl Dilasie. She often was the lone westerner living on a 'station' (mission property). During her forty-one years in India (1917-59) she lived in five different locations, doing medical, women's, and evangelistic work. She was most well-known as an educator. Burkhalter taught and was principal of the Girls School in Janjgir (Funk Memorial School, named for missioner Annie Funk who sank with the famous *Titanic* ship), was Bible School Principal at Janjgir, and taught a variety of courses at Union Biblical Seminary at Yeotmal (Church History, the Gospel of Matthew, Public Speaking, Lay Leadership, English Rhetoric and Composition). Students loved her vivid, dramatic methods of teaching, her clear conviction as a Bible teacher.

Burkhalter was known to have jumped from a two-wheeled, ox-pulled tonga in which she was riding to hail a train's engineer to stop the train, where the road crossed the tracks with the gates down, for her to board the main Bengal-Nagpur railroad line that she had missed at a station. Her minimal regard for being punctual followed an Indian cultural pattern—known as "in the mean time."

In an account from Burkhalter a child named Shushila asks her Christian mother why they were not getting lots of new clothes at Diwali celebration time as were other children. "Because Hindus worship Lakshmi the goddess of wealth with Diwali, your friends receive new saris and bracelets. You need to wait until Christmas time to receive your gift," her mother replied.

Conrad, Paul (MC), a doctor who cared for the whole person including the mind was thanked in a statement shared at the time of his death by his children and grandchildren for his "courage, humility, and simple living." When in India for fifteen years he had told his children that he was in India for his beliefs. "Not necessarily to change the beliefs of others, he tried to make one small part of the world a somewhat better place" he said.

Duerksen, Christena (Harder) **and Jacob R.** (GC) Christena's *Come with Me 19 Children's Stories*. (Newton, KS: Faith and Life Pr, 1971). Duerksens' personal diaries appear in Box 1-117, folder 2 at the Mennonite Library and Archives, Bethel College, North Newton, Kansas.
Married in 1924 the Duerksen couple left for India in 1926.

Christena describes in one children's story a period of severe lack of rain. The village *gauntize* (owner) gathered objects from villagers to offer as worship to Indra the god of thunder. He suggested that due in part to Indian Christians having left their former Hindu practices and patterns of worship, such evils had befallen them all. Duerksen describes the action taken to appease god Indra. A hole was dug with bamboo sticks dropped into it. After a canopy of mango leaves topped the sticks, stalks of a banana tree were added. Participants bathed and then gathered around the hole made into a worship place. The priest started a fire before reciting mantras and reading sacred scriptures. Clarified butter, coconut, and puffed rice were thrown into the fire before the offerings gathered by the villagers.

Ruth Unrau's chapter about Christena in *Encircled Stories of Mennonite Women*[2] reports that on occasion Christena was invited to have tea with the *rani* (queen) of Korba State. Ever interested in children, the *rani* always gave Christena a parting gift to share. Aware that Christena chose to identify with Indian women by wearing the sari, the *rani* gave her a white silk sari with a border of gold thread. At the time of Christena's death, she was buried in that white silk sari, a "symbol of love that flowed to her and from her." (221, 225)

While Jacob's tribute to early missioner P. A. Penner given at Penner's memorial service includes no reference to Hinduism, a few details from Hindu events, people, or issues appear in the Duerksen diaries. For example, from the 1933 record:

January 18 – Village Hindu folk were preparing for a feast during which Duerksens expected to hear "much *tamasha*" (hoopla, chaos, noise, confusion, and excitement).

February 19 – Christina and Dr. Ella enjoyed a visit with the Hindu *rani* (regional queen). . . . .The Saraipali area king had granted space for GC missioners to locate in 1900. Contact with royal family members continued for decades with missioners.

March 24 – Big day at the Hindu Savarak's home—the day when their little girl receives her name and eats her first rice.

March 31 – Sub Inspector 'brother' and Mahendar Singh came to talk about religion. Steps toward God, according to a Hindu, were explained—likely the doctrine of Hindu reformers *Arya Samajists*.

April 24 - Because of caste irregularities, no one was willing to help a poor woman bury her husband.

Ediger, Tina Block (GC)[3] – After returning to Kansas from work at Yeotmal Seminary, an ecumenical school in India where Mennonites attend and serve on staff, Block Ediger welcomed a Hindu Indian woman who arrived to study at Wichita State University. Their friendship deepened. The Hindu woman earned a Master's degree in City Planning. She valued teaching and learning with Block Ediger. She discussed details: from an abundance of pillows on a bed to prayer before meals and worship at church. Block Ediger learned about fatalism when the guest's friend was killed; Indian family adjustments when her friend married a man of lower caste than she; and living one's faith without "pushing" another to change her religious loyalty.

Friesen, John A. (MC) was born in 1915 in India to P. A. and Helena Friesen (Evangelical Mennonite Brethren). Lena died in India when John was a child. Friesen reports that in 1922 his father married

> **Florence Cooprider** (MC). She had completed medical school in 1914 (one of two first women to be graduated from the University of Illinois', Chicago, medical school). A missioner doctor in India from 1916-1941, she filled a great need and was known for roadside clinics for which she made use of an empty travelers 'home-built' bungalow.

Indians and missioners alike credit John with outstanding facility with the Hindi language.[4] After seventeen years as missioners with Hindus and Muslims burdened with leprosy, John and **Genevieve** (in India together from 1939-1981) moved from the Dhamtari area to Allahabad in the 1960s. They always worked to break down religious or cultural barriers faced by leprosy patients in communities.

Among Friesens' anecdotes in archival documents (HM I – 954, Mennonite Church USA Archives, Goshen, IN) appear the following:

- "In India the Pipal (pronounced "people") tree is known as a sacred tree of Hindu meditation, or a place of enlightenment and awareness of God."

- In a letter appears reference to Gopal-pur on Sea, a fishing village south of Calcutta with a large beach area but of no religious significance (compared to the Hindu city of Puri not far away). Those who swim along the coast are escorted by a *nulia* (boatman and personal 'lifeguard'). The grace of sailing boats, called catamarans, impressed Friesen at dawn as did a group of forty fishermen mending their nets spread out on the sand.

- A stranger disappeared after a Sunday worship service to appear later at Friesen's bungalow intent to talk.

  Sahib (Mister), I would like to become a Christian—but there's one thing, sir. I come from a high caste and so for me to become a Christian will involve considerable sacrifice. My relatives would no longer receive me; hence, I must be assured of some employment, and, sir, not just anything. I would not care to be a gardener or a night watchman—make me a preacher!—perhaps even a superintendent over the preachers!

  Friesen responded:

  Dear friend, you are a total stranger, but already I see that we share nothing in common in Christ. I could not baptize you. . . . Christ is to you a deal, a bargain—to me a passion. . . .Sorry!

After years of observing, Friesen humbly reflects on MC hypocrisy and Christian *persecution*. The latter is part of Christian heritage in India due to a small group of radical Hindu fundamentalists who counter religious minorities. It "signals the need to change the way we witness, educate and live so that people can be stronger in evangelism." Friesen also comments on how missioner "legalism and rigid approach" to being "strict disciplinarians" hindered a "spirit of fellowship" for MC Indian members.[5] He wishes that missioners had more wisely "fit into the total Christian witness of India."

Funk, Annie C. (GC) Not that Funk wrote about Hinduism, she is distinctly known among missioners. She left India a year earlier than planned due to her mother's poor health in the U.S. No one knew that she would travel on the prized but ill-fated *Titanic* ship that ran into an iceberg, from which many on board were drowned. A report has followed that Funk gave up her space on a life boat from the sinking ship to a young mother with her child. An effective educator, a reminder of Funk's commitment followed with the GC school at Janjgir later being named Funk Memorial School.

Funk, Irene (GC) died in India of acute leukemia. Knowing of her serious illness, many non-Christian Indians stopped to see her. A nurse and avid visitor, Irene had often stopped at their houses—slipping off her shoes and sitting cross-legged on a floor mat. She genuinely delighted in tea with peppery breads and sweetmeats. "Our children danced with joy on seeing her coming; she liked our food, the spicier the better" one Hindu reported to missioner <u>Ruth Ratzlaff</u>. Funk had been thrilled when invited to her cleaning lady's home to share a chicken; she knew that "poorer people often feel their homes are not good enough" Funk wrote. [6]

Graber, Lena (MC) told different age groups interesting stories from India when she was in the States on furlough. She reports enjoying riding by oxcart through jungles, safe from diverse wild animals. . . . Also:

- When giving nursing care for a paralyzed Hindu man with no legs, she found a man to assist with preparing his food. The helper placed the food on the man's plate but, due to caste differences, could not give him water or wash his dishes—those acts might pollute himself. . .
- Graber cared for one patient out under a tree because that patient was of a lower caste than three patients in beds in the same room inside the hospital. . . .
- Cow urine was a common treatment for sores among village folk. . . .
- Aware of Baptist missioner Dr. Edith Brown who had gone to Ludhiana, India, to train Indian woman doctors, Graber founded Schools of Nursing in Dhamtari, India (1950), and Kathmandu, Nepal (1959). She would see as many as 150 outpatients with diverse needs in a day, including religious mystics and *gurus* (teachers of sacred thought) from Nepali mountain areas. . .
- Graber describes how versatile she needed to be: "First I was the nurse, later perhaps the undertaker, and then the minister or counselor." . . .
- On the sixth day of life at the exact time declared by a horoscope a priest's task involved exposing a new Hindu infant for the first time to the sun; on the eleventh day the priest

wrote for the first time the name of the infant on a *pipal* leaf of a sacred tree. . . .

• Graber describes Christian witness in Nepal as "done only by hands and lives." When she asked a nurse midwife what influenced her to become Christian she said: "It was largely due to watching Christians at work. Nobody really asked me to become a Christian."

Haury, Samuel (GC) "Letters about the Spread of the Gospel in the Heathen World," *Mennonite Life*, (June 1979) 4-7. Also Institute of Mennonite Studies # 8, (Scottdale, PA: Herald Pr 1981) in which the Preface is dated 1877, followed by a current Introduction by <u>Wilbert R. Shenk</u> (MC).
Born in Germany and having transitioned to the USA in 1856, Haury (who later married Susie Hirschler) lived from 1847-1929. An early Mennonite mission publicist, he offered his tract (letters) to all Mennonites in North America. Haury addressed his letters to a fictitious "Dear Friend." With a strong vision for mission, he thought Mennonites lacked spiritual vitality. By contrast, his motives for a pre-modern, fundamentalist mission endeavor included: love for and debt of gratitude toward God, intent to fulfill biblical prophecy, a sense of Christ's return, and duty to "the heathen." Convinced that all mankind is God's offspring, Haury believes that each person is created by God for salvation; each seeks a redeemer. Haury explains for example, that when even a deprived person "throws himself down before an idol," that indicates the presence of "religious impulse" within. (9, 5)

Holsopple, Mary Jacie (MC) A Hindu man who had waited a long time before asking for surgical help for shrunken eyelids came to the hospital at Dhamtari. Despite his delayed appearance for help, he was disappointed not to get complete recovery at once. Without money for the operation, he offered a large brass plate instead; the plate showed hard usage. Several days later his dilemma surrounded the fact that his family's supply of rice was almost depleted. (Instead of the hospital's supplying food for diverse patient diets, a family member stayed with the patient to prepare food for him or her.) The doctor had not yet released the patient who came to suggest: "Please keep as much of the price of the plate as necessary for the operation and give the rest to me so that I can buy some rice." The plate was returned to him; patients often could not pay fees, Holsopple reports.

India Calling – A newsletter sent from General Conference Mennonite Missioners active at locations named Surguja, Korba, Champa, Janjgir, Mauhadi, Jagdeeshpur, and Saraipali in Central Provinces in India.

Printed at the Mission Press (Methodist) in Jubbulpore, India, copies were mailed from Newton, Kansas, ("10 cents per copy per year including postage") to North American subscribers, from 1940-onward. The writer scanned newsletters from 1957-71 for references to Hinduism. (*Themes* appear in *italics*.)

- A missioner refers to a "long *tuft of hair*" on the top of each Hindu boy's head. 11-15-41. . . "A lad's long tuft of hair expresses his hope of salvation; by means of which he believes that the gods will carry him home to heaven." Summer 1956
- For the first time some Hindu boys made an urgent request to attend the *mission Middle School*, though they lived near to a government middle school. 1-30-42, p. 1
- A case of *suttee*, the Hindu rite in which a widow throws herself (or is forced) upon the pyre of the burning corpse of her dead husband, was witnessed by hundreds in Champa. p. 3
- A Hindu woman who was a patient in the Jagdishpur hospital for a serious condition *gifted* the board chairman with *Rs. 5.00*— enough, at that time, to pay three men for nine day's labor— toward building a new church. Missioner Jacob Duerksen directly responded with a prayer of thanks.
- Although missioners move around freely, conditions are not "normal" due to heavy *war clouds*. 4-15-42
- To kill a "baby beef" prompts ire so fierce among Hindu neighbors that a culprit's usefulness might end. Gandhi suggests that *reverence for a cow* compares to that for a mother.
- Hindus never allow a loved one to *die* on a bed; the one dying is put on the floor. 8-15-43
- Gandhi – "*Conversion* is the deadliest poison that ever sapped the fountain of truth." 2-20-45, p. 1 . . . India denounces conversion. In many places the one who changes faith awaits a jail sentence. 10-46, p. 3
- "You can find almost every *doctrine* in Hinduism that Christianity proclaims, but ethics and holiness are winked at or ignored." 10-46, p. 3
- Many missioner anecdotes reflect realities of the *caste system*:
  - A caste *guru* (religious leader) faulted a man for continuing to eat with his granddaughter whose father had become a Christian.
  - An employer said to a newly baptized person: "You have dishonored the caste and blotted our religion. Leave work immediately."
  - A critical situation transpired in a Mennonite boarding school when caste Hindu boys moved out because an outcaste fellow began to eat and live among them.

- Caste restrictions are crumbling, especially in cities, but a rural, orthodox Hindu may go thirsty rather than accept water from a lower-caste person.
11-15-41; 1-30-42; 6-47; 3-19-56.
- *Woodstock School* – where children of most GC missioners attend boarding school. At times entire issues of *India Calling* are devoted to Woodstock (as 1-24-62). Not about Hinduism, many children emulate their parent's commitment, their returning to India to serve God. . . . Family "separation is often harder on the parents than on children." 1-22-60.
- **Wenger, Adah** [7] "Christmas in India." Fall 1951, 3-4.
Wenger writes about Indians' love for *festivals*. With many gods to remember or serve, Hindus have countless religious festivals. By contrast, Christians celebrate few holidays. Hindus, with religious significance attached to most every act of life, ever celebrate, Wenger writes. Non-Christians celebrate through fasting and feasting, decoration, processions, drumming, dancing, dramas, ceremonial bathing, offerings to gods, gift-giving, lights and fires, and through pilgrimage to distant, holy places. Christians need more events or joyous activities to replace that earlier abundance of celebration, Wenger believes.
- Due to a developing steel industry at Korba, the local GC Mennonite congregation becomes *ecumenical*. Worshippers might include Anglican, recent Roman Catholic converts, Nepali Christians, a few non-Christians, and people from the Mar Thoma church of south India. 1-27-64 (Mar Thoma is a group perhaps founded by Jesus' disciple St. Thomas who, with traders, went to India to preach the gospel; they were later known as Syrian Christians.) *IC* Winter 1950
- In the village of Boirmal Hindus urged the Indian Christians to join them in making *offerings to Hindu gods*. When the Christians explained why they could not cooperate, Hindus grew angry and severed friendship and business ties with those Christians, causing, for some, critical financial problems. 1-29-66
- When Indian Christians invited Hindus to their *Thanksgiving Service*, as usual the Hindus refused. Negotiations for reconciliation took place that afternoon until 2 a.m. when friendship was restored. Together Christians and many Hindus gathered the following day to celebrate Harvest bringing along peanuts, sugarcane, eggs, chickens—whatever to express joy and thanks to God.
- The September 1947 issue of *India Calling* includes reports from *August 15, India's Independence Day*. The public holiday lengthened into three days with parades, public programs,

sporting and tree-planting events, speeches and unfurling the tri-color flag. The flag has horizontal orange, white, and green stripes to symbolize sacrifice, peace and well-being with a dark blue spinning wheel symbol in the very center.

- The first page of the December 1947 issue of *IC* includes notice of Dr. **Ella Bauman's** receiving letters from New Delhi asking her to help with medical work among *Hindu refugees*—two camps of 60,000 each—in Punjab State. The request expressed need "for strong doctors who can cope with such a situation." A note adds that a Mr. M. Diener worked among refugees in Amritsar.
- On the occasion of Mahatma *Gandhi's death* a memorial service was held in Bilaspur for people of that region to attend. Readings from three great religions present in the area of Central Province were included—portions from the *Gita* were read in Sanskrit, from the *Koran* in Arabic or Persian, and from the *Bible* (Sermon on the Mount and I Cor. 13) in English. Twenty tributes were given; hymns and chants were sung in English, Hindi, or Urdu. A closing statement expressed the principles for which Gandhi lived and died. March 1948
- *Homes* of non-Christians consist of an elderly couple with their married sons and families— "joint family living." Spring 1951
- A *pregnant* Hindu mother was mistreated, perhaps in less-than-clean conditions by a less-informed caregiver, while trying to give birth at her home. After complications developed she was brought to the GC Mennonite hospital. With such circumstances the mother often needs to stay longer than Christian women who trust the institution for care. Spring 1955, 3-4
- In *"The Basic Beliefs of Hinduism"* J. N. Banerjea explains a photo of the god form named Krishna as "a divine youth playing on the flute while ravishing the hearts of his companions— cowherd boys and lasses, even cows.". . . A Hindu is heard to have said on hearing the story of the Cross: "If God is like that, He can have my heart." . . . A prominent Hindu lady in South India said, "Rama and Krishna adorn the wall; Jesus abides in the heart." Spring 1958, 8-9
- GC missioner **Helen Kornelsen** tells the story of **Jai Singh Bagh's** writing "Village Man for Village Task." Jai Singh Bagh was from a family of *snake charmers*, magicians, and spirit worshipers. Already at the age of fourteen he had a thorough knowledge of Hindu scripture taught by his grandmother. She was his good teacher of both occult arts and Hindu mythology. Jai Singh had been introduced into the world of magic and spirits soon after a cholera epidemic caused thirty-six area deaths. Rites and incantations proved to be of little help to appease the angry

spirits. Such lack of power frightened Jai Singh, a firm blow to his faith in spirits. When several years later Jai Singh learned of an itinerant Christian *sadhu's* (holy man) visit to a nearby village, he became curious. A large crowd had gathered in the village of Cana when Jai Singh, his wife and two children arrived. Impressed with the preaching and prayer, he chose to become a Christian. Eventually his wife, father and later mother were also baptized. After being trained in scripture Jai Singh (having added the name Bagh) returned to his village of Boirmal to share his changed experience with his own people. 30-2-67

- **Hakim B. Singh Rahi** and two other graduates from the ecumenical *seminary* at Yoetmal went to the Phuljhar region to work among Hindus, Sikhs, and Jains in general and the reformed Hindus called Satnamis in particular. Among the thousand folk who listened to the gospel, prompt results in homes were not visible. But to observe Hindus listening to the message and singing Christian songs encouraged the former students. Fall 1970, p. 11

India Mission News is a newsletter sent from Mennonite Church missioners in India to subscribers in North America.

- Gangadashura is a day for worship of the Ganges River. Some Hindus believe that King Bhagirath brought the Ganges down from heaven to enable salvation for ancestors. Through bathing in the river, giving alms to the poor, or pouring water on one's head the festival continues. 6-6-26

- Some missioners wrote of their dislike for Holi festival; they avoided being included among the revelers. While some Hindus draw from an ancient story and practice for Holi, others see the hilarious occasion as mainly an opportunity for throwing colored powders on each other. A historic account tells of people gathering wood for a fire around which they marched, throwing sweet-smelling objects into it to purify them while singing lewd songs. All squirted deep purple color onto others.

  An original account, according to a missioner, suggests that a father, unable to persuade his son to worship the same god form as he, asked a daughter named "Holi" to sit in the fire with the son. Since the daughter, not the son, was consumed, the day is observed to remember Holi. 4-4-26

Kornelsen, Helen (GC) Tape 266.97 # 14, interviewed by James Juhnke 1977, Bethel College Archives, Newton, Kansas.
Kornelsen first went to India in 1948. Brief references to Hinduism from Kornelsen's prime focus on *education* make clear her identification with

India. Her education roles included supervision of district primary schools in Hindi medium, teaching at Jansen Memorial Secondary School, and instructor in the Christian Education department at Union Biblical Seminary in Yeotmal. Although aware of Hindu superstition and fears, plus concern for girls to marry by age 11-12 after which they remain obligated to a mother-in-law, Kornelsen encouraged that girls have opportunity for school experience. Or she trained some herself.

Kornelsen's work with women, frequently living in a tent for three-week periods, found her making friends in either Christian or Hindu homes. Often driven out from higher-caste groups, Christians lived in a separate, low-caste part of a village. Along with sharing the Christian message among whoever welcomed her, Kornelsen taught nutrition, simple medical procedures, and anti-liquor habits.

Kornelsen wrote about **Mathuria Bai** ("A Mother to Phujhar Mathuria Bai 1885-1964)" in *Full Circle Stories of Mennonite Women.* [8] Mathuria Bai's father was a "very zealous orthodox priest" who traveled extensively to holy places like Benares or the Jaganath temple near Puri. He would return from Benares with holy water from the Ganges River to use with rituals. When orphaned, Mathuria was taken to a Christian orphanage at Bilaspur where, when assigned as a boarding student to "apply cow dung to the courtyard floor," she refused. Her Brahman background limited her from doing such a task. She eventually married a Christian orphan fellow named Isa Das; they later joined the GC Mennonite Church. Despite opposition from high-caste people of the village of Sukhri, they proved to be effective leaders with Christian groups, Kornelsen reports.

Lapp, George J. (MC) Reporting about leprosy in India, Lapp credits certain tenets of Hinduism as reason for Hindu people to be indifferent. For a person to be infected with leprosy indicates that person's "appointed lot." The hope follows to be born into a more fortunate condition in the next incarnation, Lapp observes.

Lapp, Sarah (MC) tells of a Hindu man who brought his wife for care for a health condition. They had already gone to different Hindu shrines where they offered rupees plus a plot of land. They had made sacrifices to the priest who prayed and read Hindu *Shastras* on their behalf; during one period the priest read for them every day for three weeks. After Sarah's medical care and her husband Mahlon Lapp's laying hands on the woman with prayer, she healed. The couple then invited Lapps to their village to explain faith in Jesus.

Sarah Lapp also reports (*IMN* October 1931) about a widow named Parvati (name of one of the Hindu god Shiva's wives) from near the village of Balodgahan. Very committed to her Hindu religion, she had made pilgrimages to famous shrines and sacred places such as the source of the Ganges River. From Hardwar where the railroad line ends, she had walked for two weeks into the Himalaya Mountains enduring great hardship and spending over Rs. 300 for travel, gifts to priests, and idols. Near a temple she experienced a heaven-sent vision of God in the form of three idols. . . . Calling daily on God she also listens carefully when missioners speak of Jesus, Lapp says.

Mosher, Arthur (GC) describes Hindus as people of multiple religious features who share common elements of Indian origin. For most of them the will or power of God is personified in many gods and goddesses. For Hindus the water of rivers is deified and, because milk improves health, the cow is considered sacred. Beliefs in caste, spirits, and transmigration of the soul are central; with the latter a soul occupies different bodies in succession. All creatures are thought to be sacred because God is within each one.

Naik, Tushar (GC) http://www.mennonitemission.net/Stories/News/Pages/NewChristianschool; 2 pp.
Dr. Naik reports about St. Stephen's Model School begun in 2008. It is now located on the ground floor of the 50-bed Sewa Bhawan Hospital at Jagdeeshpur, the hospital where he currently is surgeon. Dr. Kanchan Naik, Tushar's wife, manages OB-GYN needs at the same location. Through English instruction by teachers of all faiths, Christian stories and morale-building stories of other faiths add to this new "seedbed" of instruction for doctors.

Ratzlaff, Harold & Ruth (GC) The Ratzlaffs served in India from 1940-76. They tell of a young man's great interest in the Gospel, who, on telling his family and friends, was persecuted and beaten in attempts to dissuade him. He begged for baptism. Further,
- Harold reports dealing with a "rash of marriage problems." Evidently some Christians had not shifted far from their experience of Hinduism to understand the sanctity of marriage.
- Ruth was convinced that "We Christians must know about Hinduism in order to make our religion effective, to know how to approach people." She wonders if missioners are at times "stumbling blocks" for confused Indians.
- A Hindu village owner's wife who had been treated at the hospital came to a church service to express thanks. She walked to the front to give Rs. 5 for the building fund.
- Observing a Hindu *mela*, Ruth concluded that most people were present to buy and sell, not for a religious purpose. On entering a nearby temple she saw gods and people making offerings to

them. "Oh my," she wrote, "there was nothing cleansing about it, nothing made them 'new' that I could see."

- Harold attended the International Missionary Conference held near Madras (Tambarum) in 1938. He received encouragement for indigenous mission areas.

- When Ruth asked her Hindu peon to bring her some eggs from the bazaar, he returned along with a woman coolie to carry the eggs. Eggs were something the peon would not touch.

- Harold's Masters Thesis is titled *Planting a Church in India*. Without references to Hinduism, it focuses on three topics: the "History of the Founding of the GC Church, the Organizational Structure of the Hindustani Conference (1922), and Future Actions for the Church Program."

Sell, Blanche (MC) When on furlough Sell spoke to diverse groups like children of 6-8th grade and the Middlebury, Indiana, annual World Day of Prayer meeting. For the latter, that year's program had been created by ecumenical women from India. She told of her "dear friends, Christian and non-Christian" in India: Kejai Bai—a Bible woman, hospital housekeeper, and prayer partner with Blanche; Lucy—a Christian peacemaker who in the hospital setting shared daily prayers with Hindu patients like Ram Shankar; and Mohinar. Mohinar, a nurse faithful to the Sikh religion, lived with Blanche when they taught nurses in Indore. They often talked and prayed together, but "Mohinar never saw a need to become Christian." Sell describes Mohinar as one who worked with people of all castes and faiths. She reported the terrible time of Partition, when she found her good Muslim neighbor dead. Mohinar had also shared with Sell how she suffered when one of her own Sikh faith killed Prime Minister Indira Gandhi.

Sell showed those who listened to her talks pictures of Hindu gods and goddesses—of Lakshmi goddess of wealth; god Shiva known as the destroyer; Parvati, Kali, Hanuman, and Ginesh. She explained Hindu worship patterns; reincarnation; yoga as one path to God, and *Sarwanaudlal*— belief that all ways lead to God (as through Jesus).

Theodore, Caroline Banwar (GC) "Saying Yes to Need Caroline Banwar
Theodore 1901-1952," in *Encircled Stories of Mennonite Women*
by Ruth Unrau. (Newton, KS: Faith and Life Press, 1986) 255-60.
Banwar Theodore, though born into an Indian, German Baptist home, moved with her parents to Champa when invited by missioner P. A. Penner (GC) to be house parents for healthy children of patients being treated for leprosy. The first, therefore overworked, doctor in the Champa dispensary, Banwar was soon joined by doctors Ella and Harvey Bauman (GC) for ten years; she often spent evenings in the Bauman

home. Unrau notes that there was no hospital for people when Banwar arrived. However, due to Hindu care for the sacred cow, two "cow hospitals" cared for old bovines.

In addition to women patients Banwar was befriended by the *rani* (queen) of Korba State, Unrau states. Not only was her family invited to stay in the palace guest house, the *rani* gifted Banwar with the village of Banjari. That meant that taxes owed by villagers were sent to Dr. "Caro." Both Christian and non-Christians attended her wedding; she married Dr. Harold Theodore who persuaded her to go into private practice. That practice offered better income; she was also free to treat both women and men. A cerebral stroke led to her death—"too soon and too cruelly" Unrau adds. (260)

Thiessen, John (GC) "Kilari" in *Fellowship in the Gospel, India 1900-50,* compiled and edited by Ruth Ratzlaff.[9]
Under a large "peepul" tree lay a bluish stone with a small red stone (referred to as the eye) on top. A goddess named Kilari was known as the protector of travelers and vehicles. People stopped to offer a coconut (often used for worship) to the image by the road. Breaking the coconut on the stone and pouring its milk over the little red stone while bowing very low three to four times, a worshipper cut the coconut into small pieces to pass around to anyone near. Eating the same kept Kilari in a good mood to protect them, Thiessen understood. For Christians nearby or riding a bus that was stopped for this rite, the question surfaced about whether to receive and eat—thereby recognize Kilari. If Kilari were offended, a bus conductor could become angry or blame any trouble en route on one who had refused the sacred gift of coconut.

Waltner, Vernelle S. (GC) "The Bethsada Homes and Hospitals" in *Fellowship in the Gospel, India 1900-1950,* compiled and edited by Ruth Ratzlaff, 76-84.
Waltner explains why a missioner who helped a person with leprosy was viewed as great. Hindus called a person with leprosy an outcaste; a person who lived with such a person was to be penalized. People with leprosy were not to make purchases in shops either, Waltner adds. (78)

Weaver, Irene Lehman (MC) "'A New Day in Mission': Irene Weaver Reflects on Her Century in Ministry," by Lynda Hollinger-Janzen in *Missio Dei* 8, (Elkhart, IN: Mennonite Mission Network, 2005).
Lehman Weaver, daughter of missioners Lydia and M. C. Lehman, reports playing inside their Dhamtari compound (property) as a three-year–old. A troop of elephants stopped when going by. A *rajah* (Indian prince) traveling with his entourage noticed her and invited her to have a ride. Seated between the *rajah* in his gold and blue chair and the

mahout (driver), she watched the latter lead the elephant by pulling its ears or prodding it with a stick. The Lehman family remained friends with that *rajah* who later sent Irene a pony.

Not with direct reference to Hinduism, Lehman Weaver, who died in 2014 at age 103, lists ten principles for ministry, the final one being to "love people into God's kingdom."

Wiens, Norma (GC) While her husband **Wendell** served as surgeon at the Sewa Bhawan Hospital at Jagdeeshpur in central India, Norma filled diverse roles: mentoring in music, community efforts, relating with Indian pastors' wives, and encouraging Indian leadership development. . . . She describes a procession to a *mela* (large gathering) and the occasion when a Hindu friend went to the city of Allahabad to scatter the ashes of her son who had died at the age of 12. That mother had "prayed to the Christian god" with the promise that if her son's health returned, his father would become a Christian.

Wiens, Peter J. (GC) "How the Gospel First Came to Phuljhar."
        Manuscript Collections Box 2, # 14 Folder, Mennonite Library
        and Archives, Bethel College, North Newton, KS.
Wiens, who served in India from 1906-37 tells about Ramadas who watched his bearded father busy weaving. Ever since the day that his parents, aunt and uncle had been baptized, their neighbors and other relatives treated them like outcastes. No longer did they offer his father water to wash his feet or provide him a seat of honor, as before. Two years earlier two strangers had come by offering several sacred books, different from their usual Hindu ones. Living some distance away, the 'pale-faced' man and Indian preacher returned only on occasion. But having understood the literature, Ramadas' father no longer felt that he needed or wanted to wear his Hindu string of beads, Wiens noticed.

Peter Wiens reports that "Hindoos often tried quack remedies" before seeing a missioner doctor. A common practice "burned out the devil that caused the disease"; bad burns only added to the disease, however. Elaborate ceremonies based on superstition were conducted at the time of a smallpox epidemic, with an offended god perhaps taken to the edge of a village.

Yoder, Jonathan G. (MC) One day Jonathan enjoyed a conversation with an educated Hindu who knew a lot about Christianity. During their next meeting Yoder asked the same man about Hinduism. He learned more about basing hope for salvation on "excellence of works." Results from personal works (merit), not prayer to God for help, would lead to an eventual response. Hinduism does not promote an idea of *grace*. Through his belief in reincarnation, the friend explained his ultimate goal of being absorbed into the Great God. Without a concept of *immortality*, the man added that although he might spend the next life as a lower animal or as a better person, he might also lose identity entirely if absorbed into Brahma, his ultimate hope.

Dr. Yoder expresses the need for Divine Strength to meet any day's experience whether with such informal encounters or saying a teary "Good-bye" to the Yoder daughters when they left for boarding school. He called the latter occasion "one of our greatest crosses." Medical situations always called for strength. Yoder met a poor Hindu patient at the hospital who had been gored by a buffalo. The man's intestines came wrapped in a dirty cloth. That patient went home 'repaired' and returned later to gift Yoder with a quart of milk along with a compliment: "Your salt has stuck to me."

Writer not identified with the following anecdotes:

While receiving medical treatment in a village clinic a Hindu man from a distant village stayed in Indian Pastor Joel's home at night. When possible he joined to hear Joel teach in a Bible school. Reporting his experiences on returning to his village, his people expressed interest that Joel and others come to their village to teach them.

Holiday Season: 28 yearly holidays are faithfully observed by Hindus.
Diwali – Features of this ten day event include: schools closed for two weeks; festival of lights: homes, shops, and temples cleaned and "lavishly" lighted with small, oil (vegetable) lamps; Lakshmi, goddess of wealth honored. Gambling could also be part of 'worship.' With the end of another financial year declared by merchants and bankers, the time to balance accounts or get new stocks followed. Banks might also wash Rs (money) in milk to express worship. Or invitations were given for *"pan supari"* (betel leaf nut) to chew at home.
Dashera - Images of Rawan being killed by Ram are set up in every village. Then, with "heathenish" delight, the same are thrown down and destroyed.
Marais – Marai events of the district (region of thirty to forty miles) are held during each week of March. A Marai is an annual religious ceremony during which decisions are made regarding the location for market places for the next year. At such times village people bring idols to the bazaar or market place to do special homage to tribal or village gods. They also may bring dancing girls with drummers to provide noise and enhance a parade, carrying flags fastened to long bamboo poles. On occasion narrow irons might be thrust through a man's tongue or cheek. At one large bazaar with a Marai in process a few Christians might sell

religious books, only to have some immediately burned. *IMN* February 1926 and January 1929.

India Mission News
Items about the *village of Balodgahan* recur:
July 1923 - Balodgahan, a village where some Hindu owners already lived, was purchased in 1905 by the MC mission to provide land for newly-converted Christians who were turned out from their own villages.
September 1924 – Today is a Hindu holiday. The priest of Balodgahan told the people that he would make his customary "security" round at midnight to all Hindu worship places in the village if ten chickens were given to him. Only seven were received, so he refused to carry out his regular service.
By 1925 twenty-eight Christian families live in Balodgahan in close proximity with Hindus among whom caste difference is very strong. There too, non-Christian farmers may pressure Christians. For example, the Hindu village cow herder, hired by all to take cattle to near-by fields for daytime grazing, may refuse to graze cows owned by Christians who choose not to give sacrifices to the village idol. A missioner could be called to work out an agreement for such a conflict.
November 1934 – Of interest, not Hinduism, Christian workers from Balodgahan and stations nearby joined for a very profitable two weeks of Bible Study. Sarah Lapp taught the class on the books of Ezra, Nehemiah, and Esther; the Indian pastor Sukhlal taught the Psalms, and Milton Vogt taught Job and Bible Doctrines.

IMN July 1923 –
An illiterate Hindu woman asked to buy a scripture portion from an MC Bible woman. She reported that her former copy was "badly worn." Although she was unable to read it, she put it under her head every night believing that it would protect her from evil spirits. Such superstition even utilizes the power of the Gospel, a reporter concludes.

IMN July 1923 – The funeral for Mahlon C. Lapp was held in the mango orchard (MC property in Dhamtari) with missioners and 800 Indians attending—Christians, Mohammedans, and Hindus. The song "Under the Mango Tree" that appears as number 223 in the (MC) *Life Songs* # 1 hymnal was sung. "This poem was written (in January 1909 by Elsie Byler) and music composed (April 10, 1910) as a memorial to Jacob Burkhard, missionary to India." Copyright by John D. Brunk.

IMN July 1923 - "Our rice crop is yielding well." This plot was given to the church by a Hindu widow who owns five villages. The land was a Thank Offering for what missioners had done for her.

IMN February 1925 – One evening in Mahodi village while we were talking with a group of twenty-five men, two Brahmans (high-caste) appeared intent to argue that "All roads lead to God—Ram, Sita, Shiva, Krishna." We explained that our interest was not to argue but to present the great Preacher, Master, and Lord. The reporter notes the contrast of this occasion with a previous one when three men had come asking, "How can we break caste or be anti-caste?"

IMN March 1926 – Twenty-six teachers and missioners were entertained in a Hindu home by several Hindu teachers of the MC schools. The beautiful, tasty meal of eighteen different vegetarian dishes was prepared and served according to high-caste Hindu customs. Those eating sat on rugs placed on the well-swept earthen floor, used banana leaves for plates, tree leaves sewn together for cups, and their fingers for eating. That barefoot, scantily dressed men served the oriental meal is also reported.

IMN August 1926 – Doctors are often called to assist when care can no longer be expected to help. In spite of such circumstances, the reputation for white, western medical personnel must gradually be "built up." Rather than permit a wife to be examined by a male doctor, some Hindu husbands would rather let a wife die. Attitudes toward cleanliness also need to be promoted. . . .Earlier MC nursing superintendent Lena Graber wrote of delivering 117 babies during a year; with 25 the birthing process was "abnormal.". . . At times when a doctor enables a patient's recovery, a relative might say, "Your God saved him or her."

IMN January 1928 – The idea of regular attendance at a specific place and time for public worship is foreign to Indian Hindu custom. Worship within Hinduism is more individualized, either in a public temple or an altar area at home. This pattern plus frequent holidays with loud, colorful confusion, plus the occasional *mela* (large gathering) become high points of Hindu worship. The annual *mela* at Rudri (not far from Dhamtari) brings all castes together. Each good Hindu bathes in the Mahanadi River before offering a coconut and ghee (clarified butter) to the priest who is active in the crude temple there.

IMN February 1928 – Many Hindus honor the snake; few will kill one. By the time a child entered the hospital, rigor mortis had set in; she had been bitten by a poisonous cobra. Some believe that complete death does not occur for at least two days with snake bites.

IMN January 1929 – After parents of mixed-caste died, several Hindus of their village brought the couple's two daughters to missioners and said: "Baptize these girls; we cannot accept them of mixed-caste origin."

IMN July 1932 – "A number of Christian widows have gone for a few days to visit among their Hindu relatives. To go back to former villages and meet old acquaintances means a great deal to them; they also use the occasion to witness for Jesus.

IMN November 1934 – A month earlier the one reporting had been to the village of Dane Sarai not far from Kurud. A Christian family owns a house there and fifteen acres of land. Eleven Hindu families that belong to the Oil-Makers Caste, some of whom relate with the Christian family, live there too. When visiting a friendly fellow named Chamru, leader of the Oil-Makers, a missioner asked about his interest in accepting Christ. Chamru responded, "What about my household? Could I be a Christian and keep my family together?" The reporter knew of his two wives.

---

[1] Published by the American Mennonite Mission, Dhamtari and printed by R. C. Davis at the Jubbalpore Mission Press (Methodist).

[2] Newton, KS: Faith and Life Press (1986) 213-26.

[3] The writer valued conversation with Block Ediger in Newton, KS, July 7, 2014.

[4] The writer tape recorded John and wife Genevieve (MC), missioners for forty-one years, as they alternate with Hindi and English to tell a delightful story about a parrot.

[5] J. Roger Kurtz "Mission in India: A Story of Three Generations," *Gospel Herald*, (October 25, 1983) 729-31.

[6] Helen Kornelsen "In Glad Service to Mankind: Irene Funk (1943-75)" in *Full Circle Stories of Mennonite Women*, Mary Lou Cummings, ed. (Newton, KS: Faith and Life Pr, 1978) 94-96.

[7] Missioner Adah went to India as the wife of Noah Burkhalter; he died there. After P. A. Wenger arrived to work in India he and Adah were married.

[8] Mary Lou Cummings, ed. 12-27. "Bai" is an honorific title given to women.

[9] Newton, KS: Mennonite Pub. Office, (1950) 58.

Theology of Religions

People who examine theology of religions—lived encounter among people and communities of diverse religions—often discuss a typology of exclusive, inclusive, and pluralist options. Each person expresses bias through any perspective. While very few of the materials annotated here directly engage Hindu thought or practice, they convey ideas prevalent among Christians who relate with Hindus and those loyal to diverse religions. Such ideas have clearly influenced interreligious rapport or discontent, including among Mennonites with Hindus. The writer's bias is that future interfaith well-being hinges on honest personal conviction alongside openness to the Wisdom of difference.

Adrian, Victor. (MB) "Jesus and the Religions of the World," *Direction* (23, no. 1 Spring 1994) 29-43.
Along with evangelical Christians' need to understand other religions, "we need to know what we believe about Jesus and how He relates to world religions" declares Adrian. He describes *syncretism* as an attempt to create a universal religion without due attention to unique aspects. While Adrian's view negates religious pluralism and inclusivism, some pluralists or inclusivists might question segments of his descriptors of their stance. Ideas for readers to endorse, critique, or question:
>Cooperation among world religions is difficult if one religion claims an absolute savior.
>New insight into world religions may cause Christians to credit values of other religions.
>World religions have centered more on human efforts to save themselves—self-redeem, self- justify, self-sanctify—than on *God's* efforts to save.
>Pluralists move from a distinct understanding of God's revelation in Jesus Christ to a theocentric view where God becomes distant, a mystery that makes relative a claim for Jesus as the only way to that Mystery.
>The logic of pluralism has ended in despair about any true knowledge of God!
>There is something radically exclusive in the Christian claim that Jesus is the only way to God, that outside of Him there is spiritual darkness and death.

Brunk, George III. (MC) "The Exclusiveness of Jesus Christ," in *Jesus Christ and the Mission of the Church, Contemporary Anabaptist Perspectives.* Erland Waltner, ed. (1990) 1-23, plus responses.

Finger, Thomas. (MC) "A Mennonite Theology for Interfaith Relations," in *Grounds for Understanding Ecumenical Resources for Responses to Religious Pluralism.* S. Mark Heim, ed. (Grand Rapids: Eerdmans 1998) 69-92.
Finger reviews the 1994 Mennonite conference on religious pluralism, an event sponsored by Mennonite Central Committee. Annotations offer background for understanding frequent Mennonite resistance to religious pluralism, to their seeing Hinduism as "other." Finger presents four historic Anabaptist Affirmations that shape thought toward other religions. To those four he adds three more current, Mennonite guidelines for interfaith relations. Then follow two issues that Finger himself identifies for the context of interreligious dialogue. In the process he suggests that three of the main conference speakers—John Toews (MB), J. Denny Weaver (GC), and Gayle Gerber Koontz (GC) who primarily presented John Howard Yoder's (MC) material—endorsed a more traditional view of Jesus as norm while Gordon Kaufman (GC) presented an open, more pluralist stance. The Affirmations begin:

1. Jesus Christ, including his specific teachings, example, and way of life, provides the ultimate norm for all human living.
2. Peace, sharing, and justice are central to this normative way.
3. Jesus' way generally appeals more to the oppressed, marginalized, and poor than to others.
4. The greatest opposition to Jesus' normative way comes not from non-Christian religions but from perverted Christianity.
5. Approach other religions with open willingness to learn.
6. Emphasize and embody chiefly Jesus' story and his way.
7. Emphasize witness and respectful, open relationships in particular settings, not intent to discern or hasten history's overall course.
8. Can one seriously participate in interfaith relations without deep normative commitments?
9. "Kenotic lordship" (Finger's language and preference) functions within a Trinitarian dynamic.

Finger, Thomas N. (MC) "Mission Amid Other Religions and World-views," in *Christian Theology an Eschatological Approach*, Vol. II, by Thomas Finger. (Scottdale, PA: Herald Pr, 1989) 297-319.
Finger's two main sections in this chapter are titled: I. Approaches to the World Religions (*continuity* or *discontinuity*) and II. Christian Truth and Other Truths. (298, 308) If missioners were to connect with Hindus

on points where agreement already exists, such as that Jesus was a prophet, engagement would not lead to conversion, Finger says. Questions follow: whether the intent would be for Hindus to become more like Christians in common social tasks or whether each Hindu becomes a better Hindu. (302)

Without disclosing personal views, Finger gives extensive attention to Hendrik Kraemer's theology of fifty years earlier; that theology in turn builds on Karl Barth's. Kraemer concludes that God's presence in non-Christian religions does not lead directly to Christ. Although points of contact exist, Kraemer finds "no salvific continuity" between Christianity and Hinduism. Total intertwining between major religions and Christianity are impossible he says. (304, 306-07) Since some people ask if all religions might be moving toward a point of convergence or if any religion's basic claims might be compatible, Finger names possible patterns of unity through questions. Responses reflect bias: "Major religions are fundamentally incompatible. Christianity has a fullness which the others need and lack. 'Religious experience' is too varied to identify any common core among them. Jesus' lordship sets him primarily in opposition to other claims to ultimate truth." (310-14)

Finger, Thomas N. (MC) "What are Mennonites Saying about Religious
Pluralism?" *Mission Focus Annual Review* (vol. 1, 1993) 33-37.
Finger informs readers that, as the MC and GC representative to a study group with inter-faith concerns for the Faith and Order Commission of the US National Christian Council of Churches, he surveyed six Mennonite mission and service organizations. [1] His discussion of findings presents organizations from "apparently less to apparently more positive evaluations of pluralism."

Rosedale Mennonite Missions affirms that while non-Christian religions may hold and convey worthy ideas, they "do not provide a way of salvation." Only Christ saves.

The *Mennonite Brethren Board of Missions and Services* affirms "no other name but Christ's for salvation." It credits religious pluralism for both more tolerance as well as "destructive relativism." It commends exchange with Muslims, Hindus and Buddhists who are becoming neighbors "as long as the Gospel's uniqueness is not compromised."

Eastern Mennonite Missions affirms that since God works within other world religions, all people have knowledge of God. With conviction that other religions fail to provide salvation, EMM personnel, through word and deed, move toward their goal of "bringing together all things under Christ's rule." They therefore proclaim that "Jesus Christ is the only Savior and Lord." Finger notes EMM's dialogue in 1984 between Jewish and Mennonite scholars on themes of: salvation, Messiah, land, and covenant.

The *GC Mennonite Church's Commission on Overseas Mission* (COM) affirms Jesus Christ as "the only Saviour and Lord" while noting that to evangelize deals also with social issues like poverty or ecology, notes Finger. Study papers have shaped COM insight. Roelf Kuitse, Dutch Mennonite seminary professor of mission, endorses a theocentric (that God is ultimate, not Christ) and an "interreligious ecumenical" approach. It recognizes different Christologies within the potential for religious pluralism. Another paper that COM officials note was by Saphir Athyal, Indian seminary professor. It affirms Jesus' unique and final features alongside diverse ways that Asian Christians, with integrity, value religious pluralism and interreligious dialogue that avoids being evangelistic.

MC Mennonite Board of Missions affirms Jesus alone as "savior and lord of all people." It also notes that the Bible contains both insight into ultimate salvation in Jesus Christ and "the universal scope of God's salvation." Further, it credits what is positive in other religions. A paper by <u>Calvin Shenk</u>, MC missioner and professor, affirms: God's presence everywhere, "sparks of truth in all religions," and sensitive dialogue that does not abandon commitment to Christ. He comments on both cultural and religious pluralism, Finger says. All cultures are to be valued; none will be absolutized, Shenk says. He does not clarify his view of religious pluralism as "total relativization of ultimate religious truth-claims."

The agency *Mennonite Central Committee* 's purpose centers on service with disadvantaged folk, not starting churches as is true for the above agencies. Its workers expect to learn from those with whom they work, to promote increased dignity and self-reliance. Earl Martin, earlier MCC spokesman in Asia, affirms that because God is already present, where workers serve is Holy Ground. Workers intend to communicate through local people of faith and life traditions, even when they differ from those of MCCers. While Martin finds God's shalom embodied in Jesus, MCC "calls Jesus the fullest revelation of God."

Finger observes in conclusion that Mennonites seem open to work, dialogue, and find truth with adherents of other religions. While "they appear open to acknowledge various paths to Christ, Christ still seems to be the one saving path to God."

Friesen, Duane K. (GC) "A Discriminating Ethic in the Context of Religious Pluralism" in *Artists Citizens Philosophers Seeking the Peace of the City*. (Scottdale, PA: Herald Pr, 2000) 259-78. Friesen's article which reflects on his book appears in *Mennonite Life* (55, no. 1, March 2000).

A teacher of a course on Eastern Religions at Bethel College, Newton, Kansas, Friesen critiques two points of Hinduism: how some of its forms "legitimate a static social system (caste)" and the belief that "all religions (many paths) point to the same goal." Presumably his writing about religious pluralism refers indirectly to Hinduism and other specific religions through more general statements. Annotations nearly quote Friesen's ideas that shape a person's view of a religion like Hinduism.

- The world has always been religiously pluralistic. (258)
- The presence of pluralism generates the growth of religious *"fundamentalism,"* a phenomenon practiced in most religious traditions. Friesen notes four dimensions of a fundamentalist worldview: belief in the infallibility of one's own scriptures or dogma; desire to create a disciplined community often organized in patriarchal and hierarchical order; desire to convert other people to one's own, presumed "true" belief system; resistance to modernization and lack of tolerance for religious diversity. . . . Authoritarian fundamentalism—which asserts the truth of one's own faith and falsity of other faiths— and relativism are similar in many ways Friesen adds. (259, 261)
- We can learn from and respect others as others without absorbing them into our own system. . .
  Relating with people of other faiths depends upon the acceptance and affirmation of one's own particularity, not a denial of it. (262)
- The church's task is to be faithful, to "sow seeds," not convert others. . . . People become Christians when they are inwardly convinced by the truthfulness and significance of the story of God's restoration of life in all dimensions. (263)
- The church begins relating to people of other faiths with repentance (as for failure to recognize wisdom in their faith, for anti-Judaism, or for valuing Constantine's Christianity). (264-5)
- Through listening to and seeing God in the other we connect our particular vision of life with the vision, practice, and truthfulness of others. (268-9)

Friesen, Duane K. (GC) "The Discernment of Wisdom in the Encounter between the Christian Faith and People of Other Religious Faiths," *Mission Focus: Annual Review*, (vol. 8, 2000) 119-37.
Segments from the previous article appear here too. Although pluralism has been part of the world scene for centuries, more Mennonites have come to *new awareness* of it, Friesen observes. (120) He explains principles in succinct ways: how similar authoritarianism and relativism can be; how good relationship across religions respects the mystery of the other person; how, for Christians, Jesus Christ becomes the metaphor for understanding God. He notes what Christian mission is not—intent to convert others, to persuade others of their need for salvation through confession of Jesus, or their need to believe a set of

doctrines. He nudges Christians to listen to, learn from, and see God in the other; to use reason to faithfully repent of or test their own paradigms in conveying the story of God's action in Christ, and to rely on God's spirit to transform each person's life—their own and other's.

Theology of religions prompts distinct features: different methods of dialogue to know and complement difference, claiming and confession of paths and practices, change perspectives, and growth in the ability to judge what is valid or authentic. As Friesen might critique the law of karma, doctrine of reincarnation, or potential for stagnancy within the caste system of Hindu practice, he calls Christians to assess their own stereotyped treatment of "the Jews." He with vision explains what being "in Christ" is: "to enter into a relationship of love with another in which both parties are open to the possibility of being changed by one's engagement with the other." (136)

Harder, Gary. (GC) "The Uniqueness of Christ," *Mennonite Reporter* (April 16, 1990) 9-10.

Koontz, Gayle Louise Gerber. (GC) *Confessional Theology in a Pluralistic Context: A Study of the Theological Ethics of H. Richard Niebuhr and John Howard Yoder*. PhD Dissertation, Boston University 1985. Gerber Koontz drew heavily from this study of Yoder (MC) in her lecture published as "Evangelical Peace Theology and Religious Pluralism: Particularity in Perspective," *The Conrad Grebel Review* (14, no. 1 Winter 1996) 57-89.

Theologian professor Gerber Koontz' admits that neither Niebuhr with a more open Theocentric focus nor Yoder with conviction for a Christocentric, more exclusivist, bias has had "extensive academic or personal encounter" with religious pluralism. (15, 187) Each, similar to Gerber Koontz, has given prime attention to the world of Christianity; none of the three has lived with nor presumed to directly engage Hinduism. Yet Gerber Koontz notes principles for relating with people of diverse religions from Yoder's writing. He prompts Christians to avoid saying to people of another culture that their culture or religion is fulfilled by yours. Avoid thinking that any culture fully satisfies all who experience it, and recognize that other religions (including presumably Hinduism) are superior at certain points without trying to prove that yours is better, Yoder suggests. Then too, Christians need not "talk about either uniqueness or displacement." They are to proclaim the grace of God in Christ, Gerber Koontz endorses from Yoder. (371-74)

Other writers have examined Yoder's view of world religions and pluralism. Joon-Sik Park[2] comments that Gerber Koontz rightly argues that what is crucially important to fruitful interreligious exchange for a confessional orientation like Yoder's is the passionate confession of religious convictions and an underlying, corresponding commitment to defenseless dialogue, which Yoder strongly called for, Park suggests. (22) Duane K. Friesen explains that, for Yoder in "*The Jewish-Christian Schism Revisited,* neither Jesus nor Judaism rejected the other.[3]

Koop, Karl. (GC) "Christianity and the Other Religions," *Mission Focus: Annual Review* (vol. 9 2001) 86-91.
Koop notes in discussing the theology of religions typology—exclusive, inclusive, pluralist—that those who have been in contact with different religions might admit that "the moral character of a Muslim, Hindu or Buddhist may be equal or even superior to that of a Christian." (87) He suggests that those holding an inclusive stance may, through God's grace mediated via a non-Christian religion, experience salvation whether or not Jesus Christ is confessed as Savior and Lord. Noting biblical texts that claim that both Jesus (John 17, Hebrews 1) and other faiths (Acts 10:34-36) provide ways to salvation, Koop cautions either refuting God's presence and work among people of other faiths or idealizing religions. (89)

Nyce, Dorothy Yoder. (MC) "Appendix: Texts of Influence," *Multifaith Musing: Essays and Exchange,* 139-48.
Yoder Nyce has written about the theology of religions typology in several places including pages 30-33 in *Multifaith Musing.* She looks into biblical texts like John 14:6 and Act 4:12 in the Appendix. Drawing on serious commentary by numerous writers she examines the important metaphors of Way, Truth, and Life and probes "Why" Mennonites (and Christians more broadly) have "needed" (chosen) to endorse a posture of "better than, final, only" in presenting Jesus the Christ. With biblical scholar Samartha who lived most of his life among Hindus she agrees:
> To claim salvation in no one other than Christ negates and judges neighbor religions. It divides people into "we" and "they" in ways that disrupt common tasks. . . Exclusive claims for one's own faith put fences around God's mystery. (145)

Pankratz, James N. (MB) "Mennonite Identity and Religious Pluralism," in *The Church as Theological Community Essays in Honour of David Schroeder*, Harry Huebner, ed. (Winnipeg: CMPC, 1990) 301-13. Reference to this resource appears in the *Introduction.*

Shenk, Calvin. (MC) Annotations from Shenk's exclusivist stance from his book *Who Do You Say that I Am?* appear in *Later Era.*

Shenk, Wilbert R. (MC) "Christian Witness in a Religiously Plural World," and "Christological Foundations for Evangelizing in a Pluralist

Society" in General Papers File at AMBS Library –
S54/Rev050504, 11 pp.

In the first article missiologist, historian, and professor Shenk explains that in every generation attitudes and understandings of cultures and religions appear on a continuum. He adds that many nineteenth century missioners had limited knowledge of other religions; presumed that they served the cause of truth, not error like others; and that the number of believers of other religions, like Hinduism, would decline. Among several traditional thinkers, Shenk introduces J. N. Farquhar (1861-1929) and Hendrik Kraemer (1888-1965). While the former called missioners to have genuine sympathy for and accurate knowledge about Hinduism, he concluded that only Christ could "crown or fulfill" Hindu longing. Shenk describes Kraemer as empathetic toward people of any faith and convinced that only God judges women and men justly.

Shenk's second article clarifies the terms *pluralism, plurality and pluralist*. Among other comments he suggests that *pluralism* "implicitly and often explicitly questions the possibility of making truth claims" and that pluralists "privilege ideas more than living relationships." (7) The bulk of the piece contains Shenk's responses to his summary of George R. Brunk III's fourteen theses central to Brunk's article mentioned, not annotated, above titled "The Exclusiveness of Jesus Christ."

Toews, John E. (MB) "Toward a Biblical Perspective on People of Other
Faiths," *The Conrad Grebel Review*, (Winter 1996) 1-23.
Professor Toews' article was first discussed at the 1994 MCC consultation titled "Peace Theology and Relating to People of Other Faiths." He notes caution among evangelicals to deal with religious pluralism; they fear Christ's exclusive uniqueness being questioned. Toews chooses to focus on New Testament content. He examines the core Christian confession "Jesus is Lord" and texts like John 14:6 and I Cor. 8-10, along with key texts in Acts and Romans. He sees the confession "Jesus is Lord" as both exclusive and inclusive; the latter approach needs to be applied to missional contexts. Toews encourages Christians to be "cautious and gracious" when relating with people of other faiths.

Among numerous quotes to annotate from this article:
God is present in the religious histories of all people and completely in
Jesus Christ.
All people must repent and turn to the living God.
The one God is revealed finally and fully in Messiah Jesus.
The exclusivity of the confession "Jesus is Lord" is designed to be
inclusive. The lordship of Jesus does not negate the presence of God
in other cultures and religions.
God is just and impartial in dealing with all people.

William Klassen, writer and theologian, presented a "Response" to Toews' paper (*Conrad Grebel Review*. (24-32). Some key comments:
Tension emerges in confessing "Jesus is Lord" alongside
affirming God's desire that all people be saved. While the former axiom is exclusive the latter is inclusive. Christianity, even at its most exclusive, requires that there be others, not Christians [alone] . . .
The command to "convert" the sinner or heathen is never given to Christians in the New Testament. Preaching repentance is different from converting people, Klassen explains.
There is no dialogue between religions; there is only dialogue between members of different faiths. When we are in an interfaith dialogue, we are the Christ to the partner in dialogue. That is a rare privilege and great honor, Klassen confesses.

Van Hoogstraten, Marius M. "Restoring Difficulty: How Theology of Religions Seeks to Avoid the Fragility of Encounter and Why We Need to Reclaim It," *Anabaptist Witness*, (2, nol. 1 April 2015) 11-30.

Weaver, Alain Epp. (GC) "Parables of the Kingdom and Other Faiths, How should Christians relate to people of other religions, or of no religion?" in *What Mennonites are Thinking 2001*, Merle & Phyllis Pellman Good eds., (Intercourse, PA: Good Books, 2001) 160-65. See also *The Mennonite* (April 25, 2000) 4-5.

Weaver, Alain Epp. (GC) "We all Drink from the Same Stream," *Mennonite Life* (March 1997), 10-18.

---

[1] Finger does not indicate what specific questions he posed nor how the Faith and Order Commission wished to use survey findings. Theologian Finger was hand-picked by another MC theologian for the Faith and Order task; that assignment has been passed on to theologian Gayle Gerber Koontz (GC).
[2] "'As You Go': John Howard Yoder as a Mission Theologian," Note # 63 of 23 pp. http://physix.goshen.edu/mgr/pastissues/july04park.html;
[3] The book with segments of Yoder's writings is by Michael G. Cartwright and Peter Ochs, eds. (Grand Rapids: Eerdmans Publ Co, 2003). See also Mark Thiesen Nation "And Those of Other Faiths?" in *Mennonite Patience, Evangelical Writers, Catholic Convictions*. (Grand Rapids: Eerdmans Publ Co, 2006) 102-08.

Appendix

Writers who are not Mennonite have published or prepared resources that Mennonites used to understand and write here about Hindu thought and practice; the writer had hoped to prepare annotations. With space limits, accept my apology for failure to include full citations.

Aleaz, K. P. *Theology of Religions Birmingham Papers and other Essays*.
Das, R. C. "The Study of Hinduism," *Christian Monitor*, 12/47, 370-71.
Fishman, A. T. *Culture Change and the Underprivileged. A Study of Madigas in South India under Christian Guidance,* 1941.
Jurji, Edward J. "The Phenomenon of Hinduism," Lecture. AMBS Library
Mar Gregorios, Paul. "The Challenge of Hinduism What Can Christians Learn from It?" in *Christianity among World Religions,* 38-45.
Rao, R. R. Sundara. *Bhakti Theology in the Telugu Hymnal*, 1983.
Sharma, Bal Krishna. "Funerary Rites in Nepal: Cremation, Burial and Christian Identity" (Oxford Center for Mission Studies) 2010.
Sudaker, Paul. "Evangelism among Hindus," *National Evangelical Graduate Fellowship Bulletin*, April 1970.
Taneti, James. *Caste, Gender, and Christianity in Colonial India: Telugu Women in Mission*. Thesis, Western Theological Seminary 2013.

About the Author

Ever since living in India from 1962-65, plus during eight further assignments there, Yoder Nyce has been drawn to study and absorb the richness of multi-faiths alongside Christian loyalty. She learned about engagement with Hindu people through friendship with Mennonite missioners like Fyrne, Ramoth, Thelma, and Esther and reading Indian theologians named Aleaz, Ariarajah, Panikkar, Selvanayagam, Sharma, and Thangaraj. Her Doctor of Ministry thesis focused interreligious dialogue. Through observing and conversing with loyalists who practice diverse expressions of Hinduism she, a teacher and researcher, values conveying to others intriguing and meaningful insight. To prove that she is not alone in such interest, this annotated bibliography emerged. Ten or more books plus numerous articles by her preceded this study. Family ties with two adult daughters and husband (along with Southeast Asia college student guests) combine curry meals with interfaith talk.